Steward of God's Mysteries

Steward of God's Mysteries

Paul and Early Church Tradition

Jerry L. Sumney

WILLIAM B. EERDMANS PUBLISHING COMPANY
GRAND RAPIDS, MICHIGAN

Wm. B. Eerdmans Publishing Co.
2140 Oak Industrial Drive NE, Grand Rapids, Michigan 49505
www.eerdmans.com

© 2017 Jerry L. Sumney
All rights reserved
Published 2017

ISBN 978-0-8028-7361-3

Library of Congress Cataloging-in-Publication Data

Names: Sumney, Jerry L., author.
Title: Steward of God's mysteries : Paul and early church tradition / Jerry L. Sumney.
Description: Grand Rapids : Eerdmans Publishing Co., 2017. |
    Includes bibliographical references and index.
Identifiers: LCCN 2017014595 | ISBN 9780802873613 (pbk. : alk. paper)
Subjects: LCSH: Paul, the Apostle, Saint—Theology. | Bible. Epistles of Paul—
    Criticism, interpretation, etc.
Classification: LCC BS2651 .S86 2017 | DDC 227/.06—dc23
    LC record available at https://lccn.loc.gov/2017014595

For Tim Stevens,
long-suffering college roommate
and lifelong friend

Contents

Foreword: Paul's Place in Christian Tradition, by Patrick Gray — viii

Preface — xi

Abbreviations — xii

1. Thinking about Paul's Place in the Early Church — 1
2. "Christ Died for Us": The Meaning of the Death of Jesus — 20
3. "Jesus Is Lord": The Identity of Jesus — 41
4. "For Our Sins": Understandings of Salvation — 70
5. "The Coming of the Lord": Envisioning the Kingdom — 96
6. "In Remembrance of Me": The Lord's Supper — 133
7. "I Handed On to You . . . What I Received" — 159

Bibliography — 175

Index of Authors — 196

Index of Subjects — 200

Index of Scripture and Other Ancient Texts — 203

Foreword: Paul's Place in Christian Tradition

"Death," Paul tells his Corinthian correspondents, "is the last enemy to be destroyed" (1 Cor 15:26). At the time of his own death, Paul's enemies had only just begun their work. Few contemporary scholars know more about Paul's enemies than Jerry Sumney. In *Identifying Paul's Opponents: The Question of Method in 2 Corinthians* (1990) and *Servants of Satan, False Brothers, and Other Opponents of Paul* (1999), he calls attention to the importance of correctly identifying the adversaries against whom Paul is writing in order to understand his letters. Since the time of F. C. Baur and the Tübingen School in the 1830s, an emphasis on conflict has been central to a dominant approach to the study of Paul and of early Christianity more broadly. Even scholars who question key components of this model find it hard to break free from it. In these works and in subsequent essays, Sumney has shown that opposition to Paul during his lifetime was not simply a function of tensions between Jewish and Gentile factions within the early Christian movement and, furthermore, that a focus on the specific situation behind individual letters is a more reliable way of understanding opposition to Paul than is reliance on tenuous reconstructions cobbled together from multiple sources.

Perhaps one should therefore qualify this assessment of Sumney's research by saying that few scholars know more about what can and cannot be known about Paul's enemies. What we know about this opposition comes almost exclusively from Paul's own letters, especially 2 Corinthians, Galatians, and Philippians. His ostensible opponents in these letters may not necessarily think of themselves as such, which may also be true of "the ignorant and unstable" who twist Paul's words "to their own destruction" (2 Pet 3:16). Acts, too, reflects traditions that are negative in their assessment of the apostle, though these perspectives are not those of its author. Those who took issue with Pauline teachings or pastoral practices in his own day have left behind nothing in writing. To be sure, the Letter of James is often taken as a polemic against the notion that faith without works might merit salvation, whether the author's target is Paul or exaggerated or misunderstood versions of Pauline teaching. The Letter of Jude has likewise been read as making an allusion to Paul and implying that an excessive emphasis upon grace encourages a libertine attitude to morality. Still others see Jesus's statement in the Sermon on the Mount that he has not come to abolish the law or the prophets but to fulfill them as covert criticism of putative Pauline antinomianism. Some go even further, claiming that when Matthew has Jesus conclude that whoever breaks one of the least of the commandments "will be called the least in the kingdom of heaven" (5:19), he is taking a dig at Paul's self-identification as "the least of the apostles" (1 Cor 15:9). Such conjecture can be quite clever, but as often as not too clever by half.

In this volume, Sumney turns his attention to the modern heirs of Paul's ancient enemies. Pitting Paul against Jesus is one of the oldest attested forms of criticism. It appears as early as the second century with the Ebionites and can be found in a wide range of contexts ever since. Pagans from late antiquity, medieval Jews and Muslims, British Deists, Enlightenment rationalists, philosophers, feminists, poets, playwrights—these and many other observers have charged Paul with unwittingly grafting alien elements on the faith of Jesus or betraying him outright. Sumney continually circles back to three popular iterations of this basic argument—Hyam Maccoby's *Mythmaker: Paul and the Invention of Christianity* (1987), Barrie Wilson's *How Jesus Became a Christian* (2008), and James D. Tabor's *Paul and Jesus: How the Apostle Transformed Christianity* (2012)—though he might have selected many other examples from the last several decades. And these are only examples of book-length critiques written by scholars. The list of luminaries who have compared Paul unfavorably with Jesus in other forms reads like a veritable who's who of the last two centuries: Thomas Jefferson, Ralph Waldo Emerson, Friedrich Nietzsche, Leo Tolstoy, H. G. Wells, H. L. Mencken, Martin Buber, Mahatma Gandhi, Adolf Hitler, and Carl Jung, to name only a few.

Adjudicating the question of Paul's fidelity to Jesus and the faith of his earliest followers requires more than simple comparison of the primary account of the apostle's teaching in his letters with the secondary accounts of Jesus's teachings found in the Gospels. It is not that any such comparison is a self-evidently misguided task. Rather, subjectivity and confirmation bias inevitably affect the process in such a way that Paul's supporters and detractors each find only what they seek. Instead, Sumney proposes to compare Paul's teachings with those of the early church from which, in his own telling, he received the faith.

But in the same way that we are dependent on Paul for information about Paul's enemies, we have few other sources from which to reconstruct the chain of tradition linking Paul to the early church and thus to the earliest followers of the one he calls Lord. Only in rare instances does he document his sources. Painstaking analysis of the extant forms of this tradition embedded in the letters is required in order to bring some control to the process. In the pages that follow, Sumney does much of the methodological and exegetical heavy lifting that is too often taken for granted. He lays out the criteria he uses in isolating preexisting creedal, confessional, liturgical, hymnic, and other kinds of tradition, enabling the reader to understand the basis on which comparative data might be generated. In so doing, he also makes possible some informed judgments about Paul's "originality" or creative fidelity with respect to Jesus and the primitive church in such areas as Christology, soteriology, eschatology, and the meaning of the Lord's Supper.

It is much easier to make facile claims about Paul "founding" Christianity, by accident or by design, or "inventing" this or that aspect of Christian theology than it is to engage in close, critical, dispassionate analysis of the primary texts. The devil is in the details. Sumney will have succeeded if his examination of these details makes it more difficult to invoke pat answers that do little to illuminate the origins of Christianity and Paul's role in it.

PATRICK GRAY

Preface

This book got its start in an invitation to contribute to the 2008 Theological Diversity in Early Christianity section of the Society of Biblical Literature. When I received that invitation to present a paper in their group, I had no idea that I would give so much attention to form-critical analysis of the Pauline letters. But it sparked my interest in examining the ways that Paul was dependent upon the traditions that the church formed before he was a member and outside his sphere of influence. I am grateful for the response to my initial foray into this work by Jennifer Knust at that session. I received good advice on other parts of the work at a session of the 2015 Society for New Testament Study meeting and from Carl Holladay's response and the comments of others, especially Greg Sterling, to a presentation of parts of it at the 2016 Christian Scholars Conference. I am grateful for all the responses at those meetings and from the faculty colloquy of Lexington Theological Seminary. I am particularly grateful for the conversations about this work that I had with O. Wesley Allen. The thoughts of all of these parties have improved this work in significant ways. Of course, the faults that remain are of my own making.

I owe a special debt of gratitude to Maryann Wellman, who was so helpful in combing through and organizing research materials for this project.

Parts of chapters 1 and 2 were published previously in " 'Christ Died for Us': Interpretations of Jesus' Death as a Central Element of the Identity of the Early Church," in *Reading Paul in Context: Explorations in Identity Formation: Essays in Honour of William S. Campbell*, edited by Kathy Ehrensperger and J. Brian Tucker (Edinburgh: T. & T. Clark, 2010), 147–72. This material is used by permission of Bloomsbury Publishing Plc. I thank them for their gracious permission to use it.

Abbreviations

AB	Anchor Bible
AGJU	Arbeiten zur Geschichte des antiken Judentums und des Urchristentums
ANTC	Abingdon New Testament Commentaries
BBR	*Bulletin for Biblical Research*
BETL	Bibliotheca Ephemeridum Theologicarum Lovaniensium
Bib	*Biblica*
BibInt	*Biblical Interpretation*
BibInt	Biblical Interpretation Series
BJRL	*Bulletin of the John Rylands Library*
BNTC	Black's New Testament Commentaries
BZ	*Biblische Zeitschrift*
BZNW	Beihefte zur Zeitschrift für die neutestamentliche Wissenschaft
CBQ	*Catholic Biblical Quarterly*
CNT	Commentaire du Nouveau Testament
ConBNT	Coniectanea Biblica: New Testament Series
EB	Études bibliques
EHS	Europäische Hochschulschriften
EKKNT	Evangelisch-katholischer Kommentar zum Neuen Testament
ETS	Erfurter theologische Studien
ExAud	*Ex Auditu*
FRLANT	Forschungen zur Religion und Literatur des Alten und Neuen Testaments
GTJ	*Grace Theological Journal*

HBT	*Horizons in Biblical Theology*
HDR	Harvard Dissertations in Religion
HNT	Handbuch zum Neuen Testament
HNTC	Harper's New Testament Commentaries
HR	*History of Religions*
HTKNT	Herders theologischer Kommentar zum Neuen Testament
HTS	Harvard Theological Studies
ICC	International Critical Commentary
Int	*Interpretation*
JAAR	*Journal of the American Academy of Religion*
JAC	*Jahrbuch für Antike und Christentum*
JBL	*Journal of Biblical Literature*
JETS	*Journal of the Evangelical Theological Society*
JSNT	*Journal for the Study of the New Testament*
JSNTSup	Journal for the Study of the New Testament Supplement Series
JSPHL	*Journal for the Study of Paul and His Letters*
JTI	*Journal of Theological Interpretation*
JTS	*Journal of Theological Studies*
KEK	Kritisch-exegetischer Kommentar über das Neue Testament
LCL	Loeb Classical Library
LNTS	Library of New Testament Studies
Neot	*Neotestamentica*
NewDocs	*New Documents Illustrating Early Christianity,* ed. G. H. R. Horsley and Stephen Llewelyn. North Ryde, NSW: Ancient History Documentary Research Center, Macquarie University, 1981–
NGS	New Gospel Studies
NIB	*The New Interpreter's Bible,* ed. Leander E. Keck. 12 vols. Nashville: Abingdon, 1994–2004
NICNT	New International Commentary on the New Testament
NIGTC	New International Greek Testament Commentary
NovT	*Novum Testamentum*
NovTSup	Novum Testamentum Supplements
NTL	New Testament Library
NTS	*New Testament Studies*
NTTS	New Testament Tools and Studies
Pillar	Pillar New Testament Commentary
PRSt	*Perspectives in Religious Studies*
PS	Pauline Studies
QD	Questiones Disputatae

RNT	Regensburger Neues Testament
RTL	*Revue théologique de Louvain*
SBLDS	Society of Biblical Literature Dissertation Series
SBLMS	Society of Biblical Literature Monograph Series
SBLSP	Society of Biblical Literature Seminar Papers
SBT	Studies in Biblical Theology
SemeiaSt	Semeia Studies
SHAW	Sitzungsberichte der Heidelberger Akademie der Wissenschaft
SNT	Studium zum Neuen Testament
SNTSMS	Society for New Testament Studies Monograph Series
SNTW	Studies of the New Testament and Its World
SP	Sacra Pagina
STDJ	Studies on the Texts of the Desert of Judah
StPatr	Studia Patristica
SUNT	Studien zur Umwelt des Neuen Testaments
TDNT	*Theological Dictionary of the New Testament,* ed. Gerhard Kittel and Gerhard Friedrich, trans. Geoffrey W. Bromiley. 10 vols. Grand Rapids: Eerdmans, 1964–1976
THKNT	Theologischer Handkommentar zum Neuen Testament
TPINTC	Trinity Press International New Testament Commentaries
TynBul	*Tyndale Bulletin*
TZ	*Theologische Zeitschrift*
VC	*Vigiliae Christianae*
WBC	Word Biblical Commentary
WMANT	Wissenschaftliche Monographien zum Alten und Neuen Testament
WUNT	Wissenschaftliche Untersuchungen zum Neuen Testament
ZNW	*Zeitschrift für die neutestamentliche Wissenschaft*
ZST	*Zeitschrift für systematische Theologie*
ZTK	*Zeitschrift für Theologie und Kirche*

CHAPTER 1

Thinking about Paul's Place in the Early Church

In this book we will search Paul's letters for preformed traditions that he did not formulate. We will look for occasions when he uses such traditions as a means to persuade his churches to believe a particular doctrine or act in a particular way. We will observe what kinds of theological claims these traditions make and look for points of continuity and points of difference in relation to Paul's theology. The point of this examination is to bring some light to a slice of the church's history in its first few decades, particularly where Paul's teachings stand in relation to those in the church before him and those in other branches of the church during his ministry. We will try to identify where some distinctive theological claims about Christ, his death, the nature of salvation, and eschatology first seem to appear. We will also examine the traditions about the Lord's Supper to gain some insight into how they developed.

One view of Paul's relationship to those in the church before him that is resurrected every twenty years or so claims that Paul is the inventor of "Christianity" or that Paul is the one who invented the divine Christ; before him, the church had simply followed the ethical teaching of a human Jesus. Among the more recent such works are those of Hyam Maccoby (*The Mythmaker: Paul and the Invention of Christianity*, 1987), Barrie Wilson (*How Jesus Became Christian*, 2008), and James Tabor (*Paul and Jesus: How the Apostle Transformed Christianity*, 2012). Modern versions of this thesis go back at least as far as Joseph Klausner (1943), and before him to Adolf Harnack and William Wrede. A similar view of Paul's relationship to the earlier and non-Pauline branches of the church appears in scholars who see the Q community or others

1

holding to the teaching of Jesus without the christological and soteriological beliefs of the later (post-Pauline) church.[1]

It is interesting to note that when Wrede called Paul "the second founder of Christianity," he meant it as a compliment.[2] He meant that Paul turned the church into a universal religion. What Wrede claimed as something good has become an accusation in those who now claim that Paul invented Christianity.[3] The tales of how Paul single-handedly took over the church have become more elaborate in these recent claims. The tone and methods of these works are more those of conspiracy theory writings than those of careful history.

In this chapter we will review some aspects of these studies. We begin by looking at some assertions of those who contend that Paul invented Christianity. They identify a number of things about Paul and his teachings that they claim are shocking. We will then make some observations about the methods of historical research they employ. The brief glimpses at these studies will help clear the table before we begin to explore whether or how Paul is dependent on earlier church teaching. We will survey the diversity of views within the early church that Paul's letters evidence. Finally in this chapter we will set out a method for identifying preformed material in Paul's letters. This method will guide the work in the rest of the study to try to see what beliefs were held by those outside Paul's influence.

Assertions That Paul Invented Christianity

The assertion that the religion of Paul was not the religion of Jesus is often claimed to be a radical and hidden idea.[4] This claim is correct in many ways and not surprising. Jesus was never a Christian and was never a member of the church. The church does not begin until some followers of Jesus experience

---

1. For example, Burton Mack argues that Q and the Gospel of Thomas are evidence that there were people who see Jesus as a teacher but give no emphasis to his death (*A Myth of Innocence: Mark and Christian Origins* [Philadelphia: Fortress, 1988], 78–123). See 98–100 for his vivid description of Paul as one who was devising the Christ cult over against the Jerusalem Jesus movement.

2. William Wrede, *Paul*, trans. Edward Lummis (London: Green, 1907), 179. He also called him the "real creator of Christian theology" (177).

3. For a thorough review of the accusations that have been made about Paul from the second century to the present, see Patrick Gray, *Paul as a Problem in History and Culture: The Apostle and His Critics through the Centuries* (Grand Rapids: Baker Academic, 2016).

4. For example, in Barrie Wilson, *How Jesus Became Christian* (New York: St. Martin's, 2008), 3.

his resurrection and then have the experience of feeling that the risen Christ is in some way facilitating the presence of God in their midst. The church is composed of those who believe that God vindicated the message and ministry of Jesus through the resurrection. Even by the Gospel accounts, no one believed this before Jesus was crucified. The rest of this book will help one see what kinds of claims this experience led them to make about Jesus. Of course, in the earliest days all church members remained observant Jews. They saw no contradiction between making claims about what God had done in Christ and being faithful Jews.

There is now debate among Pauline scholars about how long the church continued to see itself as a group wholly within Judaism. Some contend that Paul's churches, which had mostly gentile members, continued to be a subgroup within the local synagogues at least as long as Paul was alive. Even if many of those churches were separate from the local synagogues, as I think they were, Jewish members of those churches would have remained members of their synagogues. The list of troubles Paul says he endured in 2 Cor 11:21b–29 includes chastisements received from synagogue authorities. He continues to submit to the authority of synagogue officials even as he is a missionary of the church. So while Paul is a member of the church and Jesus never was, Paul maintains, at least in some ways, his observance of Judaism. So both Jesus and Paul were adherents of Judaism, but only Paul was a church member. Paul is, then, a member of a different religious movement than Jesus, even though both were observant Jews.

Some who claim that Paul invented Christianity say that he shifted the movement away from an emphasis on the teaching of Jesus to an emphasis on teaching about the Christ.[5] There is here an important truth that, again, is not really shocking or new. The church from its beginning was not just about passing on the teachings of Jesus. It was a movement that made claims about who Jesus was and, as we will see, began calling him Messiah/Christ very early. Wilson also claims that it is unusual to say that Paul's religion emerged from a different revelation than that of Jesus.[6] Of course, since the risen Jesus was the speaker in the Acts accounts of Paul's revelation, this is hardly surprising news. Indeed, it has to be true.

---

5. See Wilson, *How Jesus Became Christian*, 2–3. James Tabor asserts that the church before Paul's time did not see Jesus as the Son of God, have a dying and rising savior, practice baptism into Christ, or have the kind of Eucharist seen in Paul and the Gospels (*Paul and Jesus: How the Apostle Transformed Christianity* [New York: Simon & Schuster, 2012], 25). We will address each of these topics in later chapters.

6. Wilson, *How Jesus Became Christian*, 3–4.

The claim that there was this shift from the teaching of Jesus to teachings about him, though, contains an internal fallacy; it presents readers with a false dilemma. The move to proclaiming things about Jesus's identity does not need to signal that his teachings are being ignored. In places it is clear that Paul expects members of his churches to know stories of the life of Jesus and to know his teachings (e.g., 1 Cor 7:10). As we will see, for Jesus's followers to have a reason to continue to think about his teachings, they had to formulate an understanding of his identity in the wake of his execution as an insurrectionist. So they had to begin proclaiming things about his identity that made him worth remembering, not just remember his teachings. Further, as Elisabeth Schüssler Fiorenza points out, the Jesus traditions were formative for the urban non-Palestinian churches because the first people to take the message outside Palestine were Jews who went to other Jews and synagogue adherents. These missionaries led those who listened to adapt the Jesus tradition to their different cultural settings.[7]

Wilson makes what he also seems to see as a shocking revelation when he says that the "New Testament is not a neutral collection of early Christian writings."[8] This is also true and nearly self-evident. It is clearly a collection intended to help the church maintain its belief in Christ and to guide its behavior. The collection intends its readers to believe certain things about Jesus and to reject other claims. What Wilson and Maccoby want to claim beyond this is that the whole New Testament is the product of the Pauline branch of the church, which is dramatically different from the earlier, Palestinian church.[9] Looking at traditions in Paul's letters will help us evaluate whether the divide between the predominantly Jewish churches and those Paul founded is as wide as those who charge Paul with inventing Christianity contend.

Historical Methods

Beyond the sensationalizing of some assertions about the early church, there are also serious questions about the historical methods employed in some of these studies. A prime example is Maccoby's view of Paul's psychological

---

7. Elisabeth Schüssler Fiorenza, *In Memory of Her: A Feminist Reconstruction of Christian Origins* (New York: Crossroad, 1983), 100.
8. Wilson, *How Jesus Became Christian*, 3.
9. Hyam Maccoby, *The Mythmaker: Paul and the Invention of Christianity* (New York: Harper & Row, 1987), 4. Here Maccoby conflates the writing of the Gospels and the process of canonizing the books of the New Testament.

motivation to invent Christianity. He notes that the Ebionites say that rather than being a Pharisee, Paul was a gentile who converted to Judaism to marry a priest's daughter. When the marriage was refused, he turned against the law. Maccoby argues that the truth behind this story is that Paul was in love with Judaism itself. As a deputy of the high priest who persecuted believers in Christ, Paul converted to Judaism. But when his ambitions within Judaism were thwarted, he became involved with the "Jesus movement" and became the creator of a savior religion.[10]

To weave this tale, Maccoby relies on a fourth-century text, the *Panarion* of Epiphanius. In this work, Epiphanius describes and argues against various understandings of Christianity that he rejects. In his account of the teachings of the Ebionites, Epiphanius says they tell this story of the conversion of Paul and the failed marriage. Maccoby acknowledges that this is not historical, but then chooses elements of it he needs to create his version of Paul. So Maccoby's view of Paul is based on a psychologizing of an admittedly nonfactual account of Paul's life that appears in a polemical account of the group whose beliefs contain the story. This is hardly solid historical methodology.

Similarly, Tabor looks to Jerome, who wrote in the late fourth and early fifth century, to support his version of Paul's biography. While Tabor acknowledges that Paul was Jewish and a Pharisee (and so not as much of a liar as Maccoby charges), he was not from Tarsus but from Gischala in Galilee. While this does not directly contradict what Paul says about himself, neither is it good evidence. Still, Tabor at least does not change what his source says to construct an otherwise unsupported biography of Paul.

Maccoby identifies the Ebionites as the "authentic successors" of the Jerusalem church.[11] It seems likely that the Ebionites were, indeed, a group that grew out of the Palestinian church. The Ebionites continued to be a Torah-observant church, as the Jerusalem church was. But calling them that church's "authentic successors" is a value judgment, not a historical statement. Maccoby means that he likes what they taught better than he likes Paul. Maccoby says their beliefs were consistent with the Jerusalem church because they believed, among other things, that Jesus was just a human and that he intended to establish an earthly kingdom.[12] But these beliefs are not really what Epiphanius reports about the Ebionites. Epiphanius does say that *some* Ebionites believe Jesus was born a human, but he also says that others say he was an archangel

---

10. Maccoby, *Mythmaker*, 182–83. See Epiphanius, *Pan.* 2.30.8–9.
11. Maccoby, *Mythmaker*, 17.
12. Maccoby, *Mythmaker*, 17.

(2.30.16.4–5; 2.30.14.4; see other options in 2.30.3.4; 2.30.17.6). Other Ebionites say he was not a human because when his family came to talk with him (Matt 12:46–50) Jesus said that his family members are those who do the will of God (2.30.14.5). Those who do think he was born a human seem to have an adoptionist Christology, though Epiphanius says they do not agree among themselves (2.30.3.4–6; 2.30.18.5–6). If Maccoby is right about what the Jerusalem church believed, the Ebionites did not remain faithful to it. Indeed, Ephiphanius says that the Ebionites even say that Jesus commanded his followers to reject the temple sacrifices (2.20.16.4–7). The Ebionites, then, do not reflect what Maccoby wants to find when we look at the full description in Epiphanius.

When Maccoby moves from constructing a story of Paul's life, he describes Paul's religion as a combination of Gnosticism, mystery religions, and Judaism.[13] Scholars from the nineteenth and first half of the twentieth century often pointed to elements in those religions as the sources for the teachings of the early church. More recent scholarship acknowledges that there was no fully formed pre-Christian Gnosticism. This means it could not have been a source for Paul. Interpreters are also now more careful about saying that parallels indicate dependence. That is, similarities do not automatically show that one religion was dependent on the other.

Maccoby's kind of construction of history is also evident in his means of supporting the idea that Paul was a gentile. He identifies Paul as the source of Christian anti-Semitism. This means that Paul had to be a gentile, he argues, because there were no self-hating Jews in the first century. Jewish self-hatred is the product of Christian anti-Semitism.[14]

The idea that Jews were not subjected to vehement anti-Semitism before Paul is historically unsustainable. As Pieter van der Horst notes, "Most anti-Jewish material from Greek and Latin authors is pre-Christian."[15] From a more academically oriented resource, Louis Feldman states that from 270 BCE on, the constant view of Jews among Greek and Roman authors is negative.[16] In

---

13. Maccoby, *Mythmaker*, 197, 220n7.
14. Maccoby, *Mythmaker*, 203.
15. Pieter van der Horst, "The Egyptian Beginning of Anti-Semitism's Long History," Jerusalem Center for Public Affairs website, http://jcpa.org/article/the-egyptian-beginning-of-anti-semitism's-long-history; accessed 4/11/2016.
16. Louis H. Feldman, *Studies in Hellenistic Judaism*, AGJU 30 (Leiden: Brill, 1996), 289. In addition to Manetho, he cites Lysimachus, Posidonius, Apollonius, Apion, and Tacitus, among others. See also the collection of comments about Jews from ancient authors in Théodore Reinach, *Textes d'auteurs grecs et romains relatifs au Judaïsme* (Hildesheim: Olms, 1963).

the first century, Josephus (*Contra Apion* 1.161) and Philo (*In Flaccum* 1–107 and *Legatio ad Gaium* 114–39) tell of the abuse of Jews by both riots and government programs.

One clear evidence that this anti-Semitism led some Jews to a desire not to be identified as Jewish is the operation to remove the evidence of circumcision called epispasm. The textual evidence for the practice as a means of trying to appear like a gentile comes from as early as stories of what led to the Maccabean Revolt (1 Macc 1:11–15) and continue through the Mishnah and into the era of the Talmud.[17] There is, then, an abundance of evidence for both anti-Semitism and its effects on how Jews think of themselves before the influence of Paul.

Maccoby, Wilson, and Tabor all cite the Didache as evidence for a type of church that was not influenced by Paul. This document promises to be much more relevant to understanding Paul and the early church than a fourth-century polemical tract. This manual of church teaching and instruction seems to have been written in the late first or perhaps early second century. Interpreters are nearly unanimous in identifying it as a document produced by Jewish church members who remained Torah observant. It represents a branch of the church different from the Pauline churches. While Tabor draws on it for evidence of a number of beliefs, Maccoby and Wilson cite it primarily in discussions of the meaning and practices of the Lord's Supper. They see great differences between its supper and that in the Pauline churches. Tabor contends that the Didache's teaching goes back to Jesus and was then perpetuated by James.[18] But there is no textual or historical evidence for these connections beyond the recognition that it does belong to a predominantly Jewish branch of the church. That does not provide any certainty that it comes from James and certainly none that it goes back to Jesus. Still, since this work does come from the early church, it provides significant evidence for the teaching and practices of some churches in that early time. Thus we will give attention to it throughout this study. We will note where there are commonalities and differences between it and what we find in Paul and in the traditions he cites.

These studies that accuse Paul of inventing so many doctrines of the church fall victim to another fallacy of historical research. They seem to assume that because Paul is the first extant evidence of an idea or belief, then he must be its originator. It is certainly good historical method not to assume that ideas or institutions existed in the time before there is extant evidence. But it

---

17. See Pirqe Abot 3:16 and b. Yoma 85b as examples.
18. Tabor, *Paul and Jesus*, 46.

is not safe to assume that the author of the first extant evidence was also the first person to think of a particular idea or believe a specific doctrine. Authors often reflect what people in their groups think about the world, even when their writings are the first evidence for those thoughts. In this study we reject this fallacy and search Paul's letters for evidence of beliefs of those who were in the church before him and who were influential before he was.

A final point about historical method demands attention. Those who argue that Paul invented Christianity adopt what one can call a "Great Men" model of history; Cynthia Briggs Kittredge calls it the "heroic model."[19] In this model, all important developments (whether good or bad) are the result of the one powerful personality who is the reason and originator of each development. For Pauline scholars who adopt this model, "the origin and energy of the theological process is Paul himself." Such an interpretive model finds little room for social context or for dialogue among competing views.[20]

Feminists have been among the critics of this model of history for understanding the early church. Schüssler Fiorenza sees this as an "androcentric historiography" that is unable to integrate all the information in these texts.[21] She and others encourage interpreters to see Paul in the context of a movement that existed before he joined and did not revolve around him.[22] Paul's letters themselves are evidence that his authority and teachings were disputed. His congregations were not just passive; they were "active and engaged in formulating what is coming to be the tradition."[23] These and other interpreters encourage a reading that allows other voices to be heard within the text. As Kittredge argues, readers must allow that the authors of traditions are "the collective Christian community in worship, which includes individuals whose names the letters of Paul do not reveal."[24]

This way of envisioning the development of beliefs in the early church seems inherently more probable than seeing Paul impose his will on nearly the entire movement. It certainly does more justice to the evidence of the Pauline letters. In them we see Paul in conversation about what the church

---

19. Cynthia Briggs Kittredge, "Rethinking Authorship in the Letters of Paul: Elisabeth Schüssler Fiorenza's Model of Pauline Theology," in *Walk in the Ways of Wisdom: Essays in Honor of Elisabeth Schüssler Fiorenza*, ed. Shelly Matthews, Cynthia Briggs Kittredge, and Melanie Johnson-Debaufre (Harrisburg, PA: Trinity Press International, 2003), 319.

20. Kittredge, "Rethinking Authorship," 322.

21. Schüssler Fiorenza, *In Memory of Her*, 70.

22. Schüssler Fiorenza, *In Memory of Her*, 101–2.

23. Kittredge, "Rethinking Authorship," 326–27.

24. Kittredge, "Rethinking Authorship," 325.

should believe and practice. Some of those conversation partners see him as an authority, others reject his authority. His churches are clearly theologizing in his absence. Sometimes he thinks they reach conclusions contrary to the gospel, other times they come to views he can accept. This study adopts a model of history that allows "the existence and participation of other leaders in the communities before Paul and during Paul's ministry and identif[ies] them as 'authors' of the Christological hymns or baptismal formulas."[25]

Differences and Opponents

In favor of Paul's use of, even reliance on, preformed traditions are important commonalities among the different branches of the church. These commonalities do not support the idea that some original orthodoxy possessed a clearly articulated theology. The Pauline letters, and even Acts, are evidence for differences in beliefs and practices. The letters give evidence of people who opposed the ministry of Paul and of people, beliefs, and practices in the church that he opposed. There were arguments even among the apostles (see Gal 2). Paul perceives a need to organize a collection for the church in Jerusalem because of the friction caused by differences. The differences were real and significant; we must allow the possibility that the same was true of the commonalities.

The range of those Paul opposes in his letters demonstrates the diversity of views within the church in Paul's time. Elsewhere I have given attention to those Paul opposes in his letters and so will not repeat all the arguments here.[26] This survey of those Paul opposes begins with his earliest letter and moves through the collection in roughly chronological order.[27]

Some interpreters think Paul opposes pneumatics in 1 Thessalonians. Robert Jewett and Wolfgang Harnisch argue that these teachers claim this superior measure of possession of the Spirit because they have an overrealized

---

25. Kittredge, "Rethinking Authorship," 325.
26. See Jerry Sumney, *Servants of Satan, False Brothers, and Other Opponents of Paul*, JSNTSup 188 (Sheffield: Sheffield Academic Press, 1999); Sumney, "Studying Paul's Opponents: Advances and Challenges," in *Paul and His Opponents*, ed. Stanley E. Porter, PS 2 (Leiden: Brill, 2005), 7–58; Sumney, "The Search for the Opponents of Paul," in *Paul Unbound: New Approaches to the Study of the Apostle*, ed. Mark Given (Peabody, MA: Hendrickson, 2009), 55–70.
27. We will not treat Philemon here since Paul does not oppose any teaching or practice there. Neither will we examine the disputed letters, since any evidence we might gain from them is questionable.

eschatology, which also leads them to be antinomians.[28] Karl Donfried and Jan Lambrecht find no doctrinal controversy, but only personal attacks against Paul.[29] Perhaps the largest number of interpreters find no intruding group of teachers, but only a controversy aroused because some in the church have quit their jobs to await the imminent parousia.[30] All of these possibilities suggest that the church at Thessalonica is engaged in its own theologizing, even if its members are seeking Paul's advice.

First Corinthians is testimony to the difficulty believers had in integrating their new beliefs into their communal and social lives. Paul addresses a wide range of theological and ethical issues in his response to their letter to him and the reports he has received about them. It is on 1 Corinthians that Walter Schmithals founds his thesis that gnostics are the teachers Paul opposes in all his letters.[31] As noted, most interpreters now recognize that Gnosticism did not develop into a recognizable system or movement until sometime in the second century (if ever). Still, there is some emphasis on acquiring wisdom and knowledge through the Spirit that may be connected to wisdom traditions in Hellenistic Judaism.[32] This connection does not seem to have led the Corinthians to adopt a dramatically different understanding of Christ because Christology is not a major topic of the letter.

---

28. Wolfgang Harnisch, *Eschatologische Existenz: Ein exegetischer Beitrag zum Sachanliegen von 1 Thessalonicher 4:13–5:11*, FRLANT 110 (Göttingen: Vandenhoeck & Ruprecht, 1973), 27-37; Robert Jewett, *The Thessalonian Correspondence: Pauline Rhetoric and Millenarian Piety* (Philadelphia: Fortress, 1986), 94-106.

29. Karl P. Donfried, "The Cults of Thessalonica and the Thessalonian Correspondence," *NTS* 31 (1985): 350-51; Jan Lambrecht, "Thanksgivings in 1 Thessalonians 1-3," in *The Thessalonian Correspondence*, ed. Raymond F. Collins, BETL 87 (Leuven: Leuven University Press, 1990), 200.

30. For example, Béda Rigaux, *Les épîtres aux Thessaloniciens*, EB (Paris: Gabalda, 1956), 59; Charles Masson, *Les deux épîtres de Saint Paul aux Thessaloniciens*, CNT 11a (Neuchâtel: Delachaux & Niestlé, 1957), 32; Abraham Malherbe, " 'Gentle as a Nurse': The Cynic Background to 1 Thessalonians 2," *NovT* 12 (1970): 203-17; Raymond F. Collins, "Paul as Seen through His Own Eyes," in *Studies on the First Epistle to the Thessalonians*, BETL 66 (Leuven: Leuven University Press, 1984), 184; Sumney, *Servants of Satan*, 214-28.

31. See Walter Schmithals, *Gnosticism in Corinth*, trans. John E. Steely (Nashville: Abingdon, 1971); Schmithals, *Paul and the Gnostics*, trans. John E. Steely (Nashville: Abingdon, 1972). He continues to hold this basic position in *The Theology of the First Christians*, trans. O. C. Dean Jr. (Louisville: Westminster John Knox, 1997).

32. Birger A. Pearson, *The Pneumatikos-Psychikos Terminology in 1 Corinthians*, SBLDS 12 (Missoula, MT: Scholars Press, 1973); Richard A. Horsley, "Gnosis in Corinth: 1 Cor. 8.1-6," *NTS* 27 (1979): 32-51; Gerhard Sellin, "Das 'Geheimnis' der Weisheit und das Rätsel der 'Christuspartei' (zu 1 Kor 1-4)," *ZNW* 73 (1982): 70-71.

Thinking about Paul's Place in the Early Church

C. K. Barrett and Gerd Lüdemann are among the interpreters who follow Baur in finding teachers who demand that gentile believers undergo circumcision and observe Torah. They also argue that these teachers have some connection with the Jerusalem church.[33] Most interpreters, however, see the basic problem as one that involves a spirit of competitiveness among the Corinthians that expresses itself in various ways,[34] perhaps through their claims about possession of the Spirit that they say authorizes the various stances they take.

However many letters an editor used to compose 2 Corinthians, interpreters generally agree that the situation they address has a basic continuity—at least they all address the same opponents. As always, Baur sees opponents who demand Torah observance of gentiles,[35] and Schmithals finds gnostics. Alternatively, Dieter Georgi finds traveling Hellenistic Jewish wonderworkers, divine men, as those who oppose Paul in this text.[36] However, scholars have called into question the existence of this kind of movement.[37] The more likely view is that a group of traveling preachers has come to Corinth making claims about their possession of the Spirit that Paul finds unacceptable and incompatible with the gospel. They assert that the Spirit gives them a commanding presence, the power to perform mighty acts, and the right to be apostles. Furthermore, the Spirit authorizes them to tell of their powers and exercise them to make demands on the church. They also actively oppose Paul's apostleship. Whichever view one takes of the opponents of 2 Corinthians, it is clear that

---

33. F. C. Baur, *Paul the Apostle of Jesus Christ: His Life and Works, His Epistles and Teachings*, 2 vols. (London: Williams & Norgate, 1873–75; repr., 2 vols. in 1, Peabody, MA: Hendrickson, 2003), 1:268–320. For example, Gerd Lüdemann, *Opposition to Paul in Jewish Christianity*, trans. M. Eugene Boring (Minneapolis: Fortress, 1989), 69–80; C. K. Barrett, "Deuteropauline Ethics: Some Observations," in *Theology and Ethics in Paul and His Interpreters: Essays in Honor of Victor Paul Furnish*, ed. Eugene Lovering and J. L. Sumney (Nashville: Abingdon, 1996), 172.

34. This view follows Nils Dahl, "Paul and the Church at Corinth according to 1 Corinthians 1:10–4:21," in *Christian History and Interpretation*, ed. W. R. Farmer, C. F. D. Moule, and R. R. Niebuhr (Cambridge: Cambridge University Press, 1967), 313–35. See also Margaret M. Mitchell, *Paul and the Rhetoric of Reconciliation: An Exegetical Investigation of the Language and Composition of 1 Corinthians* (Louisville: Westminster John Knox, 1991), 297–302.

35. Baur, *Paul the Apostle of Jesus Christ*, 268–320. So also C. K. Barrett, "Paul's Opponents in 2 Corinthians," *NTS* 17 (1971): 233–54; Barrett, *The Second Epistle to the Corinthians*, HNTC (New York: Harper & Row, 1973), 28–36; Lüdemann, *Opposition to Paul*; Scott Hafemann, *Suffering and the Spirit: An Exegetical Study of II Cor. 2:14–3:3 within the Context of the Corinthian Correspondence*, WUNT 2/19 (Tübingen: Mohr, 1986).

36. Dieter Georgi, *The Opponents of Paul in Second Corinthians* (Philadelphia: Fortress, 1986).

37. See Carl Holladay, *Theios anēr in Hellenistic Judaism: A Critique of the Use of This Category in New Testament Christology*, SBLDS 40 (Missoula, MT: Scholars Press, 1977).

Paul faced powerful challenges to his authority and his understanding of the presence of God in leaders.

In Galatians, Paul is engaged in fierce polemic about the meaning of the gospel and even speaks of "another gospel." This letter clearly engages teachers who want gentiles to accept circumcision. Unfortunately, it is less clear about why they want this to happen. Most interpreters think these teachers are believers in Christ who argue that gentiles must convert to Judaism to be full members of the people of God or to be saved. Some think they are representatives of the Jerusalem church or members of an anti-Pauline movement that rejects his claim to be an apostle.[38] Some interpreters modify this view significantly, arguing that the matter of Torah observance is more about how Jews should receive gentiles in the eschatological period than about whether they can be saved without circumcision.[39] Other interpreters argue that those Paul opposes are non–Christ-believing Jews who view these gentile church members as possible candidates for full conversion to Judaism.[40] Some elements in Galatians, however, seem to assume that those Paul opposes are believers in Christ.

Though Galatians contains much autobiographical material, it seems unlikely that the people who disturb this church attack Paul's apostleship because they claim that he agrees with their position (5:11).[41] Furthermore, Paul never takes up charges against his apostleship directly, as he does in 2 Corinthians. Paul's version of his trips to Jerusalem indicates that he and the Jerusalem church agree on the core elements of the gospel—however much independence he may want to claim. He seems to think it is plausible to these readers that he maintains some relationship with the Jerusalem church.

---

38. For example, Ernest deWitt Burton, *A Critical and Exegetical Commentary on the Epistle to the Galatians*, ICC (Edinburgh: T. & T. Clark, 1921), liv–lv; Pierre Bonnard, *L'Épître de Saint Paul aux Philippiens*, CNT 10 (Neuchâtel: Delachaux & Niestlé, 1950), 12–14. Franz Mussner thinks the opponents require Torah observance for salvation but does not think they are connected with Jerusalem (*Der Galaterbrief*, HTKNT 9 [Freiburg: Herder, 1974], 12–26).

39. For example, James D. G. Dunn, "The Theology of Galatians: The Issue of Covenantal Nomism," in *Thessalonians, Philippians, Galatians, Philemon*, vol. 1 of *Pauline Theology*, ed. Jouette M. Bassler (Minneapolis: Fortress, 1991), 128–31; Francis Watson, *Paul, Judaism, and the Gentiles: Beyond the New Perspective*, rev. ed. (Grand Rapids: Eerdmans, 2007), 100–121; similarly, John M. G. Barclay, *Obeying the Truth: A Study of Paul's Ethics in Galatians*, SNTW (Edinburgh: T. & T. Clark, 1988), 54–60.

40. For example, Mark Nanos, *The Irony of Galatians* (Minneapolis: Fortress, 2002); Nanos, "Intruding 'Spies' and 'Pseudo-Brethren': The Jewish Intra-Group Politics of Paul's Jerusalem Meeting (Gal 2:1–10)," in *Paul and His Opponents*, ed. Porter, 59–97.

41. See also George Lyons, *Pauline Autobiography: Toward a New Understanding*, SBLDS 73 (Atlanta: Scholars Press, 1985).

Thinking about Paul's Place in the Early Church

If Philippians is a composite text, the letters that make it up may address multiple types of teaching and practice that Paul rejects. Many interpreters, however, see a single type of opponent. Some find an overrealized eschatology that claims a fuller measure of the Spirit than other believers possess.[42] According to some interpreters, the teachers of this view assert that God will give this gift only to those who adopt Torah observance.[43] Of course, some find gnostics as the enemy here, and some see gnostic libertines along with people who demand Torah observance for gentiles.[44] Chapter 3 does suggest that Paul knows of a movement that travels to his churches and advocates Torah observance for gentiles. He warns the Philippians about this movement, but the text does not indicate that they are having success in Philippi when he writes.

Paul's letter to the Romans is not primarily a response to teaching that he finds unacceptable, though he probably tries to dispel some ideas about what he teaches that have reached Rome.[45] While debate continues about the purposes of Romans, Paul's explication of his own understanding of the gospel is the most prominent view, albeit with some responses to views others might attribute to him or claim are consequences of his views (e.g., 6:1-2).[46]

This brief overview suggests that there are two anti-Pauline movements: one advocates Torah observance for gentiles, and the other questions Paul's apostleship because of its belief that the Spirit empowers apostles to live a powerful life that they say is missing in Paul. Paul's disputes with these groups do not involve christological issues or questions about the relationship between the earthly Jesus and the risen Christ or even the assumption that the death of Jesus is important for understanding his person or work. There is not even an argument about whether the ministry, death, and resurrection constitute an eschatological event that brings gentiles into the people of God; there is a question about *how* to admit them, but not about *whether* to admit them.

The presence of these various and conflicting theologies are evidence of

---

42. For example, Joachim Gnilka, *Der Philipperbrief*, HTKNT (Freiburg: Herder, 1968), 197; John Reumann, "Philippians 3:20-21—A Hymnic Fragment?" *NTS* 30 (1984): 593-609.

43. Helmut Koester, "The Purpose of the Polemic of a Pauline Fragment (Philippians III)," *NTS* 8 (1961/1962): 317-32.

44. Josef Ernst, *Die Briefe an die Philipper, an Philemon, an die Kolosser, an die Epheser*, RNT (Regensburg: Pustet, 1974), 25.

45. See Stanley E. Porter, "Did Paul Have Opponents in Rome and What Were They Opposing?" in *Paul and His Opponents*, ed. Porter, 149-68.

46. Stanley Porter finds five questions that have been raised about Paul in Rome: (1) they wonder why he has not come sooner; (2) they question his understanding of spiritual gifts; (3) they wonder if he has been avoiding visiting them; (4) some are concerned that he has abandoned Judaism; and (5) there may be questions about his apostolic status ("Did Paul Have Opponents").

the presence of other powerful leaders and of the active theologizing of local churches. The presence of this diversity, even if Paul wanted to eliminate some of it, indicates that Paul was not the sole voice even in the churches he founded. This at least opens the door to the possibility that Paul drew on the beliefs of the church that existed before he joined the movement. This evident diversity supports the effort to search for evidence of the thought of those others.

Other Approaches

Before setting out the method this study will use to understand the place of Paul in relation to the theology of others in the church, taking note of how some others have undertaken this task may help clarify how to proceed. David Wenham is among more recent writers who have responded to those who claim that Paul invented Christianity.[47] He approaches the question by comparing teachings of Paul with those of Jesus as they are found in the Gospels. He tries to show the similarities and points of contact between the teachings of the two. This has been the most common way interpreters have responded to the view that Paul invented Christianity or its central tenets, but it is not without its difficulties. Among those is the need to rely on the Gospel accounts of the teaching of Jesus.[48] This is problematic because we cannot be sure that the evangelists represent the emphases of the historical Jesus. Each presents a somewhat different understanding of Jesus and his teachings. In addition, Tabor claims that the Gospels are "essentially Pauline documents."[49] While nearly all New Testament scholars reject this reading of the Gospels, its assertion suggests a need for an approach that is not dependent on comparing material in the Gospels with that in the Pauline letters.[50]

The approach in this study will be quite different. Rather than comparing

---

47. David Wenham, *Paul: Follower of Jesus or Founder of Christianity?* (Grand Rapids: Eerdmans, 1995); Wenham, *Paul and Jesus: The True Story* (Grand Rapids: Eerdmans, 2002). See also V. George Shillington, *Jesus and Paul before Christianity: Their World and Work in Retrospect* (Eugene, OR: Cascade, 2011).

48. Henk de Jonge comments that it does not matter what titles Jesus may have used for himself. What is more important, he asserts, is that those who knew him and were witnesses to his life assigned those titles to him ("The Historical Jesus' View of Himself and His Mission," in *From Jesus to John: Essays on Jesus and New Testament Christology in Honour of Marinus de Jonge*, ed. Martinus C. de Boer, JSNTSup 84 [Sheffield: Sheffield Academic Press, 1993], 36-37).

49. Tabor, *Paul and Jesus*, 15.

50. However, since Tabor and Maccoby compare the account of the Last Supper in the Gospels with that in Paul, we will also compare the Pauline and the Gospels accounts of that narrative.

Thinking about Paul's Place in the Early Church

the primary account of Paul's teaching with the Gospels' secondary accounts of Jesus's teaching, this book will explore the relationship between the teachings of the earliest church and Paul's thought. We will not, then, compare the teachings of Jesus with those of Paul; rather, we will compare the teachings of other and earlier members of the church with those of Paul. This is the comparison that will show whether Paul is the inventor of teachings about Jesus or whether he adopts the teachings about Jesus that were already current in the church. The real question is not whether the teaching of Jesus and that of Paul are the same. After all, Jesus was leading a reform movement within Judaism, while the church of Paul, and we will argue the church before Paul, had a wider understanding of its mission.[51]

We will accomplish this by identifying places where the undisputed Pauline letters cite preformed traditional material and by exploring the ways that material functions. We will observe what sorts of coherence or conflict there are between it and Paul's thought and theology. Identifying traditional material in Paul can be controversial. Thus we will be cautious about identifying traditions. Given the hypothetical nature of some conclusions about the presence of traditional material, our conclusions about Paul's use of it will be cumulative rather than dependent upon a single text.

On a few occasions, Paul identifies material as traditions that have been passed to him that he in turn passes on to his churches. Among the most notable is 1 Cor 15:3-5. In this place (to which we will return in due course), Paul explicitly identifies what he writes as material that has been given to him by people who believed in Christ before him. When such explicit acknowledgment is absent, it is often difficult to identify citations of traditional or confessional material. Interpreters often disagree about whether a passage contains a preformed tradition and about just how much of the passage is from that earlier formulation.

Criteria

To bring some control to the process of isolating preformed creedal, confessional, liturgical, hymnic, and other kinds of tradition, a number of interpreters have set out criteria for identifying them. Vernon Neufeld's study of early

---

51. Schüssler Fiorenza makes this distinction between the missions of Jesus and the early church, noting that the church was "preaching an alternative religious vision and practicing a countercultural communal lifestyle" (*In Memory of Her*, 100).

confessional material sets three important criteria for isolating such material: (1) an introduction that uses *hoti* ("that"), double accusatives, and infinitives; (2) the presence of the term *homologia* ("confess") or a cognate, synonym, or antonym; and (3) use of relative clauses or participial phrases to introduce the material.[52] E. Earle Ellis adds four other criteria for identifying places at which Paul is quoting preformed material: (1) the presence of an introductory formula, (2) the passage being "self-contained," (3) the presence of vocabulary that is unusual for the author, and (4) the same piece appearing in another early writing that is independent of the text at hand.[53]

Markus Barth notes seven criteria that he considers quite reliable: (1) introductory formulae such as "just as," "for," and then a word to resume the flow of thought such as "therefore" at the end of the citation; (2) the absence of the name of the one praised; (3) a move to first person plural ("we" or "our") as the subject of the verbs of praise or confession; (4) frequent third person singular aorists with infinitives or other purpose clauses; (5) anarthrous abstract nouns, often with repetitions or pleonasms formed by synonyms or genitives; (6) identifying lines of almost an equal number of syllables or beats, which is like Semitic parallelism; and (7) features of chiasm.[54] Among other less reliable signs of the presence of a quotation he lists: summary presentation of the gospel, cosmic extension of Christ's reign, and interruption of the context.

Claus Bussmann divides the evidence for preformed material in Pauline letters into three types: linguistic arguments, literary arguments, and logical arguments.[55] His linguistic arguments are: the passage contains a New Testament hapax legomenon, words not used elsewhere by Paul and those used in a different way than the usual Pauline usage, and grammatical irregularities. Bussmann's literary arguments consist of finding a different literary style from Paul's and the presence of parallels in other early church literature. His logical

---

52. Vernon H. Neufeld, *The Earliest Christian Confesssions*, NTTS 5 (Grand Rapids: Eerdmans, 1963), 12.

53. E. Earle Ellis, "Preformed Traditions and Their Implications for Pauline Christology," in *Christology, Controversy and Community: New Testament Essays in Honour of David R. Catchpole*, ed. David G. Horrell and Christopher M. Tuckett, NovTSup 99 (Leiden: Brill, 2000), 309.

54. Markus Barth, "Traditions in Ephesians," *NTS* 30 (1984): 9-10.

55. Claus Bussmann, *Themen der paulinischen Missionspredigt auf dem Hintergrund der spätjüdisch-hellenistischen Missionsliteratur*, EHS series 23, Theologie 3 (Frankfurt: Lang, 1971), 22. Richard Longenecker offers different criteria for identifying different kinds of preformed material (*New Wine into Fresh Wineskins: Contextualizing the Early Christian Confessions* [Peabody, MA: Hendrickson, 1999]). He gives different criteria for hymns (10-11), nonpoetic confessions (15-16), and single-statement affirmations (21).

arguments include the appearance of theological ideas that are different from or not congruent with what Paul usually says, seeing that a text does not have a strong connection to the context, and seeing that Paul formulates the idea differently elsewhere. He ranks some of these criteria as more decisive than others, with words not found in Paul but present in other New Testament or early church authors highly indicative of the presence of preformed material. He sees words used differently than in Paul even more telling, while a New Testament hapax legomenon is less decisive than these two.[56] Similarly, finding thought that is different from Paul is more powerful evidence for the presence of traditional material than a passage that only formulates an idea in a different way than what we usually see in Paul.[57]

Synthesizing the criteria these earlier interpreters have enumerated, I suggest the following as criteria for identifying preformed material in Paul's letters:

1. An introductory formula. It may explicitly identify the following material as a tradition, or identify what follows as something they already know, or simply take the form of a recitative *hoti* (a "that" introducing a quotation). The presence of double accusatives and of infinitives may also constitute an introductory formula.
2. The terminology used in the section is unusual in or absent from what is found otherwise in the author's writings. If the word is used in a sense that is different from its usual use in an author, that is a strong signal that it is borrowed from another source.
3. A change to use of the first person plural ("we," "our," etc.), particularly if it is a short-term shift from second or third person with verbs of confession or praise.
4. Use of the language of confession (*homologia* and its cognates, synonyms, and antonyms) or of praise.
5. Use of a relative pronoun or clause or a participial phrase to introduce the piece.
6. The statement appears in multiple sources, particularly those not dependent on the same author or "school" within the early church.
7. The passage constitutes a self-contained assertion or statement. This is more significant if it contains material that exceeds the needs of the context.

---

56. Bussmann, *Themen der paulinischen Missionspredigt*, 22–23.
57. Bussmann, *Themen der paulinischen Missionspredigt*, 24–25.

8. The statement is not fully congruent with the author's theology seen elsewhere.
9. Interruption of the context.
10. Absence of the one named. When this occurs with the use of a relative pronoun that introduces the piece, it is particularly significant.
11. Parallelism in the rhythm of lines.
12. Presence of a word or phrase to resume the flow of the argument of the passage.
13. Various grammatical features, including anarthrous abstract nouns, pleonasm, third person singular aorists with infinitives or purpose clauses, and tightly constructed chiasms.
14. Succinct summary of the gospel that appears more than once in early Christian literature.

These criteria are arranged in order of significance. Still, there is no precise priority among contiguous criteria. On the other hand, the first ten criteria bear more weight than the remaining four because there is less room for interpreters to impose their prior assumptions on a particular text. For example, if the interpreters must remove a supposed Pauline addition or reckon with a deletion to produce parallel lines that allows them to identify a piece as traditional, that is less certain than evidence from the first ten criteria. If, however, no redaction is needed for the lines of a proposed tradition to be parallel, the eleventh criterion can bear more weight.

In addition, each proposed tradition should have at least three or four elements that meet these criteria in order to identify it confidently as a preformed piece. Of course, some element of the interpreter's judgment will remain. So we will be in conversation with the judgments of previous interpreters about whether a tradition is present in a given text.

Interpreters who identify preformed materials in New Testament writings often go on to identify the community of origin for those traditions. Various characteristics such as the vocabulary or Semitic character of the language or theological themes may suggest that particular traditions were formulated in an Aramaic-speaking environment or in a church that read the Septuagint or was influenced by the wisdom tradition or by Hellenistic Judaism. Identifying the origin of these traditions can help us understand the development of some theological tenets, but it can also be subjective. We will exercise caution in weighing the arguments put forward for locating the origins of traditions. Only when the case is strong will we rely on such determinations. It will often be clear that a tradition is non-Pauline, even when we cannot locate its originating community. The determination that it is non-Pauline will serve the purpose of demonstrating that Paul is not the first or only person in the church to advocate the view to which the tradition gives voice.

Our discussion of the traditional material embedded in the Pauline letters will identify some of them as non-Pauline, some as pre-Pauline, and some as the product of the Pauline churches. The designation *pre-Pauline* will be used for material that comes from the time before Paul was influential in the church. Such material may have been formulated before he joined the church or in the early years of his life within it, even from time he spent in the Antioch church. The label *non-Pauline* will apply to traditions that continued to develop outside the Pauline churches or without clear reference to the ways he presented the gospel.

The amount and nature of quoted or cited tradition in Paul's letters will demonstrate that he remained dependent on the theological ideas and developments that were in the church before he joined and that developed in parallel streams of the church during his ministry. He was not a Lone Ranger creating doctrines no others in the church had thought of; rather, he stayed connected to the wider church—and did so with some intentionality, if we can believe his statements about that (Gal 2:1–5, particularly his comment about not running in vain; 2:10; 1 Cor 16:1–4; 2 Cor 8–9). We will see Paul's creativity in his use of preexisting traditions to address new questions and situations more than in the creation of new doctrines or doctrinal statements.

CHAPTER 2

"Christ Died for Us"

The Meaning of the Death of Jesus

Those who argue that Paul invented Christianity often cite his understanding of the death of Jesus as one of his central inventions and one that runs counter to what the original church members believed. Hyam Maccoby contends that a failed love interest and then an inability to attain high enough status within Judaism led Paul to create the savior religion of Christianity.[1] He asserts that Paul's adoption of the myth of a descending divine savior made this invention possible.[2] In James Tabor's version of the thesis that Paul invented Christianity, it is Paul who first advocates belief in Jesus's death as a means of removing sins.[3] Barrie Wilson contends that "the Jesus Movement" saw Jesus's death and resurrection as no different from that of any other righteous person.[4] In this chapter we will examine several Pauline texts that rely on pre-Pauline and non-Pauline traditions that interpret the death of Jesus.

1 Corinthians 15:3–5

First Corinthians 15:3–5 is one of the clearest places where Paul cites a tradition. While interpreters disagree about where the citation of the tradition

---

1. Hyam Maccoby, *The Mythmaker: Paul and the Invention of Christianity* (New York: Harper & Row, 1987), 182–83.
2. Maccoby, *Mythmaker*, 184–85. Maccoby's thesis also founders because it depends on the existence of some form of pre-Christian Gnosticism.
3. James D. Tabor, *Paul and Jesus: How the Apostle Transformed Christianity* (New York: Simon & Schuster, 2012), 25.
4. Barrie Wilson, *How Jesus Became Christian* (New York: St. Martin's, 2008), 159.

ends, all agree that it includes verses 3b–5. This passage has a number of the characteristics that mark a passage as a citation of tradition. First, Paul introduces this citation with language used of passing on tradition and explicitly identifies it as material that he had received from those in the faith before him. In addition, he speaks of sin in the plural, while his almost universal use of the term outside preformed material is in the singular. This is also the only place that Paul speaks of "the Twelve" when referring to the Jerusalem apostles. Finally, Paul seldom uses the phrase "according to the Scriptures," while it appears here twice.[5] All of these unusual usages indicate that Paul did not compose these lines.

Paul's introduction of this confession asserts that it is the tradition he had received and that he passed to the Corinthians. Moreover, he says it contains the heart of the faith. This foundational statement not only sets out the centrality of the death of Jesus but also makes it vicarious. Although a number of interpreters in the early and mid-twentieth century argued that this confession originated in Hellenistic churches[6] and so was not known in Jerusalem, most now acknowledge that it arose within Palestinian circles of the earliest church.[7]

Peder Borgen, Birger Gerhardsson, and Larry Hurtado argue that the earliest Jerusalem church needed an interpretation of Jesus's death that countered and opposed the common meanings of crucifixion, including that Jesus

---

5. Also see A. M. Hunter, *Paul and His Predecessors*, rev. ed. (London: SCM, 1961), 15–16; Birger Gerhardsson, "Evidence for Christ's Resurrection according to Paul: 1 Cor 15:1–11," in *Neotestamentica et Philonica: Studies in Honor of Peder Borgen*, ed. David E. Aune, Torrey Seland, and Jarl H. Ulrichsen, NovTSup 106 (Leiden: Brill, 2003), 70.

6. For example, Hunter, *Paul and His Predecessors*, 16–17 (though he changed his mind when he revised the book in 1961; see the appendix, 117–18); Hans Conzelmann, "On the Analysis of the Confessional Formula in 1 Corinthians 15:3–5," *Int* 20 (1965): 15–25; Conzelmann, *1 Corinthians: A Commentary on the First Epistle to the Corinthians*, trans. James W. Leitch, Hermeneia (Philadelphia: Fortress, 1975), 252–54, where he denies Jeremias's claims that the passage has signs of an Aramaic origin. While he does not give attention to 1 Cor 15, Sam K. Williams argues that the Palestinian church had no need for the idea of an expiatory death to explain Jesus's death (*Jesus' Death as Saving Event: The Background and Origin of the Concept*, HDR 2 [Missoula, MT: Scholars Press, 1975], 231).

7. For example, Gerhardsson, "Evidence for Christ's Resurrection," 79–82; Martin Hengel, *Studies in Early Christology* (Edinburgh: T. & T. Clark, 1995), 11; Larry W. Hurtado, *Lord Jesus Christ: Devotion to Jesus in Early Christianity* (Grand Rapids: Eerdmans, 2003), 101. Cf. Peter Stuhlmacher, *Reconciliation, Law, and Righteousness: Essays in Biblical Theology*, trans. Everett R. Kalin (Philadelphia: Fortress, 1997), 52. See the history of the interpretation of "Christ died for" in Cilliers Breytenbach, *Grace, Reconciliation, Concord: The Death of Christ in Graeco-Roman Metaphors*, NovTSup 135 (Leiden: Brill, 2010), 83–103.

was a false messiah or that he died because of his own sin.⁸ Peter Stuhlmacher contends that the three assertions of this tradition, two of which refer to Scripture, could only be formulated "within the Old Testament–Jewish linguistic context."⁹ Gerhardsson notes, however, that this confession shows no evidence of influences from the passion narratives of the Gospels and so seems to have developed separately from them.¹⁰ Perhaps the martyrdom traditions within Judaism (e.g., those in 4 Maccabees) supplied materials that helped the Jerusalem church develop this tradition. This passage shows further that the Jerusalem church already identifies Jesus as the Messiah (because it refers to Jesus as Christ with no qualification) and gives a messianic interpretation to his death and resurrection.¹¹ Concern to identify Jesus as the Messiah makes sense only within a Jewish context. This title would have no significance for non-Jews. All of these factors point to the Palestinian or at least a predominantly Jewish church as the origin of this confession.¹²

This confessional piece also indicates that the earliest church interpreted the death and resurrection of Jesus through the lens of Scripture. Thus it was a community that gave attention to interpretation of Scripture.¹³ A number of

---

8. Peder Borgen, "Crucified for His Own Sins—Crucified for Our Sins: Observations on a Pauline Perspective," in *The New Testament and Early Christian Literature in Greco-Roman Context*, ed. John Fotopoulos, NovTSup 122 (Leiden: Brill, 2006), 18; Borgen, "Openly Portrayed as Crucified: Some Observations on Gal 3:1–14," in *Christology, Controversy and Community: New Testament Essays in Honour of David R. Catchpole*, ed. David G. Horrell and Christopher M. Tuckett, NovTSup 99 (Leiden: Brill, 2000), 346; Gerhardsson, "Evidence for Christ's Resurrection," 81–82; Hurtado, *Lord Jesus Christ*, 131. So also Oscar Cullmann, *The Earliest Christian Confessions*, trans. J. K. S. Reid (London: Lutterworth, 1949), 32; and Nils Dahl, *The Crucified Messiah and Other Essays* (Minneapolis: Augsburg, 1974), 34–35.

9. Stuhlmacher, *Reconciliation, Law, and Righteousness*, 52.

10. Gerhardsson, "Evidence for Christ's Resurrection," 80.

11. Hurtado, *Lord Jesus Christ*, 101. Such an interpretation also shows that they gave these actions an eschatological meaning. See the comments of Rudolf Bultmann, *Theology of the New Testament*, trans. Kendrick Grobel, 2 vols. (New York: Scribner's Sons, 1951–1955), 1:44; and Paula Fredriksen, *From Jesus to Christ: The Origins of the New Testament Images of Jesus*, 2nd ed. (New Haven: Yale University Press, 2000), 136–38. Similarly, Conzelmann argues that the selection of twelve as the leaders shows that the community had an eschatological outlook ("1 Corinthians 15:3-5," 22).

12. Breytenbach sees this dying formula as a conflation of Greek understandings of dying for others and "the Israelite-Jewish concept, that the ultimate consequence of sins is death" (*Grace, Reconciliation, Concord*, 69).

13. Oscar Cullmann asserts that this tradition is an interpretation of Isa 53 and its suffering servant (*The Christology of the New Testament*, trans. Shirley C. Guthrie and Charles A. M. Hall [Philadelphia: Westminster, 1959], 76). This is probably more specific than the evidence allows.

"Christ Died for Us"

scholars also assert that this confession requires a passion narrative to explain how these events occurred.[14] This may be the case even if it shows no evidence of knowing the passion accounts in the canonical Gospels.

Paul uses this confession as part of his argument about the resurrection of believers. When he mentions Jesus's resurrection, he assumes that the Corinthians believe in it. It serves as his evidence that life after death is embodied life.[15] Since it serves as evidence for a different issue, it is clear that the Corinthians believe firmly in Jesus's resurrection before this letter arrives.

One of Paul's clearest references to views of believers beyond his circle and before his admission to the church points to a community that gives sustained attention and emphasis to the death of Jesus—and this within the earliest years of the predominantly Jewish church and perhaps more specifically the Jerusalem church. This suggests that attention to the death of Jesus as salvific is neither a creation of Paul nor a result of the influence of paganism beyond Palestine. But we need to look to other passages before asserting this with full confidence.

Romans 3:24–26

Most interpreters find Paul citing a tradition in Rom 3:24–26, though some commentators reject this idea.[16] The number of Pauline hapax legomena and difficult structural elements of the sentence count in favor of Paul's use of a tradition. The three hapax legomena are *hilastērion* ("place of atonement," the NRSV option in the notes), *paresis* ("passing over" or "remission"), and *progegonota hamartēmata* ("sins committed before," with "sins" in the plural). It is also quite unusual for Paul to refer to Jesus's *blood* rather just than his death. Further, *protithēmi* appears only one other time in Paul, in Rom 1:13. There it

---

14. For example, Gerhardsson, "Evidence for Christ's Resurrection," 89–90. See also James Ware, who argues that the wording of the confession indicates that it envisioned the resurrection to be of the crucified body of Jesus ("The Resurrection of Jesus in the Pre-Pauline Formula of 1 Cor 15.3–5," *NTS* 60 [2014]: 475–98).

15. See the concise discussion of this reading of the chapter in Greg Carey, "Apocalyptic Discourse as Constructive Theology," *PRSt* 40 (2013): 19–34.

16. For example, C. E. B. Cranfield, *A Critical and Exegetical Commentary on the Epistle to the Romans*, 2 vols., ICC (Edinburgh: T. & T. Clark, 1975–1979), 1:200n1; Douglas Moo, *The Epistle to the Romans*, NICNT (Grand Rapids: Eerdmans, 1996), 220; N. T. Wright, "The Letter to the Romans," *NIB* 10:466–67; Douglas A. Campbell, *The Rhetoric of Righteousness in Romans 3:21–26*, JSNTSup 65 (Sheffield: JSOT Press, 1992), 37–57.

has the meaning of "plan" or "intend" rather than "put forward," as it means in 3:25.[17] Finally, the citation of the tradition begins with a relative pronoun, as confessions often do.[18] All of these features appear in verses 25-26. While some interpreters include verse 24 as part of the quoted citation,[19] the more secure position limits the citation to verses 25-26. All who see traditional material here agree that it includes reference to the death of Jesus as a *hilastērion*, to God's *paresis* of previously committed sin, and to God's forbearance.

While these features indicate that verses 25-26 contain traditional material, there is at least one probable insertion by Paul, the phrase "through faith" (3:25). This is a common Pauline expression, and it interrupts the flow of thought from "place of atonement" to "through his blood." Joseph Fitzmyer also contends that Paul adds "for a demonstration of his righteousness at the present" (v. 26b-c). Both the theme of righteousness and the eschatological sense of the present are regular elements of Paul's thought.[20] This phrase certainly ties the citation to the themes of Romans. So it may be that they were added by Paul rather than being language that moves Paul to use the citation.

Interpreters are divided over whether this tradition comes from the Hellenistic or the Palestinian church. Sam Williams has argued extensively that the citation is from the Hellenistic church and addresses the issue of God's lack of action against the nations for their sins.[21] He contends that the tradition's use of *hilastērion* confirms this arena for its development because its only contemporaneous use to mean expiation is found in 4 Maccabees, a document of fully hellenized Judaism. Most interpreters, however, continue to believe it originated in "Jewish Christianity,"[22] often because they understand *hilastērion*

---

17. Toan J. Do notes that this verb is used in the LXX with this meaning in Exod 29.23; 40:23; Lev 24:8; Ps 53(54 MT):5; 2 Macc 1:8, 15; and 4 Macc 8:12 ("The LXX Background of *hilastērion* in Rom 3,25," in *The Letter to the Romans*, ed. Udo Schnelle, BETL 226 [Leuven: Peeters, 2009], 653).

18. See Robert Jewett, *Romans: A Commentary*, Hermeneia (Minneapolis: Fortress, 2007), 270-71.

19. For example, Bultmann, *Theology*, 1:46. Joseph A. Fitzmyer also identifies parts of 3:24 as preformed. Among the pre-Pauline elements he identifies is the use of *charis* ("grace") (*Romans: A New Translation with Introduction and Commentary*, AB 33 [New York: Doubleday, 1993], 341-43).

20. Fitzmyer, *Romans*, 343.

21. Williams, *Jesus' Death as Saving Event*, 32-34.

22. For example, Bultmann, *Theology*, 1:47; Ernst Käsemann, *Commentary on Romans*, trans. Geoffrey W. Bromiley (Grand Rapids: Eerdmans, 1980), 95; Dahl, *Crucified Messiah*, 155; James D. G. Dunn, "Paul's Understanding of the Death of Jesus as a Sacrifice," in *Sacrifice and Redemption: Durham Essays in Theology*, ed. S. W. Sykes (Cambridge: Cambridge Uni-

to be a reference to the lid of the ark of the covenant.²³ Cilliers Breytenbach contends that this image does not introduce ideas of appeasement, but instead interprets the death of Jesus as "place of mercy."²⁴ Thus it could be used by Palestinian Jews.

Among those who identify "Jewish Christianity" as its sources, Ben Meyer and Peter Stuhlmacher assert that it comes from the Stephen circle because it includes a critique of the temple.²⁵ Although it is possible to read this confession as a critique of the temple, softer readings are also possible. Still, its clear references to the temple indicate that it is from the Jewish branch of the church that is connected to the temple. This group could include Jews outside Palestine.

For our purposes here, we do not need to settle the contested issues about whether various phrases are Pauline insertions since all agree that the tradition focuses attention on the death of Jesus as a means of dealing with sin's consequences. If it originates among believers who critique the temple, they still find its symbols meaningful. If, as Williams argues, this formula developed in the face of the conversion of gentiles, it must have its roots in the first years after Jesus's death because there were already gentiles in the church when Paul joins it.²⁶ This may point us to Antioch or perhaps Damascus as its place of origin. Whether it originates in Palestine or Syria, Paul assumes it is a known and accepted formulation of the faith. He perhaps includes it here to emphasize "the common foundation of belief he shares with the Christians in Rome."²⁷

---

versity Press, 1991), 41–43; J. Louis Martyn, *Theological Issues in the Letters of Paul* (Nashville: Abingdon, 1997), 142.

23. In Exod 25:17-22 the term is used to refer to the top of the ark of the covenant. Dahl argues that the tradition alludes to the Akedah as well (*Crucified Messiah*, 155).

24. Breytenbach, *Grace, Reconciliation, Concord*, 66. See also Alexander Weiss, whose study of the use of the term outside Judaism indicates that it may refer to a votive offering rather than a sin offering ("Christus Jesus als Weihegeschenk oder Sühnemal?" *ZNW* 105 [2014]: 294–302).

25. Ben F. Meyer, "The Pre-Pauline Formula in Rom. 3.25-26a," *NTS* 29 (1983): 198–208; Stuhlmacher, *Reconciliation, Law, and Righteousness*, 99–104. This position is very similar to that of Williams. Without identifying the sources as the Stephen group, Breytenbach also identifies this use as a polemic against the temple (*Grace, Reconciliation, Concord*, 66).

26. Paula Fredriksen asserts that the message about Jesus was in Diaspora synagogues within two years of Jesus's death (*From Jesus to Christ*, 135). It may even have happened within the first year.

27. Hengel, *Studies in Early Christology*, 140.

Romans 4:25

Most interpreters think Paul cites another tradition to describe the work of Christ in Rom 4:25.[28] Its introduction with a relative pronoun and its use of *paradidōmi* ("handed over"), language known to be used in traditional formulations, suggest that it is preformed material. It also consists of two parallel clauses with the verbs in the third person aorist passive indicative (*paredothē* ["handed over"] and *ēgerthē* ["raised"]), each followed by the preposition *dia*, each line concluding with the pronoun *hēmōn* ("our"). Further, when Paul speaks of something being done "for our trespasses," or similar phrases, he uses the preposition *hyper*, but here we find *dia*. Importantly, this verse uses *dikaiōsis* ("justification") to describe the effect of Jesus's resurrection (or better the single event of his death and resurrection). Surprisingly, this noun appears only one other time in Paul (Rom 5:18).[29] These features all suggest that this verse comes from the tradition.[30] Interpreters are unanimous in holding that the language of being "handed over" comes from Isa 53:12.[31] The use of the preposition *dia* also seems to be drawn from this Isaiah passage.[32] This passage is clear evidence that the originators of this confession drew on Isa 53 to interpret Jesus's death.

Largely on the basis of its citation of Isa 53, Stuhlmacher follows Joachim Jeremias in identifying this confession as the product of the Jerusa-

---

28. So, e.g., Käsemann, *Romans*, 128; Cranfield, *Romans*, 1:251; James D. G. Dunn, *Romans 1–8*, WBC 38A (Waco: Word, 1988), 224; Hurtado, *Lord Jesus Christ*, 128; Martyn, *Theological Issues*, 142. Dunn calls it a "well established formulation in earliest Christianity" (*Romans 1–8*, 224). Victor Furnish comments that it is generally agreed that Paul is citing a tradition ("'He Gave Himself [Was Given] . . .': Paul's Use of a Christological Assertion," in *The Future of Christology: Essays in Honor of Leander E. Keck*, ed. Abraham J. Malherbe and Wayne A. Meeks [Minneapolis: Fortress, 1993], 109–10). Furnish notes that variations of this tradition are found in Rom 8:32; Gal 1:4; 2:20; Eph 5:2, 25; 1 Tim 2:6; Titus 2:14; 1 Clem. 21.6; 49.6 (109). Douglas Moo is less certain it cites a tradition but acknowledges this as a possibility (*Romans*, 288). Jewett thinks that the language is from the tradition, but that the style is Paul's (*Romans*, 342).

29. This is noted by Hunter, *Paul and His Predecessors*, 32; and Wright, "Romans," 503n162.

30. See Hunter, *Paul and His Predecessors*, 30–31; and Käsemann, *Romans*, 128, who adds that v. 24 provides a "solemn introduction." Vernon Neufeld adds that the antithesis of death and resurrection is also a common sign of traditional material (*The Earliest Christian Confessions*, NTTS 5 [Grand Rapids: Eerdmans, 1963], 45–47).

31. Stuhlmacher, *Reconciliation, Law, and Righteousness*, 55; Joachim Jeremias, *New Testament Theology* (New York: Scribner, 1971), 295–96; Fitzmyer, *Romans*, 389; Leander Keck, *Romans*, ANTC (Nashville: Abingdon, 2005), 132; Jewett, *Romans*, 342. Cranfield asserts that the language of "justification" also comes from Isa 53:11 (*Romans*, 1:251–52).

32. Jewett, *Romans*, 342.

lem church.[33] Rudolf Bultmann also identifies this as a formula that existed before Paul came into the church and as evidence that the earliest church saw Jesus's death as expiatory.[34] While not convinced that it can be traced to Jerusalem, Fitzmyer thinks it comes from the Hellenistic Jewish church.[35] This branch of the church would also be familiar with Scripture and think that understanding Jesus through it was important. Whether from the Palestinian church or the church as it moved outside Palestine, we see that the idea that Jesus's death dealt with the consequences of sin arose among the earliest believers[36] and that they made sense of the idea with their interpretations of Scripture.

The use of *dikaiōsis* ("justification") in this confessional statement is particularly significant. It shows that the tradition before Paul did interpret Jesus's death as providing "justification." J. Louis Martyn argues at length that the theme of justification was present and accepted by all Jewish church members.[37] Thus as important as justification is to Paul's exposition of the gospel in Romans and Galatians, it is an element he has taken over from the tradition—though he does of course develop it in his own way.[38]

Note again that Paul does not work to convince the readers of what this confession asserts. In some ways it pushes beyond the needs of the argument since Paul's central point at the end of this paragraph focuses on "the one who raised Jesus our Lord." The addition of the soteriological confession does not

---

33. Stuhlmacher, *Reconciliation, Law, and Righteousness*, 55. In this he accepts as evidence the Semitisms Jeremias identifies.

34. Bultmann, *Theology*, 1:46, 82. Dahl sees another allusion to the Akedah here (*Crucified Christ*, 157, 188). Breytenbach rejects the language of expiation here. He contends that this expression and other traditions Paul cites speak of abolishing the consequences of sin but not expiation (*Grace, Reconciliation, Concord*, 71).

35. Fitzmyer, *Romans*, 390. Breytenbach sees in this text, as he does in 1 Cor 15:3–5, a merging of Greek traditions of dying for others with a Jewish understanding of the consequences of sin (*Grace, Reconciliation, Concord*, 69). He argues this on the basis of the LXX translation of the Isaiah text from which the tradition drew its language (83–94).

36. Furnish maintains that of the four citations of this tradition in Paul, this is the only place Paul uses it to affirm the tradition's identification of Jesus's death as expiatory. On the other hand, he always uses it to speak of the "soteriological significance" of that death ("He Gave Himself," 120–21).

37. Martyn, *Theological Issues*, 141. He is commenting on Paul's citation of a tradition in Gal 2:16 when Martyn identifies the theme of justification as one that was accepted by all Jewish Christ-believers. See his discussion of evidence for this theme in the Jewish church's tradition and how justification could be understood within the context of Judaism (141–53).

38. Cf. Keck, who mentions this possibility (*Romans*, 132).

contribute directly to the church's distinctive understanding of God's identity as the one who raised Jesus (rather than, for example, the God of Abraham). Its mention of *dikaiōsis* ("justification") does, however, provide a verbal link to the beginning of the next paragraph.

Philippians 2:6-11

Philippians 2:6-11 is among the most widely recognized preformed sections in the New Testament. Its style is clearly elevated and it has multiple parallel clauses. As do many preformed pieces, it begins with "who" (*hos*) and a participle. It also clearly stands apart from the surrounding text as a separate unit. It is often called a hymn, even though it does not conform precisely to the structure of Greek hymns. Thus John Reumann suggests that it is better to call it an encomium.[39] Reinhard Deichgräber contends, however, that the plerophoric language points toward identifying it as a hymn.[40] This type of language is as much at home in an encomium as in a hymn, so this factor may not help us determine which is the better category. Whether it was "sung" in the early church is unclear, but its form does indicate that it was part of the church's liturgy, and its placement in Philippians shows that it was known by the recipients of that letter.

Against the standing consensus, some have argued that Paul was the author of this piece.[41] But its non-Pauline vocabulary weighs heavily in favor

---

39. John Reumann, *Philippians: A New Translation with Introduction and Commentary*, AB 33B (New Haven: Yale University Press, 2008), 361-62.

40. Reinhard Deichgräber, *Gotteshymnus und Christushymnus in der frühen Christenheit: Untersuchungen zur Form, Sprache und Stil der frühchristlichen Hymnen*, SUNT (Göttingen: Vandenhoeck & Ruprecht, 1967), 110-11.

41. For example, Gordon D. Fee, "Philippians 2:5-11: Hymn or Exalted Prose?" *BBR* 2 (1992): 29-46; Adela Yarbro Collins, "Psalms, Philippians 2:6-11, and the Origins of Christology," *BibInt* 11 (2003): 361-72. Joseph H. Hellerman does not present an argument against a pre-Pauline origin for the piece; he simply moves forward as though it is from Paul, arguing that Paul shaped it with his experience of suffering recorded in Acts 16 ("Vindicating God's Servants in Philippi and in Philippians: The Influence of Paul's Ministry in Philippi and upon the Composition of Philippians 2:6-11," *BBR* 20 [2010]: 85-102). Susan Eastman also seems to assume that Paul is the author of this poetic material ("Philippians 2:6-11: Incarnation as Mimetic Participation," *JSPHL* 1 [2011]: 1-22; see, e.g., 18n80). While Collins and Eastman are notable exceptions, Bonnie Thurston notes that this position is advocated largely by evangelicals (*Philippians and Philemon*, SP [Collegeville, MN: Liturgical Press, 2005], 86). Ben Witherington III is also an exception to that characterization. He attributes the aversion to seeing

"Christ Died for Us"

of non-Pauline authorship. In the space of just six verses the words *morphē* ("form"), *harpagmos* ("grasp"), *hyperypsoō* ("highly exalted"), and *katachthonios* ("under the earth") all appear. This is the only place in Paul that they appear and the only place in the New Testament that the last three appear.[42] Additionally *hypēkoos* ("obedient") appears only one other time in Paul, 2 Cor 2:9. Beyond this non-Pauline language, it is notable that the death of Christ leads to his exaltation rather than to his resurrection and return, as is usually the case in Paul.[43] Such considerations indicate that Paul is not the author of this liturgy.

Reumann suggests that the author is a member of the Philippian church. This is why the theology bears a resemblance to Paul's, but the language does not.[44] Few interpreters offer such a precise provenance for the piece, and its reference to exaltation rather than resurrection counts against it. The parallelism seen throughout indicates to many interpreters that the author was Semitic.[45] Ernst Lohmeyer goes so far as to identify it as a eucharistic liturgy of the Jerusalem church.[46] More cautiously, Markus Öhler identifies is as a pre-Pauline piece formed in the context of the Jewish wisdom tradition.[47]

Other interpreters see the liturgy as the product of the Hellenistic church. Ralph Martin concludes that the author was influenced by both the "Hebraic and Hellenistic thought-world."[48] It is more difficult to discern whether it comes from within the Pauline sphere of influence or is from an earlier time or from another segment of the church. Cynthia Kittredge insists that the

---

it as pre-Pauline to a fear that it has an Adamic Christology (*Paul's Letter to the Philippians: A Socio-Rhetorical Commentary* [Grand Rapids: Eerdmans, 2011], 132).

42. Charles B. Cousar finds this vocabulary evidence decisive (*Philippians and Philemon*, NTL [Louisville: Westminster John Knox, 2009], 52–53). See also the treatment of these terms in Witherington, *Philippians*, 140–42.

43. Cousar, *Philippians and Philemon*, 52–53.

44. Reumann, *Philippians*, 333, 361–62.

45. For example, Ernst Lohmeyer sees the phrase "being found as a human" as evidence of Semitism because of its unusual use of the participle and *hōs* (*Kyrios Jesus: Eine Untersuchung zu Phil. 2,5–11*, SHAW [Heidelberg: Winter, 1928], 39–40). See the summary of Lohmeyer's observations about Semitic elements in Ralph Martin, *Carmen Christi: Philippians ii. 5–11 in Recent Interpretation and in the Setting of Early Christianity*, rev. ed. (Grand Rapids: Eerdmans, 1983), 38–40. Witherington also recognizes the presence of these features (*Philippians*, 135).

46. Lohmeyer, *Kyrios Jesus*, 67.

47. Markus Öhler, "Bausteine aus frühchristlicher Theologie," in *Paulus Handbuch*, ed. Friedrich W. Horn (Tübingen: Mohr Siebeck, 2013), 499.

48. R. Martin, *Carmen Christi*, 297.

theology is different enough from Paul's that it is pre-Pauline (at least in the sense that it is not influenced by Paul) and had a functional life before its use in Philippians.[49]

Whatever its origins, Paul draws it into Philippians because he thinks the readers will accept it as support for the point he wants to make. He uses it to support his exhortation to unity and humility within the church. He does not draw out the theological points that have been the object of so much debate and discussion from the second century on. These theological assertions can, however, help us to see what Paul thought the church to which he was writing already believed about Jesus's death.

Verse 8 of this poetic liturgy focuses attention on Jesus's death as the central feature of his earthly life. No other element of his life or ministry receives mention. Granting the assertion of various interpreters that "even death on a cross" is a Pauline insertion[50] does not diminish the pivotal role this tradition gives to Jesus's death. Although the original setting may have dictated this emphasis (if it was developed for use at the Eucharist or baptism as some have thought), this liturgy still demonstrates how important this event was in the life and theology of the church that used it. One should also note that this piece associates Jesus's death and his exaltation (v. 9) through its use of Ps 110, the psalm quoted most often in the New Testament.[51]

This preformed text may go back to the Aramaic-speaking church. Ralph Martin notes that Lohmeyer argues on the basis of its language and style that it is the product of an author whose first language is Semitic (though Martin thinks it is the product of Hellenistic Christianity).[52] Following this lead, Fitzmyer has produced an Aramaic version of it.[53] If it has an Aramaic *Vorlage* or an author with Aramaic as his first language, this liturgy probably indicates that the earliest Jerusalem church had the death of Jesus as a central focus of

---

49. Cynthia Briggs Kittredge, *Community and Authority: The Rhetoric of Obedience in the Pauline Tradition*, HTS 45 (Harrisburg, PA: Trinity Press International, 1998), 75-77.

50. So, e.g., Ulrich B. Müller, *Der Brief des Paulus an die Philipper*, THKNT 11.1 (Leipzig: Evangelische Verlagsanstalt, 1993), 105; Deichgräber identifies this as the dominant view (*Gotteshymnus und Christushymnus*, 125). However, a number of recent commentators reject this, e.g., Thurston, *Philippians and Philemon*, 83; and Morna Hooker, "Philippians," *NIB* 11:509. Both see the mention of the cross as something of a climax for the first part of the piece.

51. See the work of David Hay on the importance of this psalm for the early church (*Glory at the Right Hand: Psalm 110 in Early Christianity*, SBLMS 18 [Nashville: Abingdon, 1973]).

52. R. Martin, *Carmen Christi*, 27-28.

53. Joseph A. Fitzmyer, "The Aramaic Background of Philippians 2:6-11," *CBQ* 50 (1988): 470-83.

"Christ Died for Us"

their understanding of Jesus. Others, however, think it was composed within Hellenistic Christianity[54] and draws on pagan or gnostic ideas. That it is an adaptation of an earlier hymn or was first composed from a gnostic outlook are the least likely options. As Morna Hooker comments, the idea that it has a gnostic origin "has almost nothing to be said for it."[55]

If those who argue that Paul composed this material for this letter are correct, then it shows us only Paul's teaching that he expects his church to affirm before the arrival of this letter. While this seems rather unlikely, it may be best, with Deichgräber, to acknowledge that we know too little about the early church to identify the original *Sitz im Leben* of this piece.[56] Its various parts seem to point to elements that many attribute to different specific groups within the early church. Perhaps this by itself should caution us about making those distinctions within the church too large and too firm. Since some argue that it was composed in a Pauline church, we must be careful not to give significant weight to it as we try to determine what beliefs were present in the church before Paul's influence. While this view is held by few, its possibility demands this caution. Still, we find no assertions about the death of Jesus here that do not appear in other more certainly non-Pauline traditions.

The citation of this liturgy does not advance an argument about Christology or the meaning of the death of Jesus. In the context of Philippians generally and of chapter 2 in particular, it grounds a central exhortation of the letter. The incarnation and death of Jesus provide the example of the way believers are to relate to one another. They are to adopt the pattern of life seen in Jesus; they are to put the good of others above their own good (2:3–5). Again, then, Paul does not argue for the meaning of the death of Jesus found here—he simply assumes that the Philippians already believe it.

Romans 8:32, 34

In Rom 8:32–34 Paul says that God gave his Son "for us" and raised him to God's right hand. A number of interpreters find at least fragments of liturgical or confession material in verses 32 and 34.[57] The language of *paradidōmi*

---

54. For example, Jean-François Collange, *The Epistle of Saint Paul to the Philippians*, trans. A. W. Heathcote (London: Epworth, 1979), 92.
55. Hooker, "Philippians," 501.
56. Deichgräber, *Gotteshymnus und Christushymnus*, 132.
57. For example, Hurtado, *Lord Jesus Christ*, 129; Hengel, *Studies in Early Christology*

("handed over") and *hyper* ("for") in verse 32 support this identification. Dunn comments that the use of *paradidōmi* echoes "a well-established Christian theological understanding of Christ's death."[58] Nonetheless, the extent of the quoted material is debated. Käsemann asserts that the phrase "handed him over for us all" is certainly a liturgical fragment,[59] but Jewett argues that Paul has added "for us all" out of his concern to include gentiles.[60] This concern for gentiles, however, really only applies to "all." Still, the decision about this could affect one's view of the piece's provenance. A number of interpreters also find an allusion to the Akedah in verse 32.[61]

Verse 34 certainly alludes to Ps 110. Conforming to this psalm, this is the only place where Paul uses the expression "right hand of God."[62] The verb *entynchanō* ("intercede") appears only three times in Paul, all in Romans (8:27, 34; 11:2). This is the only place in which Christ is the one interceding for others. Jewett sees the three parallel clauses that all begin with *hos* ("who") as good evidence that this is traditional material.

The short nature of the expressions Paul takes up here does not allow us to identify what part of the church produced these expressions. This passage does, however, demonstrate that believers other than Paul connected Christ's death and exaltation while maintaining a view of his death that makes it atoning. The possible reference to the Akedah and the certain allusion to Ps 110 point to believers who are familiar with Scripture and think it is important to understand Jesus's death through Scripture. This suggests that the formulators were Jewish. This may be particularly the case if Jewett is correct about the Pauline addition of "for us all." Whether Paul added it or not, Jewett may correctly discern that its intention is to include gentiles into the sphere of those for whom Christ's death is effective. If so, the formulation points to a time when gentiles are being brought into the church.

139–40; Neufeld, *Earliest Christian Confessions*, 45–47; Hay, *Glory at the Right Hand*, 59, 131; James D. G. Dunn, *Christology in the Making: A New Testament Inquiry into the Origins of the Doctrine of the Incarnation*, 2nd ed. (Grand Rapids: Eerdmans, 1989), 35; Fitzmyer, *Romans*, 532; Furnish, "He Gave Himself," 117–19.

58. Dunn, *Romans 1–8*, 497.
59. Käsemann, *Romans*, 247.
60. Jewett, *Romans*, 538.
61. For example, Moo, *Romans*, 540n18; Wright, "Romans," 610. Jewett, however, finds this unlikely because the evidence is insufficient to assert that the Akedah had been interpreted as an atoning event in the first century (*Romans*, 537).
62. We will discuss the significance of the citation of this psalm in ch. 3.

"Christ Died for Us"

2 Corinthians 5:21 and Galatians 3:13

Interpreters often find elements of an early confession in 2 Cor 5:21[63] and Gal 3:13.[64] These passages interpret the work of Jesus as an event that brings reconciliation with God by having Christ take up the sins of others. Though neither mentions the death of Jesus directly, it is undoubtedly in view. This is particularly clear in Galatians, where a reference to the crucifixion immediately follows. The death of Jesus is also an element of the context of 2 Cor 5. The material in 2 Cor 5:21 stands apart from its context and is self-contained. It provides support for the assertion that is really the point Paul is making. It uses the prepositional phrase *hyper hēmōn* ("for us"), which occurs in preformed material in Paul but seldom outside it in this kind of context. Further, while Paul often uses the expression "the righteousness of God," only here is it seen as a characteristic that believers possess. So it stands out as an uncharacteristic usage.[65] If, as many think, the phrase "made to be sin for us" is drawn from Isaiah's Suffering Servant sayings (ch. 53), it is also evidence that Paul is not the original composer of this interpretation of Christ's work because he never cites this motif except in quotations of traditional material.[66]

In his discussion of Gal 3:13, Hans Dieter Betz sees Christ becoming a curse "for us" as comparable to Christ becoming "sin for us" in 2 Cor 5:21. He asserts that these ideas go back to pre-Pauline Jewish Christianity. He contends that the church drew on ideas of sacrificial and meritorious death that already existed within Judaism as it tried to understand Jesus's death. When Paul uses it in this context, Betz comments, he may be the only one that understands the vicarious death of Jesus also to mean the end of the

---

63. Dunn (*Christology in the Making*, 121), Victor P. Furnish (*II Corinthians*, AB 32A [Garden City, NY: Doubleday, 1984], 340), and Ralph Martin (*2 Corinthians*, WBC 40 [Waco: Word, 1986], 156–57) assert that Paul is quoting traditional material here. Among the reasons for seeing a citation of traditional material are the use of *hyper* in the expression "for us" and its unusual use of *hamartia*, which may include punishment here.

64. Dunn (*Christology*, 121) and Hans Dieter Betz (*Galatians: A Commentary on Paul's Letter to the Churches in Galatia*, Hermeneia [Philadelphia: Fortress, 1979], 150–51) see traditional material in this verse.

65. R. Martin also argues that it runs against Paul's anthropology (*2 Corinthians*, 140).

66. R. Martin, *2 Corinthians* 140, citing R. H. Fuller, *The Mission and Achievement of Jesus*, SBT 1/12 (London: SCM, 1954), 57. Martin finds much more of 2 Cor 5:18–21 to be drawn from preformed material (138–41). Frank Matera also raises a similar possibility, commenting that the *hōs hoti* ("as that") may serve to introduce the known traditional formula (*II Corinthians: A Commentary*, NTL [Louisville: Westminster John Knox, 2003], 140).

law.⁶⁷ Betz argues that the sinless nature of Christ's sacrifice made it "uniquely meritorious" within the thought of Judaism.⁶⁸ While this generalization about Judaism is too broad, it may well substantially capture the thought of early believers in Christ who were influenced by both the sacrificial system in Jerusalem and martyrdom traditions within Judaism.

The formulation in 2 Cor 5:21 indicates that the earliest believers gave significant attention to interpreting the death of Jesus. We cannot locate the origin of its formulation with certainty, though. It does belong within a community that knows Isaiah and gives attention to Scripture. This points to a segment of the church that is predominantly Jewish.

Romans 14:9 and 1 Thessalonians 4:14

In chapter 5 we will see that Rom 14:9 contains a tradition. Similarly, in chapter 4 we will show that 1 Thess 4:14 also incorporates preformed material. Here we will note that both refer to the death and resurrection of Christ to focus attention on the parousia. In the former, Paul establishes Christ's place as judge of all; in the latter, he assures the readers that the deceased will participate in the resurrection through their association with Christ. These Pauline interpretations seem to rest on a known tradition that assigns Jesus's death an eschatological meaning by associating it with his resurrection. We will return to this meaning of Jesus's death in chapter 5.

Other Possible Citations

A number of other passages contain what many interpreters think are fragments of formulaic traditions that refer to Jesus's death. These do not meet enough criteria to admit them as good evidence for what the church outside the Pauline sphere believed. Still, these possible citations are worthy of attention.

---

67. H. Betz, *Galatians*, 151. He also identifies Gal 3:13 as a place where Paul draws on traditional material. But the evidence for identifying it as preformed is not strong enough for us to be certain. While it has the noun *katara* ("curse") that appears only here and in 3:10 (where it may appear by attraction) and the prepositional phrase "for us" with *hyper*, these two indicators are not sufficient to identify it with certainty as a traditional formulation.

68. H. Betz, *Galatians*, 151.

Romans 6:3[69] and 1 Cor 6:11[70] may cite traditions that relate the death of Jesus to baptism.[71] Paul even introduces the Rom 6 citation with what some see as a recitative *hoti*.[72] The preceding phrase, "don't you know," may also indicate that Paul is about to cite a known formula.[73] The use of *apolyō* ("wash") in 1 Cor 6:11 is a hapax legomenon in Paul, and it appears only one other time in the New Testament (Acts 22:16), where it also refers to baptism. Its use in the passive suggests to many interpreters that it is already technical language for baptism.[74] Since Paul does not use this metaphor to describe the effects of baptism elsewhere, it seems likely that he is not the originator of this interpretation. Raymond Collins notes that in addition to the singular use of "washed," the phrase "our Lord Jesus Christ" is another traditional phrase.[75] (We will give attention to the development of such identifications of Jesus in ch. 3.) The verb *hagiazō* ("to make holy") is also relatively rare in Paul. As often as he uses the cognate noun "saints" to describe believers (at least twenty-three times), he uses the verb only six times. It is related directly to baptism only in 1 Cor 6:11. So this is an unusual use for Paul, especially when compared to its two uses in 1 Cor 7:14, where an unbeliever is made holy through association with a believing spouse. There is then significant, but not decisive, evidence that Paul is citing or alluding to preformed tradition in Rom 6:3 and 1 Cor 6:11. If he is

---

69. So Moo, *The Epistle to the Romans*, 359; Keck, *Romans*, 158; Cranfield, *Romans*, 1:300; John A. Ziesler, *Paul's Letter to the Romans*, TPINTC (Philadelphia: Trinity Press International, 1989), 156.

70. So Hans Conzelmann, *1 Corinthians: A Commentary on the First Epistle to the Corinthians*, trans. James W. Leitch, Hermeneia (Philadelphia: Fortress, 1975), 107; Raymond F. Collins, *First Corinthians*, SP (Collegeville, MN: Liturgical Press, 1999), 237-38.

71. Lars Hartman (*"Into the Name of the Lord Jesus": Baptism in the Early Church*, SNTW [Edinburgh: T. & T. Clark, 1997], 71) and David Hellholm ("The Impact of the Situational Contexts for Paul's Use of Baptismal Traditions in His Letters," in *Neotestamentica et Philonica: Studies in Honor of Peder Borgen*, ed. David E. Aune, Torrey Seland, and Jarl H. Ulrichsen, NovTSup 106 [Leiden: Brill, 2003], 155-59) find a tradition in these passages. First Corinthians 6:11 is one of the passages J. Louis Martyn cites as evidence that Jewish Christianity developed the theme of justification before Paul took it up (*Theological Issues in the Letters of Paul*, 143).

72. Robert Jewett, however, sees this *hoti* as an element of the style of diatribe rather than as recitative (*Romans*, 396).

73. Ziesler notes that Paul uses similar expressions to introduce traditional material (*Romans*, 156). Keck comments that this introductory expression shows that Paul can assume that his understanding of being baptized "into Christ" is shared by believers he had not taught (*Romans*, 158-59). Similarly, Cranfield, *Romans*, 1:300; Dunn, *Romans 1-8*, 312.

74. Conzelmann, *1 Corinthians*, 107, who is following Joseph Ysebaert, *Greek Baptismal Terminology* (Nijmegen: Dekker & Van de Vegt, 1962), 6.

75. R. Collins, *First Corinthians*, 237-38.

citing traditional material in either passage, it indicates a pre-Pauline (or at least non-Pauline) view of baptism understood as a rite that incorporated the baptized into the death of Christ. Furthermore, this interpretation of baptism assumes that Jesus's death is "for us" and has a salvific effect.

Second Corinthians 1:7b also may contain an early tradition.[76] Paul introduces his statement about the Corinthians being sharers in his difficulties and in his comfort with "knowing that."[77] If it is a preformed tradition, this passage indicates that the church had begun to interpret the difficulties its members endured because of their new faith as an identification with the death of Jesus. This might suggest that even the thoroughly Pauline theme of suffering as part of identification with Christ has a significant predecessor in the tradition rather than being uniquely or originally Paul's idea.

Interpreters commonly see Rom 5:8; 14:15; 1 Cor 8:11; 2 Cor 5:14; and 1 Thess 5:9-10 as passages that contain citations of preformed confessional declarations or that draw on formulaic language.[78] They all contain statements about Christ's death for others using a form of *apothnēskō* ("die"; three of them in the aorist third person singular) with *hyper* ("for").[79] In all three the subject

---

76. So E. Earle Ellis, "Preformed Traditions and Their Implications for Pauline Christology," in *Christology, Controversy and Community: New Testament Essays in Honour of David R. Catchpole*, ed. David G. Horrell and Christopher M. Tuckett, NovTSup 99 (Leiden: Brill, 2000), 309. Seeing a citation of a tradition here, Victor P. Furnish comments that discussion of the "travail of the Messiah" was a "concept in the earliest church" (*II Corinthians*, 119-21).

77. Ellis gives this passage as his example of such phrases introducing a tradition ("Preformed Traditions," 309).

78. See Jewett, *Romans*, 361-62. Others who identify the material in these passages as traditional include: for Rom 5:8, Victor P. Furnish, *Jesus according to Paul*, Understanding Jesus Today (Cambridge: Cambridge University Press, 1993), 12-13; Käsemann, *Romans*, 137-38; for 14:15, Käsemann, *Romans*, 376; for 1 Cor 8:11, Anders Eriksson, *Traditions as Rhetorical Proof: Pauline Argumentation in 1 Corinthians*, ConBNT 29 (Stockholm: Alqvist & Wiksell, 1998), 159-66; for 2 Cor 5:14, Furnish, *Jesus according to Paul*, 12-13, 34-35; Ralph P. Martin, *2 Corinthians*, WBC 40 (Waco: Word, 1986), 130-31 (where he ties this formulation to a baptismal liturgy); for 1 Thess 5:9-10, Ernest Best, *A Commentary on the First and Second Epistles to the Thessalonians*, BNTC (London: Black, 1972), 218. While rejecting the idea that v. 9 draws on a baptism liturgy, Abraham J. Malherbe acknowledges that the "for us" participial phrase draws on "the earliest strata of Christian tradition" (*The Letters to the Thessalonians: A New Translation with Introduction and Commentary*, AB 32B [New York: Doubleday, 2000], 298-99). Henk de Jonge, however, lists 1 Thess 5:10 as one of the sure places that Paul is citing the pre-Pauline dying formula ("The Original Setting of the *Christos apethanen hyper* Formula," in *The Thessalonian Correspondence*, ed. Raymond F. Collins, BETL 87 [Leuven: Leuven University Press, 1990], 235).

79. Raymond Collins says that the use of "for us" in 1 Thess 5:10 is "[t]he first time that Jesus' death is interpreted soteriologically in Christian literature" ("Paul's Early Christology," in *Studies on the First Letter to the Thessalonians*, BETL 66 [Leuven: Leuven University Press, 1984], 263).

"Christ Died for Us"

of the verb is the name Christ. These citations seem to be abbreviated versions of the same tradition Paul quotes in 1 Cor 15:3–5. The multiple places this form of the phrase appears supports the idea that it is a known formulation. While the citation is too brief in the passages outside 1 Cor 15 to speculate about a provenance, its presence in three letters suggests that the formula was used widely. This is particularly the case for the Romans occurrences because this is a church in which Paul has not taught, yet he seems to expect them to recognize the allusion.[80] Robert Jewett agrees with Karl Kertelge's assessment that the repeated appearance of this formula shows that on this point there was "broad terminological and substantial agreement between Paul and pre-Pauline traditions in interpreting Jesus's death."[81] Even while the multiple appearances of the formula suggest that this is a set expression, its appearance in these verses fulfills fewer of our criteria for identifying traditional material than any other passages we have admitted as evidence. Fortunately, they contribute nothing distinctive beyond providing more examples of the church seeing the death of Jesus as benefiting others.

Finally, "Christ crucified" or "Jesus Christ crucified" may be a preformed encapsulation of the gospel that Paul takes up from the early church.[82] Paul uses the verb *stauroō* ("crucify") only eight times. Three of those (1 Cor 1:23; 2:2; Gal 3:1) seem to reflect this set confession. Galatians 3:1 identifies "Jesus Christ crucified" as a core element in the initial proclamation of the gospel. Other instances of the verb assume familiarity with this motif, and some assume that the crucifixion has become a pattern for understanding existence as a believer (2 Cor 13:4; Gal 5:24; 6:14). If this is a pre-Pauline formula, its form may suggest that it arose as the earliest believers had to make sense of the very paradox to which this formula gives expression: a crucified messiah. At the same time that it makes this seemingly absurd claim, it identifies that messiah as Jesus. Believers would have formulated this statement in a context

---

80. Again, this consideration may be less important if Francis Watson is correct in asserting that the Roman congregation is already a Pauline church, even though Paul had not been there. See his *Paul, Judaism, and the Gentiles: Beyond the New Perspective*, rev. ed. (Grand Rapids: Eerdmans, 2007).

81. Jewett, *Romans*, 362, citing Karl Kertelge, "Das Verständnis des Todes Jesu bei Paulus," in *Der Tod Jesu: Deutungen im Neuen Testament*, ed. Karl Kertelge, QD 74 (Freiburg: Herder, 1976), 123–24.

82. Furnish finds Paul's use of the phrase in 1 Cor 2:2 and Gal 3:1 to be uses of a tradition (*Jesus according to Paul*, 24). Hans Dieter Betz calls "Jesus Christ crucified" an "abbreviated form of the 'kerygma' " and notes the parallels in 1 Cor 1:23 and 2:2 (*Galatians*, 132n40). Other passages he seems to think make use of this tradition include 1 Cor 1:13, 17, 18; 2:8; 2 Cor 13:4; Gal 5:11, 24; 6:12, 14, 17; Phil 2:8; 3:18.

where other interpretations of Jesus's death were more common.[83] Thus if it is a previously formed proclamation, it may take us to the earliest times after Jesus's death as those who experienced the resurrection brought the paradox of their faith to expression.

If "Christ crucified" is a formulation that Paul adopts, such a shorthand of the kerygma assumes that this event is a focal point of the church's message. If the inclusion of the name Jesus suggests that this formulation developed in Palestine, it provides further evidence of the importance they give that form of death in their interpretation of Jesus. This is particularly significant because many New Testament interpreters think of Paul as the one who introduced "cross" language into the church. If "Christ crucified" is a preformed confession, then Paul would be dependent on the tradition for even this expression of the faith. But if Paul formulated this expression, it shows only that his churches know it as the core of his preaching.

Conclusion

Our examination of citations and allusions to traditions Paul cites offers no evidence that there were branches of the church that did not give a central place to interpreting the death of Jesus. On the contrary, they indicate that the church developed clear lines of interpretation of Jesus's death in its earliest days. Paul's citation in 1 Cor 15:3-5 shows that the Jerusalem church made Jesus's death a prominent feature of its message and saw that death as in some way vicarious.[84] Breytenbach argues that this and other traditions about Jesus's death do not give it an expiatory meaning. He argues this because he understands that meaning to suggest that God had to be appeased. He instead contends that these texts assert that Jesus's death abolishes the consequences of sin.[85] If expiation necessarily includes appeasement, Breytenbach seems correct. Given the common inclusion of appeasement in expiation, it may be better to speak of the death of Jesus as vicarious when we speak of it as the means by which sin and its consequences are dealt with.

The assertions about Jesus's death in the tradition in 1 Cor 15:3-5 seem

---

83. Ernst Käsemann (*Perspectives on Paul*, trans. Margaret Kohl [Philadelphia: Fortress, 1969], 35) describes a "theology of the cross" as a necessarily polemical formulation.

84. Henk J. de Jonge comments that it is the consensus of studies of the use of formulae that the phrase "Christ died for us" is pre-Pauline and that it grew out of Jewish martyr theology ("The Original Setting of the *Christos apethanen hyper* Formula," 230-31.

85. Breytenbach, *Grace, Reconciliation, Concord*, 66-72.

to have emerged in the face of alternative interpretations of that death and in conjunction with the claim that Jesus was the Messiah. It also indicates that these ideas were developed through the church's interpretation of Scripture. If Paul is being honest about his reception of this tradition, then it was formulated within the very first years of the church's existence.

The tradition Paul cites in Rom 3:25–26 provides clear evidence that the death of Jesus was central in the pre-Pauline church. When this tradition interprets Jesus's death as a *hilastērion* ("place of atonement" or "mercy seat"), it clearly points to Jewish believers because of the way this term is used in the Septuagint for the lid of the ark of the covenant. Whether from Palestine or Syria, it comes from a community in which temple imagery is meaningful. Further, if part of the tradition's function is to explain the admission of gentiles (though this remains less secure), then it may have been formulated within months of their entering the church. That would imply that this image and this formulation make their way into the church within two or three years of its founding.

Even the liturgical material of Phil 2 provides evidence of the pivotal role of Jesus's death in the thought of the early church. In a recitation of the exalted place of Jesus before the incarnation and after his resurrection, the only part of his ministry that receives mention is his death. But since it is possible, though it does not seem probable, that this liturgy was composed within the Pauline sphere, we will not consider its evidence about the church outside Paul's influence as certain. In what it says about the death of Jesus, however, it adds nothing that we have not seen in traditions that more certainly developed outside Paul's influence.

The allusions to Isa 53 in the tradition Paul cites in Rom 4:25 confirm what we saw in 1 Cor 15, that at least some who made Jesus's death a central element of their interpretation of him were also among those who gave extended attention to understanding him through Scripture. Indeed, Scripture (at least as remembered by the disciples) may have been one of the most important resources for the earliest church as it came to terms with the death of Jesus.

We have seen that some traditions Paul cites about Jesus's death as a sacrifice fit well within Jewish thought of the time. The hypothesis that the church had to move out of Palestine or beyond Jewish thought to Hellenistic thought before such understandings of Jesus's death were possible finds no support in the evidence. Just the opposite: some of the church's interpretations of Jesus's death grow out of ideas associated with the temple. The possibility that such ideas were enabled by martyrdom theologies seems likely. And while the evidence of 4 Maccabees for the interpretations of martyrs' deaths is direct evidence only for Hellenistic Judaism, it seems unlikely that those ideas had no currency in the Palestine of Roman occupation.[86] While it is clear that the death of Jesus was interpreted as an event that deals with sin, the language of forgiveness is not used. As Breytenbach observes, the noun *aphesis* ("forgive") does not appear in the undisputed Paulines.[87] Furthermore, the cognate verb *aphiēmi* appears only five times, and only in Rom 4:7 where Paul is citing Ps 32:1 does it mean "forgive." What has now become a dominant metaphor for the meaning of Jesus's death, then, was not central in the tradition Paul cites or in his thought.[88]

It may be important to observe that many of Paul's citations of traditions about Jesus's death appear in Romans. Here he is writing to a church he did not found and had never visited. His citations serve to ground the content of his message that goes to a church that has less reason to trust him than his own churches have.[89] If the members of this church do recognize these allusions and citations, which Paul's use of them assumes, they are evidence that this emphasis on, and these interpretations of, Jesus's death are widespread, if not universal, within the church. If they are not so widespread or well known, Paul thinks they are; and so he thinks he stands well within the church's tradition on this matter. The traditions Paul cites suggest that there existed a broad agreement about the centrality of, and the vicarious and salvific effect of, Jesus's death. It seems to be Paul's expectation that all who identify themselves with the church agree about this matter, at least in these general ways.

---

86. See Breytenbach's discussion of the Greek ideas of dying for others being present in Hellenistic Judaism (*Grace, Reconciliation, Concord*, 115–19).

87. Breytenbach, *Grace, Reconciliation, Concord*, 63. Breytenbach also suggests that Rom 4:7 is part of a tradition Paul is citing (64).

88. Breytenbach notes that forgiveness language is prominent in the Gospel's presentation of the teaching of Jesus (*Grace, Reconciliation, Concord*, 63).

89. Even if, as Francis Watson proposes, we should consider the Roman church a Pauline church, they still may need assurances about his grounding in the tradition they received from his emissaries (*Paul, Judaism, and the Gentiles*).

CHAPTER 3

"Jesus Is Lord"
The Identity of Jesus

Those who claim that Paul invented Christianity often point to the Christology of his letters for evidence. They name Paul as the person who introduced ideas about divine sonship, about Jesus as exalted Lord, and about Christ's descent from heaven. Thus they contend that Paul turned the human Jesus into a divine being. In this chapter we will explore texts that contain non-Pauline or pre-Pauline formulae involving exalted claims about Christ.

Before turning directly to christological traditions, we should note that Paul draws on preformed traditions when affirming the central theological tenet of both Judaism and the earliest church: belief in the oneness of God. Vernon Neufeld identifies the "God is one" formula that appears in Rom 3:30; Gal 3:20; 1 Cor 8:4; and Eph 4:6 as a preformed tradition.[1] Its appearance in so many places and its clear reliance on the Shema indicate that it is a known formula.[2] Some also identify the doxology of Rom 11:36 as dependent upon a preformed hymn because of its style and the absence of beliefs held only by the church (once the citations have been deleted).[3]

---

1. Vernon H. Neufeld, *The Earliest Christian Confessions*, NTTS 5 (Grand Rapids: Eerdmans, 1963), 44-45.

2. Richard Bauckham also notes that Rom 3:30 is an allusion to the Shema (*Jesus and the God of Israel* [Grand Rapids: Eerdmans, 2008], 95).

3. See Robert Jewett, *Romans: A Commentary*, Hermeneia (Philadelphia: Fortress, 2007), 713-14.

Romans 8:11; 4:24; 10:9; Galatians 1:1; and 1 Thessalonians 1:10

Another early tradition identifies God as the one who raised Christ from the dead. While it appears with variations, the original form seems to have used *theos* ("God") as the subject or used a pronoun or an articular participle without an explicit subject. Each appearance of the formula uses the verb *egeirō* ("awaken, raise") in the aorist, then a reference to Jesus in the accusative, and the anarthrous prepositional phrase "from the dead" (*ek nekrōn*).[4] Variations of this formula appear in Rom 8:11a, b; 4:24; 10:9; Gal 1:1; 1 Thess 1:10; Eph 1:20; Col 2:12; Acts 3:15; 4:10; 13:30; 1 Pet 1:21; Ign. *Trall.* 9.2; Pol. *Phil.* 2.1; 12.2 (*egeirō* is in the passive in Rom 6:4).[5] Werner Kramer argues that Rom 8:11; 10:9; and Gal 1:1 are part of a *pistis* formula, as Rom 10:9 demonstrates with its use of *homologeō* ("confess").[6] In 2 Cor 4:14, "the one who raised the Lord Jesus" follows the widely used introductory formula, "knowing that."[7] Paul uses the formula here to support his assertion that God will vindicate the faithful through resurrection with Jesus.[8] He assumes that the Corinthians know and

---

4. Jewett, *Romans*, 477. Klaus Wengst describes the formula he finds in Rom 8:11; Gal 1:1; and 2 Cor 4:14 more simply, seeing it as an affirmative declaration and a predication in participial form with God as subject, Jesus as object of the act, *egeirō* in the aorist, and the phrase "from the dead" (*Christologische Formeln und Lieder des Urchristentums*, SNT 7 [Gütersloh: Gütersloher Verlagshaus, 1972], 32).

5. So Jewett, *Romans*, 477. James Dunn identifies "God raised him from the dead" as one of the five types of formulae that appear in Paul's letters. He finds this formula in Rom 4:24–25; 7:4; 8:11; 10:9; 1 Cor 6:14; 15:4, 12, 20; 2 Cor 4:14; Gal 1:1; 1 Thess 1:10 (*The Theology of Paul the Apostle* [Grand Rapids: Eerdmans, 1998], 175). Wesley Hill identifies Rom 4:24; 8:11a, b; and Gal 1:1 as citations of traditions and comments that this gives them importance in "Pauline discourse" (*Paul and the Trinity: Persons, Relations, and the Pauline Letters* [Grand Rapids: Eerdmans, 2015], 52–53).

6. Werner Kramer, *Christ, Lord, Son of God*, trans. Brian Hardy, SBT 1/50 (London: SCM, 1966), 22. Martin Hengel also identifies Rom 4:25 as a confessional formula ("Confessing and Confession," in *Earliest Christian History: History, Literature, and Theology: Essays from the Tyndale Fellowship in Honor of Martin Hengel*, ed. Michael F. Bird and Jason S. Maston, WUNT 2/320 [Tübingen: Mohr Siebeck, 2012], 612).

7. Rudolf Bultmann, *Theology of the New Testament*, trans. Kendrick Grobel, 2 vols. (New York: Scribner's Sons, 1951–1955), 1:122; Victor P. Furnish, *II Corinthians*, AB 32A (Garden City, NY: Doubleday, 1984), 258; Margaret E. Thrall, *A Critical and Exegetical Commentary on the Second Epistle to the Corinthians*, ICC (Edinburgh: T. & T. Clark, 1994–2000), 1:342n1055. Furnish comments that *eidotes hoti* "frequently introduces a formulation that a writer may presume to be familiar to his readers" (*II Corinthians*, 258). Paul Barnett lists 2 Cor 1:7; 5:6; 1 Cor 15:58; Gal 2:16; Jas 3:1; and 1 Pet 1:18 as examples of its use (*The Second Epistle to the Corinthians*, NICNT [Grand Rapids: Eerdmans, 1997], 242n17). See the further argument for identifying material in 2 Cor 4:14 as tradition in ch. 5 below.

8. Ralph P. Martin, *2 Corinthians*, WBC 40 (Waco: Word, 1986), 89.

accept the tradition because it is the grounds he gives for his willingness to accept weakness for the good of his churches.

The earliest forms of this tradition probably named Jesus as the object of God's act (as in Rom 8:11a),[9] but soon the titles *Christ* and *Lord* were added or used as alternatives (as in 2 Cor 4:14 and Rom 8:11b, respectively). Markus Öhler identifies this formula as the essential confession of earliest church preaching because there would have been no continuation of the movement without belief in Jesus's resurrection.[10] Furthermore, C. E. B. Cranfield observes that its use of a title to describe God in relation to God's mighty works is a characteristic of Jewish prayers and hymns that the church adopted in its earliest days.[11] These factors indicate that this tradition originated in the earliest Palestinian churches. It is no surprise, then, that Paul could expect the Roman church to recognize it.

One of the most ubiquitous titles for Jesus in Paul's letters is *Christ*. It appears so often that some have proposed that it functions as a name rather than a title among the members of Paul's churches.[12] This title and understanding of Jesus come from a time before Paul joined the church. Neufeld notes that it

---

9. Wengst envisions two forms for this tradition, one that uses the noun *theos* as the subject and one that has only the participial form of *egeirō* (*Christologische Formeln*, 33).

10. Markus Öhler, "Bausteine aus frühchristlicher Theologie," in *Paulus Handbuch*, ed. Friedrich W. Horn (Tübingen: Mohr Siebeck, 2013), 499. So also Brendan Byrne, *Romans*, SP (Collegeville, MN: Liturgical Press, 1996), 61.

11. C. E. B. Cranfield says, "the use of titles describing God by reference to His mighty works or His attributes are both characteristics of Jewish and early Christian prayer and hymnody" (*A Critical and Exegetical Commentary on the Epistle to the Romans*, 2 vols., ICC [Edinburgh: T. & T. Clark, 1975–1979], 1:390–91). Bauckham describes this text as a Jewish description of God's unique relationship to the cosmos (*Jesus and the God of Israel*, 103). The passive form of this tradition ("died and was raised") appears in 2 Cor 5:15. It may be a development from the form that names God as the subject or it may have arisen simultaneously as a response to the belief in the resurrection. Neufeld also identifies the proclamation of Jesus as Messiah as the earliest kerygma (*Earliest Christian Confessions*, 23). Traugott Holtz contends that Jesus had understood his mission as messianic, so that this understanding goes back to Jesus himself ("Das Alte Testament und das Bekenntnis der frühen Gemeinde zu Jesus Christus," in *Christus Bezeugen: Festschrift für Wolfgang Trilling zum 65. Geburtstag*, ed. Karl Kertelge, Traugott Holtz, and Claus-Peter März, ETS 59 [Leipzig: St. Benno, 1988], 56).

12. For example, Kramer, *Christ, Lord, Son of God*, 67. James Dunn asserts that Christ has become a name in Paul ("How Controversial Was Paul's Christology?" in *From Jesus to John: Essays on Jesus and New Testament Christology in Honour of Marinus de Jonge*, ed. Martinus C. de Boer, JSNTSup 84 [Sheffield: JSOT Press, 1993], 151). Similarly, Joseph A. Fitzmyer, "The Christology of the Epistle to the Romans," in *The Future of Christology: Essays in Honor of Leander E. Keck*, ed. Abraham J. Malherbe and Wayne A. Meeks (Minneapolis: Fortress, 1993), 83.

is the basic confession about the identity of Jesus in the Johannine literature and in Acts, where it appears only in Jewish contexts.[13] He identifies it as the earliest kerygma.[14] The absence of any defense of its use indicates that Paul thinks the claim that Jesus is Christ is a given in the church.[15] If the comment in Acts 11:26 preserves a historically accurate impression, it shows that *Christ* was a dominant title for Jesus in the Antioch church.[16] As we will see below, the title *Christ* appears in conjunction with other titles in traditional material.

Romans 4:24

Romans 4:24 may allow us to see another development through the "God raised Jesus" tradition with its use of the title *Lord*. This verse speaks of "those who believe in the one who raised Jesus our Lord." The confession of Jesus as Lord is another of the church's earliest confessions.[17] It appears in multiple sources (Rom 10:9; 1 Cor 12:3; Phil 2:11; Acts 5:14) and in Rom 10:9 is introduced with a form of *homologeō* ("to confess" or "to believe").[18] In Rom 4:24 it follows a form of *pisteuō* ("to believe"), and the phrase's subject, God, is named with a substantive participle. So it seems at least to echo the traditional formula we have already seen used. Paul uses the phrase to identify God in his discussion of the relationship between Abraham's faith and that of believers in Christ. He does not argue for this understanding of God; he assumes that

---

13. Neufeld, *Earliest Christian Confessions*, 105, 120, 122–23.
14. Neufeld, *Earliest Christian Confessions*, 123. Robin Scroggs asserts that "Christ" was one of the titles for Jesus used in the Palestinian church (*The People's Jesus: Trajectories in Early Christianity* [Minneapolis: Fortress, 2001], 80). See also Karl Kertelge, "Jesus Christus verkündigen als den Herren (2 Kor 4,5)," in *Christus Bezeugen*, ed. Kertelge, Holtz, and März, 233.
15. So Dunn, "How Controversial Was Paul's Christology?" 151–52.
16. Öhler is among recent interpreters to accept this testimony ("Bausteine aus frühchristlicher Theologie," 501). He also argues that "in Christ" language is pre-Pauline and may have been in use in Antioch (503–4).
17. So also Neufeld, *Earliest Christian Confessions*, 43–45; Bultmann, *Theology*, 1:293; Oscar Cullmann, *The Earliest Christian Confessions*, trans. J. K. S. Reid (London: Lutterworth, 1949), 28; Byrne, *Romans*, 321–22; Cranfield, *Romans*, 2:527; John Ziesler, *Paul's Letter to the Romans*, TPINTC (Philadelphia: Trinity Press International, 1989), 262. Dunn identifies this statement as one of the five basic confessional formulae of the early church (*Theology of Paul*, 175).
18. Wengst cites Rom 10:9 as an example of the way Paul cites tradition because it has authoritative force (*Christologische Formeln*, 28). So also Michael Theobald, "Die Briefe des Paulus: Römerbrief: Literarische Kennzeichen des Schreibens," in *Paulus Handbuch*, ed. Horn, 220–21.

this church accepts it and that it will not detract his audience from his larger argument about faith and the law.

Romans 10:9

Reinhard Deichgräber identifies the brief "Jesus is Lord" that appears in Rom 10:9 as an Ur-formula from the resurrection witnesses.[19] Somewhat similarly, Oscar Cullmann identifies it as the basic confession of the church that was in general liturgical use before the time of Paul.[20] At the same time he notes that it was not the earliest understanding of Jesus, but was the idea that gave coherence to other claims about him.[21] It seems correct that proclamation of the resurrection preceded and served as the grounds for the acclamation of Jesus as Lord.[22] Still the assignment of the title *Lord* to Jesus comes from the Aramaic-speaking church, as the expression *Maranatha* (1 Cor 16:22) demonstrates.[23] Ferdinand Hahn argues further that the use of "Lord" to refer to the arriving groom in the parable of the ten maids shows that this title was in use in the Aramaic church because this parable depends on Palestinian wedding customs.[24] Thus both the confession of the resurrection and that of identify-

---

19. Reinhard Deichgräber, *Gotteshymnus und Christushymnus in der frühen Christenheit: Untersuchungen zur Form, Sprache und Stil der frühchristlichen Hymnen*, SUNT (Göttingen: Vandenhoeck & Ruprecht, 1967), 112.

20. Oscar Cullmann, *The Christology of the New Testament*, trans. Shirley C. Guthrie and Charles A. M. Hall, NTL (Philadelphia: Westminster, 1959), 216-17.

21. Cullmann, *Christology*, 236.

22. Neufeld, *Earliest Christian Confessions*, 67; David du Toit, "Theologische Themen: Christologische Hoheitstitel," in *Paulus Handbuch*, ed. Horn, 297.

23. While Reginald Fuller contends that calling Jesus "Lord" could not develop in the Aramaic-speaking church because they could not call Jesus *YHWH-kyrios* (*The Foundations of New Testament Christology* [New York: Scribner's Sons, 1965], 186), the evidence of the *Maranatha* formula shows otherwise. Larry W. Hurtado also argues that this confession originated in the earliest Jerusalem church (*Lord Jesus Christ: Devotion to Jesus in Earliest Christianity* [Grand Rapids: Eerdmans, 2003], 197-200). Hengel even argues that "Jesus is Lord" and the *Maranatha* call were used before the formulation of the "God raised Jesus" confession ("Confessing and Confession," 608).

24. Ferdinand Hahn, *The Titles of Jesus in Christology: Their History in Early Christianity*, trans. Harold Knight and George Ogg (New York: World, 1969), 91-92. While it is possible that the title could have been added to the telling as the parable moved into the Greek-speaking world, the combination of the Palestinian customs in the parable and the independent evidence of the use of "Lord" in Aramaic with its eschatological connections make it more probable that the title was used in early Aramaic versions of the parable.

ing Jesus as Lord come from the earliest church, a time before Paul joined the movement.

This acclamation of Jesus as Lord could have a range of meanings. Even during Jesus's lifetime some may have referred to him as "lord" to designate him as their master or teacher.[25] But following the experience of the resurrection, it took on new meanings that extended from identifying Jesus as the one who is God's agent of the eschaton to one who serves as a viceroy of God, and perhaps to identification of Jesus with the LORD, the God of Israel. The earliest acclamation of the lordship of Jesus in the Palestinian church was probably related to his resurrection and the expectation of his return.[26] Whether the *Maranatha* call was related to a communal meal or was a plea for the return of Jesus,[27] there is an eschatological element in its use. These elements of the church's affirmations assume he is at least an agent in God's eschatological plan and almost certainly accord him an exalted position.[28] The ubiquity of references to Ps 110:1 (109:1 LXX) to describe the position of Jesus shows this to be the case.

Psalm 110 is quoted or alluded to more frequently in the New Testament than any other passage of the Hebrew Bible.[29] The more than twenty citations

---

25. So Hahn, *Titles of Jesus*, 102.

26. Neufeld asserts that the church proclaimed Jesus as Lord because he was resurrected (*Earliest Christian Confessions*, 67). So also Hahn, *Titles of Jesus*, 102. Wengst, however, rejects this broad consensus. He argues that since the acclamation of Jesus as Lord includes the idea that he is over the powers, it must come from the Hellenistic church (*Christologische Formeln*, 133). The more likely explanation of its use to refer to Christ's position of power over the powers is that it is a new explication of that earlier acclamation. The use of Aramaic in the formula makes it more probable that the movement is from the Aramaic church to other uses rather than that a Greek-speaking church was the origin of the Aramaic expression. The Qumran texts at times use *māraya'* to replace the name of God and so shows that this usage was current in first-century Judaism. See the evidence in Joseph Fitzmyer, "The Semitic Background of the New Testament *Kyrios*-Title," in *A Wandering Aramean: Collected Aramaic Essays*, SBLMS 25 (Missoula, MT: Scholars Press, 1979), 115–42. This essay is cited by Hurtado, who concurs with this evaluation (*Lord Jesus Christ*, 109). Hengel and Anna Maria Schwemer argue that the combination of the recollection of Jesus and the presence of the Spirit as the eschatological gift of the exalted Lord made the titles *Mara* and *Adonai* inseparably applied to Jesus (*Paul between Damascus and Antioch: The Unknown Years*, trans. John Bowden [Louisville: Westminster John Knox, 1997], 34).

27. Chris Tilling identifies *Maranatha* as "an early communal prayer" addressed to the risen Christ and as evidence of a divine Christology in Paul (*Paul's Divine Christology* [Grand Rapids: Eerdmans, 2012], 179).

28. David DuToit asserts that calling Jesus "Lord" conveys to him the power and lordship of God ("Theologische Themen: Christologische Hoheitstitel," in *Paulus Handbuch*, ed. Horn, 297).

29. David Hay lists the following as references to Ps 110: Matt 22:44; 26:64; Mark 12:36; 14:62;

"Jesus Is Lord"

of Ps 110:1 appear in the Synoptic Gospels, Acts, Ephesians, Colossians, Hebrews, and Revelation.[30] Paul cites it in Rom 8:34 (see the discussion in ch. 2) and 1 Cor 15:25. This list demonstrates that citation of this psalm is present in all the major lines of traditions in the New Testament, with the exception of the Johannine literature[31] (unless Revelation is included in it). Hengel notes that three of these citations (1 Pet 3:18-22; Eph 1:20-22; Rom 8:34b) appear in fragments of traditional material.[32] It is also cited in 1 Clem. 36.5; Pol. *Phil.* 2.1; Barn. 12.10; Apoc. Pet. 6; Sib. Or. 2.243; and Apoc. Jas. 14:30.[33] The sparse use of this tradition in Paul indicates that he is not the source of its extensive use throughout so many branches of the church. The widespread and regular use of this psalm indicates clearly that it was used early, including in pre-Pauline times, as a means to interpret the resurrection but current absence of Jesus.[34]

The importance of the citation of this psalm becomes even more obvious when we note that it was not used in Second Temple Judaism outside the church in connection with any messianic figure. Other enthronement psalms were used in this literature with messianic meanings, but not this one, which contains the only reference in the Hebrew Bible to being exalted to God's right hand.[35] The only possible allusion to Ps 110:1 appears in the T. Job 33:3, as part of a defense speech of Job that has no messianic overtones.[36] The church's

---

16:19 (part of the later addition to Mark); Luke 20:42-43; 22:69; Acts 2:33, 34-35; 5:31; 7:55-56; Rom 8:34; 1 Cor 15:25; Eph 1:20; 2:6; Col 3:1; Heb 1:3; 8:1; 10:12-13; 12:2; 1 Pet 3:22; Rev 3:21 (*Glory at the Right Hand: Psalm 110 in Early Christianity*, SBLMS 18 [Nashville: Abingdon, 1973], 163-64).

30. In addition to these citations of v. 1, Hay lists ten places that Hebrews cites Ps 110:4: Heb 5:6, 10; 6:20; 7:3, 8, 11, 15-17, 21, 24-25, 28 (*Glory at the Right Hand*, 163-64).

31. So Richard Bauckham, *Jesus and the God of Israel* (Grand Rapids: Eerdmans, 2008), 21.

32. Martin Hengel, *Between Jesus and Paul: Studies in the Earliest History of Christianity*, trans. John Bowden (Philadelphia: Fortress, 1983), 85-86. Hay argues that the change in wording from the LXX to the wording in these three texts demonstrates that the authors are citing a traditional formula (*Glory at the Right Hand*, 35-40). The LXX has *en deixōn*, while these texts have *en dexia*.

33. These are identified by Hay, *Glory at the Right Hand*, 164-65.

34. So also Hay, who asserts that it helps explain how Jesus can be the Messiah but not have an earthly kingdom (*Glory at the Right Hand*, 34). Cullmann also notes that it must have been important for the early church (*Christology of the New Testament*, 222-23). Hay speculates that Mark 12:35-37 and its Synoptic parallels may show that it was used with reference to Jesus during his lifetime (*Glory at the Right Hand*, 157).

35. So Hengel, *Between Jesus and Paul*, 86.

36. The reference to an everlasting kingdom in the context (T. Job 33:9) may suggest that this passage does have an eschatological orientation. But it may only indicate that Job's vindication will be after his present life and in a heavenly realm. Bauckham comments that this passage is only possibly, not certainly, an allusion to Ps 110 (*Jesus and the God of Israel*, 22).

widespread use of this psalm stands in stark contrast to its absence from other contemporaneous Jewish literature. It indicates that a segment of the church that was familiar with the Psalms proclaimed the ascension of Christ to God's throne as one of its earliest confessions about Jesus. Richard Bauckham suggests that this usage indicates that the church was interested in saying something about Jesus that the rest of Second Temple Judaism was not interested in saying about anyone.[37] It clearly shows that the church before the time of Paul applied the title *Lord* to Jesus and in connection with it asserted that Jesus had assumed a place of power at the throne of God. While recognizing that the church did not have a single, uniform interpretation of the psalm, Hay argues that it "was an unusually apt vehicle for expressing the ultimacy of Jesus."[38]

The designation *Lord* for Jesus also appears in the Didache. James Tabor and Barrie Wilson identify the Didache as one of the few documents from the early church that is not dominated by Pauline thought.[39] In its description of the requirements for those who participate in "the Eucharist," it says that they must have been baptized in the name of "the Lord." It then immediately quotes a saying of Jesus as something that "the Lord" said (9.5). Thus it is clear that "the Lord" here is Jesus and that he is the one in whose name one is baptized. Such a usage demonstrates that this church gives Jesus an extraordinary place in its liturgy, a place that assumes an exalted position for him. This is confirmed by its concluding prayer of the meal that ends with "*Maranatha*. Amen" (10.6). Such an expression assumes the exaltation of Jesus and accords him a place as God's agent of the eschaton.[40]

Dunn contends that using the title *Lord* for Jesus suggests veneration.[41] He points to Hahn's situating of this acclamation in the context of worship. Hahn sees the *Maranatha* prayer as evidence for a liturgical context.[42] At the same time, he asserts that the title took on still more exalted meanings as it

---

37. Bauckham, *Jesus and the God of Israel*, 22.

38. Hay, *Glory at the Right Hand*, 16. Fitzmyer asserts that when Paul says "Jesus is Lord" he "along with the rest of the early church acknowledged that Jesus was on a par with YHWH of the Old Testament" ("Christology," 84).

39. James D. Tabor, *Paul and Jesus: How the Apostle Transformed Christianity* (New York: Simon & Schuster, 2012), 46; Barrie Wilson, *How Jesus Became Christian* (New York: St. Martin's, 2008), 156–57.

40. Note also the curious expression "the Lord's Day of the Lord" (*kyriakēn de kyriou*), in 14.1. Bart Ehrman translates the phrase, "the Lord's own day" (*Apostolic Fathers*, 2 vols., LCL [Cambridge: Harvard University Press, 2003], 1:439).

41. Dunn, *Theology of Paul*, 257.

42. Hahn, *Titles of Jesus*, 96, 102. For our purposes at this point, it does not matter whether it arose as an acclamation or as a prayer used in connection with the Lord's Supper.

moved into the Hellenistic church.⁴³ Those familiar with the Septuagint must have found the first hearing of "God raised the Lord" (1 Cor 6:14) rather jarring. This statement follows the form of the tradition that proclaims that God raised Jesus, but the use of the title *Lord* by itself in the formula is exceptional. Interpreters note that this statement is an example of, or at least echoes, the traditional formula.⁴⁴ It may be, however, as Kramer contends, that the title *Lord* here is a Pauline addition.⁴⁵ Yet it is an addition that Paul does not think will be controversial because he uses the tradition as a proof in his argument about the resurrection of the believer's body. Richard Longenecker notes that such usages mean not only that Paul was not the first to call Jesus "Lord," but also that "he believed his proclamation of Jesus as Lord was in direct continuity with the proclamation of the earliest church."⁴⁶ The association of this title with Ps 110 demonstrates that the church before Paul understood Jesus to have ascended to an exalted position at the throne of God.

Larry Hurtado argues that Paul's use of and passing on of the *Maranatha* formula shows that Paul and the Aramaic-speaking church have a "shared religiousness."⁴⁷ Further, it suggests that "Paul sought to align the christological terms and devotional practices of his converts with those of earlier circles of Jewish Christians."⁴⁸ Hurtado presses the point, saying that the use of *Maranatha* in the Pauline churches shows that Paul was promoting "a shared liturgical practice between Paul's Gentile churches and their Aramaic-speaking, Jewish Christian coreligionists and predecessors in the faith."⁴⁹ Paul's use of *Abba* to refer to God in Gal 4:6 and Rom 8:15 supports this understanding of Paul's practice. Notably, he expects the Roman church to recognize this Aramaic title for God.⁵⁰

---

43. Hahn, *Titles of Jesus*, 68.

44. Dunn sees it as an example (*Theology of Paul*, 175). Those who see it as an echo include Victor P. Furnish, *The Theology of the First Letter to the Corinthians*, New Testament Theology (Cambridge: Cambridge University Press, 1999), 22; and Raymond F. Collins, *First Corinthians*, SP (Collegeville, MN: Liturgical Press, 1999), 246. Hans Conzelmann notes the dependence on the tradition (*1 Corinthians: A Commentary on the First Epistle to the Corinthians*, trans. James W. Leitch, Hermeneia [Philadelphia: Fortress, 1975], 111n19).

45. Kramer, *Christ, Lord, Son of God*, 24.

46. Richard N. Longenecker, *The Christology of Early Jewish Christianity*, SBT 2/17 (Naperville, IL: Allenson, 1970), 127.

47. Hurtado, *Lord Jesus Christ*, 111.

48. Hurtado, *Lord Jesus Christ*, 111.

49. Hurtado, *Lord Jesus Christ*, 111. Such an understanding is supported by the recent recognition that Paul remained an observant Jew who attended synagogue services and maintained Torah observance in settings that did involve excluding gentile church members.

50. Joseph Fitzmyer observes that no passages in the Hebrew Bible use this title for God. There

Romans 8:3 and Galatians 4:4

Another title for Jesus that appears in church tradition before Paul is that of "son." We saw in chapter 2 that Rom 8:3 contains preformed material. The phrase "God sent his own Son" seems to be part of that citation of a tradition.[51] This sending language appears in multiple sources and is particularly prominent in the Johannine materials.[52] It is, however, very unusual in Paul.[53] Further, the insertion of this statement makes this verse rather awkward.[54] Despite these characteristics, Jewett follows Keck in questioning whether this is the citation of a completely formed traditional piece. They prefer to see it as a traditional model or pattern that Paul repeats here.[55] This understanding of the expression still recognizes that Paul is drawing on a prior and widely known understanding of Christ.

This sending formula that identifies Jesus as God's Son also appears in Gal 4:4, where it is more certainly part of a preformed piece. Here it surfaces within what Hans Dieter Betz and J. Louis Martyn identify as a tradition that speaks of both the identity of Jesus and his soteriological function.[56] Martinus de Boer follows Calvin in noting that the poetic structure of 4:4–5 suggests that Paul is citing an existing formula.[57] H. Betz identifies the longer piece as traditional because it contains material that is irrelevant to the argument of Galatians, particularly the assertion that Jesus had a human mother. In addition, the assertion that Jesus was born under the law must originally have been

---

are, however, some uses of its Hebrew form in the Qumran literature (*Romans: A New Translation with Introduction and Commentary*, AB 33 [New York: Doubleday, 1993], 498–99).

51. For example, Hengel ("Confessing and Confession," 607; *Between Jesus and Paul*, 40), Fuller (*Foundations of New Testament Christology*, 195), Kramer (*Christ, Lord, Son of God*, 115), and Hans Dieter Betz (*Galatians: A Commentary on Paul's Letter to the Churches in Galatia*, Hermeneia [Philadelphia: Fortress, 1979], 205n38) see the longer section of Rom 8:3–4 that has elements of Christology and soteriology as a citation of a preexisting formula.

52. Douglas Moo, *The Epistle to the Romans*, NICNT (Grand Rapids: Eerdmans, 1996), 478n40.

53. Moo, *Romans*, 478n40; Byrne, *Romans*, 242.

54. Jewett observes that many interpreters note this awkwardness (*Romans*, 482).

55. Jewett, *Romans*, 482, citing Leander Keck, "The Law and 'The Law of Sin and Death' (Rom 8:1–4): Reflections on the Spirit and Ethics in Paul," in *The Divine Helmsman: Studies on God's Control of Human Events, Presented to Lou H. Silberman*, ed. J. L. Crenshaw and S. Sandmel (New York: Ktav, 1980), 43–44.

56. H. Betz, *Galatians*, 205–8; J. Louis Martyn, *Galatians: A New Translation with Introduction and Commentary*, AB 33A (New York: Doubleday, 1997), 389–90.

57. Martinus C. de Boer, *Galatians: A Commentary*, NTL (Louisville: Westminster John Knox, 2011), 262.

positive, even though it is seen negatively in the argument of Galatians.[58] Thus the original thrust of the tradition was to assert the humanity and Jewishness of Jesus.[59] Such an assertion indicates that this way of speaking of Jesus came from a church in a thoroughly Jewish context. Betz comments that the Christology of Gal 4:4-5 is not that of Paul, but it is acceptable to him.[60] Thus Paul can make use of it for his argument in Galatians.

Identifying Jesus as the Son of God was widespread in the earliest church, though its meaning varied. Psalm 2:7 and 2 Sam 7:14 refer to Israel's king as God's son. Allusions to this psalm that identify Jesus as God's Son appear in Acts 13:33; Heb 1:5; 5:5, and perhaps in the pronouncements at Jesus's baptism in the Synoptics. This use of Ps 2:7 in a variety of texts at least indicates that the wider church accorded Jesus an exalted status. The Q tradition in Matt 11:25-27/Luke 10:21-22 also identifies Jesus as the Son of God. Further, Paul calls Jesus the Son of God seven times in Romans and only eight times (including Gal 4:4) in all the other undisputed letters.[61] This signifies that he expects a church that he did not found to accept this identification of Jesus. These occurrences of the title *Son* in so many different places show that Paul was not the first to use it for Jesus.[62] The passages from the Hebrew Bible that call the king a son of God demonstrate the wide range of meanings it could have. So calling Jesus the "Son of God" does not necessarily indicate that he is seen as divine. It does indicate that he had a distinctive relationship with God.

Interpreters are divided over whether the sending language of Rom 8:3 and Gal 4:4 assumes that the Son was preexistent. Following Wilhelm Bousset, H. Betz rejects this understanding, noting that other ancient religions talk about divinities sending saviors without assuming that this meant they were preexistent.[63] The *religionsgeschichtliche* parallels Bousset provides are now usually seen as less than conclusive.[64] Dunn also argues that there is no ev-

---

58. H. Betz, *Galatians*, 207.
59. H. Betz, *Galatians*, 208.
60. H. Betz, *Galatians*, 208.
61. Hurtado notes that these references appear in clusters even in Romans. Thus they seem related to three points: they apply an honorific to Jesus, they give a theocentric focus on the way God acted in Jesus, and they link the salvation of believers to the status of Christ ("Jesus' Divine Sonship in Paul's Epistle to the Romans," in *Romans and the People of God: Essays in Honor of Gordon D. Fee on the Occasion of His 65th Birthday*, ed. Sven K. Soderlund and N. T. Wright [Grand Rapids: Eerdmans, 1999], 223).
62. A. M. Hunter, *Paul and His Predecessors*, rev. ed. (London: SCM, 1961), 88.
63. H. Betz, *Galatians*, 206-7.
64. See the discussion of Bousset's approach in Larry W. Hurtado, *How on Earth Did Jesus*

idence of preexistence here because this formula is a reflection of an Adam Christology.[65] Ben Witherington III counters Dunn's reading by observing that "son" language is not part of an Adamic Christology.[66] M. de Boer sees a connection between this sending and that of preexistent Wisdom in Jewish wisdom literature, but acknowledges that it does not require that the Son is preexistent.[67] Indeed, prophets are sometimes sent by God, but nothing about that suggests that they are ontologically different from other humans.[68] M. de Boer notes, however, that this expression of the church's tradition does set Jesus apart from all others and gives him a unique relationship with God because it is through him that others can receive adoption.[69] The presence of this tradition in the Johannine literature suggests that for some who use this language it does assume a preexistence for the one sent because it clearly includes that element in John 1.[70]

In both Rom 8 and Gal 4, the tradition serves as proof for important assertions. In Galatians it is support for the argument that gentiles do not need to observe the Torah as Jews do because the sending of Christ signaled a new act of God to redeem and adopt all people through Christ. In Rom 8 it provides the evidence that believers are freed from condemnation. Again, Paul expects

---

Become God? Historical Questions about Earliest Devotion to Jesus (Grand Rapids: Eerdmans, 2005), 16–18.

65. James D. G. Dunn, *Christology in the Making: A New Testament Inquiry into the Origins of the Doctrine of the Incarnation* (Grand Rapids: Eerdmans, 1996), 39–43.

66. Ben Witherington III, *Grace in Galatia: A Commentary on Paul's Letter to the Galatians* (Grand Rapids: Eerdmans, 1998), 287–88.

67. M. de Boer, *Galatians*, 263. He comments further that the preexistence of Christ is clearer in 1 Cor 8:6 and Phil 2:6-8. Frank J. Matera comments that Christ's preexistence is not stated explicitly but is probably implied (*Galatians*, SP [Collegeville, MN: Liturgical Press, 1992], 150).

68. Sam K. Williams gives Jer 7:25; Ezek 2:3; and Hag 1:12 as examples (*Galatians*, ANTC [Nashville: Abingdon, 1997], 112).

69. M. de Boer, *Galatians*, 262.

70. See also the theological argument of Heinrich Schlier, *Der Brief an die Galater*, 11th ed., KEK 7 (Göttingen: Vandenhoeck & Ruprecht, 1951), 195–96. After noting the ways that a sending formula in earlier literature could refer to a human prophet and tracing the "sent" language into wider first-century usage, Eduard Schweizer concludes that the formulaic nature of statements about the sending of Jesus show that the language is not just imagery. He asserts that "it is difficult to understand [the sent references in Paul and John] apart from assuming that Jesus was living in a filial relation to God before being sent by him" ("What Do We Really Mean When We Say, 'God Sent His Son . . .'?" in *Faith and History: Essays in Honor of Paul W. Meyer*, ed. John T. Carroll, Charles H. Cosgrove, and E. Elizabeth Johnson [Atlanta: Scholars Press, 1990], 298–306, quotation on 306).

Romans 1:3-4

Most commentators find traditional material in Rom 1:3-4.[71] These verses say that the gospel of God is about "his Son, who being born from the seed of David according to the flesh, being designated Son of God in power according to the Spirit of holiness from the resurrection of the dead, Jesus Christ our Lord." (This wooden translation helps us see some features of the passage that indicate that it contains traditional material.) A number of elements of this statement suggest that Paul is borrowing it from already existing formulations. Having a participial construction ("being born" [or "coming to be"] in v. 3 and "being designated" in v. 4) appear at the beginning of a line is common in confessional material.[72] Further, both verses 3 and 4 have the participle followed by a prepositional phrase and then a *kata* ("according to") phrase.[73] Though some would argue that "flesh" (*sarx*) has its usual pejorative Pauline sense here,[74] most contend that it is neutral; thus its contrast with the Spirit is a non-Pauline use of the term.[75] It is also uncharacteristic of Paul to make reference to the Davidic descent of Jesus; indeed, this is the only time he does so.[76] Further, the balanced formulations of Jesus's identity that have "son of

---

71. Seyoon Kim recently asserted that this is the generally accepted position ("Jesus the Son of God as the Gospel [1 Thess 1:9-10 and Rom 1:3-4]," in *Earliest Christian History*, ed. Bird and Maston, 127).

72. Jewett, *Romans*, 98n15.

73. Among those who see this parallelism as characteristic of preformed material are Neufeld, *Earliest Christian Confessions*, 50; Jewett, *Romans*, 98n16; James D. G. Dunn, *Romans 1-8*, WBC 38A (Waco: Word, 1988), 5; Ziesler, *Romans*, 60; Leon Morris, *The Epistle to the Romans*, Pillar (Grand Rapids: Eerdmans, 1988), 43.

74. James D. G. Dunn, "Jesus—Flesh and Spirit: An Exposition of Romans 1:3-4," *JTS* 24 (1973): 40-68. This essay is cited by Morris, *Romans*, 42n39, who asserts that it needs some moderation.

75. Byrne, *Romans*, 44; Moo, *Romans*, 45n28; Jewett, *Romans*, 96. We should note that Paul speaks of "Christ according to the flesh" in Rom 9:5, where it seems likely that the phrase is simply a designation of his descent rather than carrying the common Pauline connotation of existence in the realm ruled by evil. We will not discuss Rom 9:5 here even though its use of this phrase could be another echo of this tradition. The inconclusive debate over whether the following doxology honors God or Christ renders it unusable for this study.

76. Noted by Byrne, *Romans*, 44. Neufeld asserts that this is the only mention of Davidic descent in Paul (*Earliest Christian Confessions*, 50-51).

David" and "Son of God" appear in 2 Tim 2:8 and Ign. *Smyrn.* 1.1.[77] The verb *horizō* ("designated") is also rare in Paul (appearing only here),[78] as is the expression "spirit of holiness [*hagiosynē*]," which is elsewhere "Holy [*hagios*] Spirit."[79] Dunn and Ziesler designate this way of identifying the Spirit as a Semitism.[80] Finally, Paul uses the full expression, "resurrection from the dead," only to refer to the general resurrection except for this passage. Thus it seems to signal a non-Pauline and very early formula.[81] Mention of "Jesus Christ our Lord" may also echo the confession of Jesus as Lord that we have already discussed.[82]

In addition to these formal indications that Rom 1:3–4 is preformed material, many interpreters note that the wording of verse 4 may indicate that Jesus becomes the Son of God at the resurrection. If so, the verse has an adoptionist Christology.[83] Such a christological formula is clearly un-Pauline, even if Paul could use it to define his gospel in this text. The language of this formula points to a Jewish context because of its messianic interpretation of Jesus's identity and its understanding of a person being a son of God. Reginald Fuller contends that the concern about Davidic descent points to the Aramaic church in its earliest days as it used that idea to legitimate Jesus's role as eschatological judge.[84] One may also see Jewish influence in the title "son of God" being used to denote the conferring of status or office.[85] Thus it points to an emphasis on the exalted or enthroned Jesus.[86] The combination of concern about Jesus being the seed of David and being the Son of God shows that this is a confession of the Jerusalem church,[87] or at least sets it in a thoroughly Jewish

77. Dunn also notes that this dual identity is part of the tradition behind the birth narratives in Matthew and Luke (*Romans 1–8*, 5).

78. Cranfield, *Romans*, 1:57; Jewett, *Romans*, 96; Dunn, *Romans 1–8*, 5.

79. Jewett, *Romans*, 96; Leander Keck, *Romans*, ANTC (Nashville: Abingdon, 2005), 43.

80. Dunn, *Romans 1–8*, 5; Ziesler, *Romans*, 63.

81. Jewett, *Romans*, 96; Dunn, *Romans 1–8*, 5, 15–16.

82. Those who see Paul drawing on this tradition include Byrne, *Romans*, 45.

83. So Käsemann, *Commentary on Romans*, 12. See the discussion in Dunn, *Romans 1–8*, 13–14. Moo denies that Paul is relying on a traditional formula in order to avoid the possibility that an adoptionist Christology might be cited in a Pauline letter (*Romans*, 44n48). See the rebuttal of an adoptionist sense while maintaining that Paul is citing a tradition in Matthew W. Bates, "A Christology of Incarnation and Enthronement: Romans 1:3–4 as Unified, Nonadoptionist, and Nonconciliatory," *CBQ* 77 (2015): 107–27.

84. Fuller, *Foundations of New Testament Christology*, 165–66.

85. Hahn, *Titles of Jesus*, 248.

86. So also Robin Scroggs, *The People's Jesus: Trajectories in Early Christianity* (Minneapolis: Fortress, 2001), 12–13.

87. So Kim, "Jesus the Son of God," 127–28.

environment. A provenance that sets this formula within a context in which messianic identity is important indicates that it is a very early formulation, one that comes within the earliest days of the church and is not a product of a predominantly gentile church.[88]

It may be particularly important that this formulation of the content of the gospel appears at the beginning of Romans. Citing a known tradition at this point allows Paul to show the Roman church, with which he has had no direct contact, that he holds to the understanding of the gospel that they know and affirm.[89] Even more particularly, it may indicate that Paul is intimating his fidelity to the gospel of the Jerusalem church.[90] Such assurances intend to help the Roman church accept or reaffirm Paul's apostleship and authority.

This tradition shows that in its earliest days, and before Paul was a member or had influence, the church already assigned Jesus an exalted position as a messianic and eschatological figure. He is assigned the title "Son of God," a title that here includes wielding power. While a designation as God's Son could have a wide range of meanings, those meanings are narrowed significantly when they are combined with the resurrection, God's Spirit, and power. Robin Scroggs contends that this bipartite Christology (son of David/Son of God) asserts the lordship and power of Jesus so that it "means essentially the same thing as enthronement over the cosmos."[91] Paul's use of this tradition and its theological expressions is an instance of his acceptance of, and suggests his reliance on, the earlier church's traditions and beliefs. Even when the tradition is in tension with his own ways of expressing the content of the gospel, he can

---

88. Roland Denies names the early 30s as the time of its origination ("Christology between Pre-Existence, Incarnation and Messianic Self-Understanding," in *Earliest Christian History*, ed. Bird and Maston, 92).

89. So Neufeld, *Earliest Christian Confessions*, 50–51; Jewett, *Romans*, 96, who cites Calvin Roetzel (*The Letters of Paul: Conversations in Context* [Atlanta: John Knox, 1975], 20) as one who agrees.

90. So Kim, "Jesus the Son of God," 129, 138.

91. Scroggs, *People's Jesus*, 13. See the extensive discussion of the origin and original meanings of this tradition in Jewett, *Romans*, 103–8. Rejecting Jewett's reconstruction, Bates contends that Paul does not redact the tradition that he cites. He maintains that a careful reading of this tradition finds it advocating Christ's preexistence and postincarnation exaltation (Bates, "Christology of Incarnation and Enthronement," 114–25). In opposition to a reading that sees stages in this christological formula, Joshua Jipp shows that ancient interpreters of this text saw in it a two-nature Christology rather than a two-stage Christology ("Ancient, Modern, and Future Interpretations of Romans 1:3–4: Reception History and Biblical Interpretation," *JTI* 3 [2009]: 241–59).

defer to its formulation of the faith even as he offers his own interpretation of it.

Tabor contends that the church before Paul did not identify Jesus as the "Son of God."[92] His argument that every New Testament document is shaped decisively by Paul's theology could allow him to dismiss the breadth of traditions in the New Testament that assign this title to Jesus. Yet we find this identification of Jesus in the document he claims escaped Paul's influence, the Didache. When we look at that text we find that it instructs those conducting baptisms to do them in the name of "the Father, the Son, and the Holy Spirit" (7.1–3).[93] The Didache's description of the communal meal (which it calls "the Eucharist"—see ch. 6 below for discussion of this text) calls Jesus the "child" (*pais*) of God through whom knowledge of God comes and the one who exercises God's power (9.1–4; 10.2, 3). It says that the "holy vine of David" is God's "child" (*pais*), who is made known through Jesus, God's "child" (*pais*).[94] Even if we translate *pais* in these places as "servant," the title in 7.1–3 is *huios* ("son").[95] Clearly the segment of the church that produced the Didache called Jesus the "Son of God" and used that language in a way that set him apart from all other humans and identified him closely with God. Use of that title in the core ritual of baptism and placement of it between Father and the Spirit definitively demonstrate an exalted understanding of Jesus's identity.

Philippians 2:6-11

As noted in chapter 2, most interpreters identify Phil 2:6-11 as a preformed liturgical piece that Paul adopts and adapts to use in his letter.[96] Its elevated

---

92. Tabor, *Paul and Jesus*, 25. Similarly, Wilson (*How Jesus Became Christian*, 158) says, "there is no whiff of deification" of Jesus in the Didache.

93. The formula appears twice in these verses, 7.1 and 7.3.

94. Kurt Niederwimmer translates *pais* here as "servant" rather than "child," commenting that it demonstrates the ancient origins of the formula (*The Didache: A Commmentary*, trans. Linda M. Maloney, Hermeneia [Minneapolis: Fortress, 1998], 147). It is possible, though not certain, that this passage suggests that the "holy vine" that appears in Jesus was preexistent.

95. Ehrman's translation of *pais* in 9.2, 3; 10.2, 3 is "child" (*Apostolic Fathers*, 1:431, 433).

96. For example, Ulrich B. Müller, *Der Brief des Paulus an die Philipper*, THKNT 11.1 (Leipzig: Evangelische Verlagsanstalt, 1993), 90; Carolyn Osiek, *Philippians, Philemon*, ANTC (Nashville: Abingdon, 2000), 56–57. However, Gordon Fee ("Philippians 2:5-11: Hymn or Exalted Pauline Prose?" *BBR* 2 [1992]: 29–46) and Adela Yarbro Collins ("Psalms, Philippians 2:6-11, and the Origins of Christology," *BibInt* 11 [2003]: 361–72) have argued that Paul is the author of this material.

"Jesus Is Lord"

style, parallel clauses, beginning with a relative pronoun followed by a participle, and non-Pauline vocabulary all support this conclusion.[97] While the liturgy is not composed by Paul, some do think that it was composed by someone within his sphere of influence. Thus we must be careful about how we use this piece to identify what the church before and outside Paul's influence believed.

Interpreters continue to debate whether the opening lines of the liturgy assume that Christ was preexistent. Those who see a "second Adam" theology often find no belief in a preexistence.[98] Most other interpreters think the language assumes Christ's preexistence, even though it does not state this explicitly.[99] Perhaps the strongest argument against the assumption of preexistence is the final part of the liturgy in which God grants exalted status to Christ. Reumann responds to this tension by proposing that the piece brings together two Christologies in the early church without resolving their differences: a theology of a preexistent heavenly one and a theology of Jesus exalted to lordship.[100] Alternatively, Morna Hooker suggests that the conclusion has God bestow what Christ had refused to claim for himself in the opening stanza.[101] Since this is a much debated point, we will not claim preexistence as an element of the church's Christology on the basis of this passage, even though this seems

---

97. See Ralph Martin, *Carmen Christi: Philippians ii. 5-11 in Recent Interpretation and in the Setting of Early Christian Worship*, rev. ed. (Grand Rapids: Eerdmans, 1983).

98. An early formulation of this view is Charles H. Talbert, "Problem of Pre-existence in Philippians 2:6-11," *JBL* 86 (1967): 141-53. Cf. Dunn, *Christology in the Making*, 113-28, 176-96; and Dunn, *Theology of Paul*, 266-93. A recent adaptation that looks to Isaiah's fourth Servant Song is E. Di Pede and A. Wénin, "Le Christ Jésus et l'humain de l'Eden: L'hymne aux Philippiens (2,6-11) et le début de la Genèse," *RTL* 43 (2012): 225-41.

99. Among those who see a preexistent Christ in the hymn are John Reumann, *Philippians: A New Translation with Introduction and Commentary*, AB 33B (New Haven: Yale University Press, 2008), 362; Charles B. Cousar, *Philippians and Philemon*, NTL (Louisville: Westminster John Knox, 2009), 52-55 (see his succinct rejection of the Adamic Christology interpretation); Ben Witherington III, *Paul's Letter to the Philippians: A Socio-Rhetorical Commentary* (Grand Rapids: Eerdmans, 2011), 143; see also his rejection of the Adamic Christology interpretation on 133-34. A more extensive rejection of the Adamic Christology that denies any idea of preexistence here, particularly Dunn's view, is in Hurtado, *Lord Jesus Christ*, 119-26. Morna Hooker's understanding of the appearance of an Adamic Christology in the liturgy allows her to acknowledge that its opening stanza assumes a preexistence of Christ, even as this stands in tension with the second half ("Philippians," *NIB* 11:507).

100. Reumann, *Philippians*, 362.

101. Hooker, "Philippians," 507. See also the nuanced view of Samuel Vollenweider, "Der 'Raub' der Gottgleichheit: Ein religionsgeschichtlicher Vorschlag zu Phil 2.6(-11)," *NTS* 45 (1999): 413-33. He argues that the preexistent Christ had a divine form without being equal to God.

to be more probable than that the sending formula discussed above implied preexistence in its initial use.[102]

Even if this liturgy comes from the Pauline churches, it provides further explication of the meanings of the claims about the exaltation of Christ and the use of the title *Lord* in the early church outside Paul's sphere of influence. In this encomiastic liturgy, the abbreviated narrative of the incarnation of Christ leads to God's response to that obedient death: God highly exalted him and gave him a name above all names, which exaltation leads to all in the cosmos acknowledging Christ as Lord.

The name that is above all others in Phil 2:9 is spoken more directly in verse 11: Jesus Christ is Lord. We have already seen how common it was for the church to cite Ps 110:1 to speak of the exaltation of Christ to the right hand of God's throne using the title *Lord*. Philippians 2:9-11 is another example of this understanding of the title *Lord* coming to expression.[103] Jesus is highly exalted and given the name *Lord*. As it seemed possible in other settings, here possessing that name means that veneration is appropriate, even required, of all created things. All are required to acknowledge his position and rule.[104] This assertion of the lordship of Christ over all is not unique to Pauline literature or traditions. Jesus is said to rule over all things in Matt 11:27; Luke 10:22; John 3:35; 13:3; 16:15; Acts 10:36; 1 Cor 15:27-28; Eph 1:22; Phil 3:21; and Heb 1:2; 2:8.[105] The broad spectrum of currents of the church represented here indicates that Paul did not originate this understanding of Jesus's position. Again, the relatively few instances of this claim in the Pauline corpus support the notion that its origin lies elsewhere. Profession of Jesus as the Lord who is over all and an appropriate recipient of veneration, then, originates outside Paul's influence.

The confession of Christ by all creatures in Phil 2:11 is parallel with the description of the homage that all creatures pay to the lamb in Rev 5, as is the honor given to Christ in Phil 2:9. Hengel associates the Philippians and

---

102. Bultmann (*Theology*, 1:293) and Hengel ("Confessing and Confession," 607) identify 2 Cor 8:9 ("being rich he made himself poor") as a citation of another tradition that assumes the preexistence of Christ. Susan Eastman asserts that the "became" (*genomenos*) of v. 7 is decisive evidence that this liturgy assumes a preexistence for Christ ("Philippians 2:6-11: Incarnation as Mimetic Participation," *JSPHL* 1 [2011]: 2n5).

103. Reumann is among those who recognize the incorporation of an earlier traditional formula here (*Philippians*, 361).

104. In support of his view that Paul held a more Trinitarian-friendly view than most interpreters acknowledge, Hill asserts that giving Christ the divine name here means that he is God (*Paul and the Trinity*, 94).

105. See the list in Bauckham, *Jesus and the God of Israel*, 23n45.

"Jesus Is Lord"

Revelation passages with Ps 8:6–7. What was originally a statement about the place of humanity over other creatures has become a confession about Christ reigning over the cosmos. He sees Pss 110:1 and 8:6–7 brought together in the formalized traditions found in Eph 1:20–22 and 1 Pet 3:18–22.[106] The combination of these psalms grounds the claim that the exaltation of Jesus grants him the power to exercise God's reign over the cosmos. That is the tradition Phil 2:9–11 echoes.[107] Again, the combining of these psalms to describe the position of Christ seems to have come from outside the Pauline sphere since it appears in Revelation and 1 Peter.

Seeing Phil 2:6–11 as a pre-Pauline hymn, Hurtado notes how remarkable it is that Paul can use it to make such lofty claims about Jesus and attribute devotion to him without any defense.[108] Even if the piece is from a member of the Pauline community, it draws on so many older confessions and acclamations that it clearly is making no significant innovations in the church's understanding of Jesus. Scroggs also thinks this liturgy was developed outside Paul's influence. Rather than pushing a more exalted place for Christ, Scroggs contends that Paul adds "to the glory of God" in verse 11 to counter a Christology that he did not think sufficiently subordinated Christ to God.[109] On this reading, Paul is not making more exalted claims about Christ; he is working to be sure that the sovereignty of God is preserved as the church makes exalted claims about Christ.

Bauckham argues that Second Temple Judaism defined God more by calling him "creator of all" and "ruler of all" rather than by ontological definitions that described an element of God's nature. He argues that this means

---

106. Hengel, *Between Jesus and Paul*, 85–86. Bauckham notes that this combination of Pss 110 and 8 is never applied to a messianic figure in Second Temple Judaism other than by the church to Christ (*God Crucified: Monotheism and Christology in the New Testament* [Grand Rapids: Eerdmans, 1998], 30–31).

107. Hurtado (*Lord Jesus Christ*, 112) and Reumann (*Philippians*, 373) also hear echoes of Isa 45:23 in these verses. Robin Scroggs contends that seeing Christ as Cosmocrator was a belief that developed in the church outside Paul's influence ("Paul: Myth Remaker: The Refashioning of Early Ecclesial Traditions," in *Pauline Conversations in Context: Essays in Honor of Calvin J. Roetzel*, edited by Janice Capel Anderson, Philip Sellew, and Claudia Setzer, JSNTSup 221 [Sheffield: Sheffield Academic Press, 2002], 88–92).

108. Hurtado, *Lord Jesus Christ*, 112–13.

109. Scroggs, "Paul: Myth Remaker," 98–99. Hill asserts that this statement is understood better using the language of "ordering" or "asymmetry" (*Paul and the Trinity*, 98) rather than subordination. While he seems correct that this ordering is mutually defining (98), that makes it no less one of subordination on Christ's part. Indeed, Hill acknowledges that the position of Christ in 2:6–11 could be labeled subordinate (110).

that identifying Jesus as the ruler over all things draws him into the divine identity.[110] Even if that overdraws the evidence, Bauckham is correct in noting that seeing Christ exalted to the throne of God means that he participates in God's sovereignty.[111] While this understanding of Christ appears more fully in Phil 2:6-11 than in many other places, we have seen that it draws on earlier preformed traditions and so expresses a view espoused by the church that was present earlier than Paul and in areas where Paul did not have dominant influence.

1 Corinthians 8:6

Another citation of a tradition appears in 1 Cor 8:6, where the text says that all things came into existence through Christ. While a few commentators argue that this verse is an ad hoc creation of Paul,[112] most recognize it as the citation of a preformed confession.[113] Following "but for us," which Anders Eriksson

---

110. Bauckham, *Jesus and the God of Israel*, 25.

111. Bauckham, *Jesus and the God of Israel*, 28. While Tilling argues that it is more helpful to examine the relation Paul posits between himself and Christ as a way to talk about Christ's divine identity (*Divine Christology*, 61–62), this observation of Bauckham remains valid even if one finds Tilling's thesis to be persuasive.

112. Notably, Gordon Fee acknowledges that it has "a creedal ring," but thinks it is possible that Paul composed it (*The First Epistle to the Corinthians*, NICNT [Grand Rapids: Eerdmans, 1987], 373–74). Fee is reticent to recognize any citations of material other than Scripture references in Paul, yet leaves open the possibility here. Dunn sees Paul drawing together each part of the formulation from various preexisting traditions, but thinks the precise form is the result of Paul putting those together to respond to the Corinthian situation (*Christology in the Making*, 179). This position also recognizes that the views expressed here are pre-Pauline. Similarly, see Anthony C. Thiselton, *The First Epistle to the Corinthians: A Commentary on the Greek Text*, NIGTC (Grand Rapids: Eerdmans, 2000), 637. Andrey Romanov comments that it is not possible to determine whether it was fully preformed ("*Heis kyrios* and *hēmeis* in 1 Corinthians 8:6: An Investigation of the First Person Plural in Light of the Lordship of Jesus Christ," *Neot* 49 [2015]: 53n11). Erik Waaler argues that it is a composition of Paul because Paul is able to compose parallel clauses and because it fits the literary structure of the argument in vv. 1–6 (*The Shema and the First Commandment in First Corinthians: An Intertextual Approach to Paul's Re-reading of Deuteronomy*, WUNT 2/253 [Tübingen: Mohr Siebeck, 2008], 395).

113. So Deichgräber, *Gotteshymnus und Christushymnus*, 116; Wengst, *Christologische Formeln*, 136; R. Collins, *First Corinthians*, 315–18; Wolfgang Schrage, *Der erste Brief an die Korinther*, 4 vols., EKKNT 7.1–4 (Neukirchen-Vluyn: Neukirchener Verlag, 1991–2001), 2:241–42; William F. Orr and James A. Walther, *1 Corinthians: A New Translation*, AB 32 (Garden City, NY: Doubleday, 1976), 231; Conzelmann, *1 Corinthians*, 144–45. N. T. Wright, who is usually

identifies as an introductory formula,[114] the verse is a self-contained unit that has three sets of parallel lines with the uses of relative clauses and pronouns that appear in other formalized material. Elements of the formula also appear in other sources.[115] Further, its content exceeds the needs of the context and it contains assertions about Christ that are unusual in Paul.[116] Furthermore, the insertion creates an anacoluthon.[117] As Hurtado notes, this passage clearly assumes the preexistence of Christ.[118] Yet Paul is not really interested in the ideas of Christ's preexistence and his mediating of creation here. They are simply part of the tradition that he cites for a different purpose.[119] We observed at the beginning of this chapter that on other occasions Paul cites the "God is one" formula. This passage seems to be a combination and extension of the acclamations of the one God (which may be related to the Shema[120]) and of Jesus Christ as Lord. The identification of God as Father, rather than Lord as in the Shema,[121] makes room for the acclamation of Christ as Lord. The

---

skeptical of finding traditions in Paul's letters, considers this passage as an example of a place where he is citing a preformed piece (*Paul and the Faithfulness of God: Parts III and IV*, Christian Origins and the Question of God 4 [Minneapolis: Fortress, 2013], 648n104).

114. Anders Eriksson, *Traditions as Rhetorical Proof: Pauline Argumentation in 1 Corinthians*, ConBNT 29 (Stockholm: Almqvist & Wiksell, 1998), 120.

115. Conzelmann (*1 Corinthians*, 145n48) names Heb 2:10 as a place where the "through him" formula appears.

116. See Conzelmann, *1 Corinthians*, 144-45; Eriksson, *Traditions as Rhetorical Proof*, 120; R. Collins, *First Corinthians*, 316. Thiselton comments that the "compressed logic" of the statement presupposes that the Corinthians already accept this understanding of Christ (*First Epistle to the Corinthians*, 638). John Fotopoulos argues that the "strong" in Corinth use this confession to support their eating in temples of other gods ("Arguments concerning Food Offered to Idols: Corinthian Quotations and Pauline Refutations in a Rhetorical *Partitio* [1 Corinthians 8:1-9]," *CBQ* 67 [2005]: 626).

117. Thiselton (*First Epistle to the Corinthians*, 632) cites Khiok-khng Yeo, *Rhetorical Interaction in 2 Corinthians 8 and 10: A Formal Analysis with Preliminary Suggestions for a Chinese, Cross-Cultural Hermeneutic*, BibInt 9 (Leiden: Brill, 1997), 190, who notes that the anacoluthon that v. 6 creates indicates that Paul is citing a tradition.

118. Hurtado, *Lord Jesus Christ*, 125-26.

119. So Schrage, *Erste Brief an die Korinther*, 2:244. R. Collins (*First Corinthians*, 320) comments that this is the only place in Paul where Christ clearly has a role in creation. Hengel, however, thinks that Phil 2:6-11; Gal 4:4; Rom 8:3; and 1 Cor 2:7 show Christ as a mediator of creation (*Between Jesus and Paul*, 40).

120. Chris Tilling argues that the discussion of love in 8:1-4 supports associating this statement with the Shema because the Shema calls on the people to love God, not just to worship only God. Thus the fuller context in 1 Cor 8 indicates that Paul has the Shema in view (*Paul's Divine Christology*, 81, 88-89).

121. Wright, however, notes that this formula has no verbs, just as the Shema has none

tight parallel lines indicate that they were combined before the composition of 1 Corinthians. The combination of these several characteristics indicates that this is preformed material.

The formula in 1 Cor 8:6 distinguishes between God, who is the origin of all things, and Christ, who is the agent through whom creation is accomplished.[122] The wisdom literature of Judaism had earlier spoken of Wisdom as the one through whom God created the cosmos. As early as Prov 8:27-30, Wisdom speaks of her own role in creation. While this may be seen as a personification of a characteristic of God, Wisdom was seen as a hypostasis of that aspect of God in some Second Temple Jewish writings. For example, the Wisdom of Solomon speaks of Wisdom as present when God made the world and as God's agent of creation (8:4-6; 9:9). Among the more philosophically inclined, Philo also speaks of Wisdom as the one through whom God made the cosmos (*Det.* 54; *Her.* 199). These similarities point to a part of the church that is familiar with at least one of these kinds of literature as the origin of this formula or of the central elements of it.[123]

The form of the tradition cited in 1 Cor 8:6 seems to have applied such understandings of Wisdom to Christ.[124] While the earliest connections to the wisdom tradition probably saw Jesus as the one who revealed and embodied God's wisdom, the church soon saw Jesus as so close to God that he could be identified with God's power and wisdom.[125] Bauckham argues that talking

---

in its formula (*Paul*, 665). Wengst, on the other hand, does not think such a dyadic formula could develop from the Shema (*Christologische Formeln*, 138).

122. Romanov argues that calling Christ God's agent in creation is too limiting. By comparison with Rom 11:36 and 4 Ezra 6:6, he contends that the "through" (*dia*) of 1 Cor 8:6b need not have such a limited meaning. Rather, Paul intends more fully to attribute things to Christ that only God does elsewhere ("Through One Lord Only: Theological Interpretation of the Meaning of *dia* in 1 Cor 8,6," *Bib* 96 [2015]: 399-414). While he has some important observations, the intentional contrast of prepositions in this confession suggests that it wants to sustain a substantive difference.

123. Wengst (*Christologische Formeln*, 141) and Kramer (*Christ, Lord, Son of God*, 96) are among those who see it emerging in the Hellenistic Jewish church. Hurtado, however, argues that we need not look to Hellenistic Judaism because the eschatological categories to which the protology is related were Jewish eschatological categories (*Lord Jesus Christ*, 125-26). Cullmann points to the conversion of Gentiles as the context in which such a bipartite confession is needed. The first thing they must confess is the oneness of God (*Earliest Christian Confessions*, 42).

124. For a discussion of the contribution of the wisdom tradition to the development of Christology in the early decades of the church's existence, see Dunn, *Christology in the Making*, 163-212.

125. See Dunn, *Christology in the Making*, 211.

of Wisdom or Word as mediators of creation did not threaten monotheism because they were seen as intrinsic to God's nature. Thus when the church identified Christ with Wisdom or Word, he could be seen as intrinsic to the divine identity as Wisdom and Word had been without that constituting a threat to the oneness of God.[126] A number of interpreters see such a move facilitated by the connection often made between soteriology and protology. That is, since the state of salvation is often conceived as a return to an original lost ideal state (a return to conditions like those of Eden), the one who effects salvation comes to be seen as the one who also mediated the original creation.[127] Hurtado sees this connection as particularly evident in texts of apocalyptic Judaism.[128]

The move to identify Jesus with God's power and wisdom took place before Paul wrote 1 Corinthians because his use of this expression assumes that the recipients already understand Christ in this way.[129] That is why Paul does not need to offer an explanation of it and why he can use it to bolster his argument against eating in temples of other gods. Since this understanding of Christ is expressed in language that is uncommon in Paul, the formula was probably developed by someone other than Paul and outside the sphere of his influence. The connections we have seen with wisdom traditions could have taken place within either the Palestinian or Hellenistic Jewish church. There is no need to look beyond Jewish sources for the origin of these ideas about Christ's identity.[130]

Paul uses this confession to register his agreement with those in Corinth who assert that they can eat at the temples of other gods because those beings are not really gods. This tradition affirms the truth that there is only one God and one Lord, despite the outside world's devotion to other gods and lords.[131] Following this acknowledgment of the correctness of the "strong" Corinthians,

---

126. Bauckham, *God Crucified*, 38-41. Hill also argues that 8:6 completes the identity of the one God by including the Lord Jesus in it (*Paul and the Trinity*, 115).

127. See, e.g., Schrage, *Erste Brief an die Korinther*, 2:241-45; R. Collins, *First Corinthians*, 317-18.

128. Hurtado, *Lord Jesus Christ*, 124-25 and 125n111. He cites 1 En. 48:1-3; T. Mos. 1:14; 4 Ezra 12:32; 13:25-26.

129. So also Hurtado, *Lord Jesus Christ*, 123-24.

130. Dunn comments that even to speak of Jesus "in the language of pre-existent Wisdom was not particularly controversial in Jewish ears" ("How Controversial Was Paul's Christology?" 164).

131. While this passage acknowledges the existence of other beings that people call "god" and "lord," Paul asserts here that the names "God" and "Lord" apply appropriately only to the God of Israel and Christ.

Paul demonstrates that they have drawn the wrong conclusions. The assertion works best if it is already known and accepted by the Corinthians. Paul is able to draw them into his argument by confirming his agreement with a known expression of the beliefs that set them apart from those outside the church.

Other Possible Citations

As was the case in chapter 2, many interpreters identify a number of other passages as instances of Paul's use of a tradition. While these do not meet enough of our criteria to use them in this study, there is enough evidence for them that we should take note of them.

Some interpreters identify the expression "Christ died and he lives" in Rom 14:9 as a citation of a preformed piece. It has a more formal style than the surrounding prose,[132] and it uses the unusual language of "he lives" rather than Paul's customary expression "he was raised."[133] Paul uses it here as the grounds for asserting that Christ has authority over all people, living and dead. If Paul is quoting a known formulation, it shows that the title *Christ* was associated with the resurrection in teaching that the church beyond Paul knows because Paul cites it to give advice to a church he did not found.

Some also identify Rom 15:3 ("Christ did not please himself") as a citation of a tradition based on its formal style[134] and its use of "to please" (*areskō*), an unusual word in Paul.[135] This assertion about Christ grounds the exhortation that believers in the Roman church should accommodate those with weaker consciences. Whether or not it is a tradition, then, it serves the same function of providing a premise on which other exhortations or teachings are based.

Some interpreters also see the identification of Jesus as the "Son of God who loved me and gave himself for me" in Gal 2:20 as a citation of traditional formulae.[136] The passage seems to contain a version of the phrase "handed

---

132. Moo, *Romans*, 845; James D. G. Dunn, *Romans 9–16*, WBC 38B (Waco: Word, 1988), 808. Robert Jewett recognizes the elevation of style but does not identify the expression as a preformed tradition (*Romans*, 832).

133. Byrne, *Romans*, 412. Keck (*Romans*, 341) notes this unusual vocabulary without identifying the phrase as a tradition.

134. Moo, *Romans*, 868–69; Keck, *Romans*, 351.

135. Dunn, *Romans 9–16*, 838.

136. Betz, *Galatians*, 125–26; Bultmann, *Theology of the New Testament*, 1:295–96; Kramer, *Christ, Lord, Son of God*, 118. John Kloppenborg also seems to recognize it as a tradition from

over for us" that appears in Rom 8:32 (see the discussion of this text in ch. 2). If we understand the opening words of the phrase as an objective genitive ("faith in the Son of God"), it provides an interpretation that may not be immediately necessary for the argument. On the other hand, if we construe the *pistis* clause as subjective ("faith of the Son of God"),[137] then the explanatory element is crucial. Rather than seeing Paul citing preformed confessions here, some see the use of "Son of God" as a way to tie together the various elements of the argument of Galatians to this point since Paul already used it in 1:16. Whether or not Paul is citing or echoing a tradition here, we have seen elements of everything he writes here in other places where it is more certain that he is citing preformed acclamations about Christ.

In 2 Cor 4:4-5 Paul names the formula "Jesus Christ is Lord" as the content of his preaching and identifies Jesus as "the image [*eikōn*] of God." Jacob Jervell identifies this description of Christ as a quotation of a preexisting confession, noting that it is formed with a relative clause.[138] He argues further that this understanding of Christ is found in multiple sources, including Col 1:15; Heb 1:3; and John 1:1, in addition to its appearance in the preformed liturgy of Phil 2:6-11.[139] Among the passages that Jervell cites, however, the word used for "image" in 2 Cor 4:4 (*eikōn*) appears only in Col 1:15.[140] Still this description of Christ stands apart from its context as a self-contained assertion and uses vocabulary that is uncommon in Paul.[141] Some interpreters find that 2 Cor 4:4-6 may incorporate elements of a tradition, but others remain uncertain.[142]

---

its use of *hyper* ("An Analysis of the Pre-Pauline Formula 1 Cor 15:3b-5 in Light of Some Recent Literature," *CBQ* 40 [1978]: 354n24).

137. As do Frank Matera, *Galatians*, SP (Collegeville, MN: Liturgical Press, 1992), 100-103; and Sam Williams, *Galatians*, ANTC (Nashville: Abingdon, 1997), 75.

138. Jacob Jervell, *Imago Dei: Gen 1,26f. im Spätjudentum, in der Gnosis und in den paulinischen Briefen*, FRLANT 58 (Göttingen: Vandenhoeck & Ruprecht, 1960), 198.

139. Jervell, *Imago Dei*, 209.

140. However, Jervell points to gnostic interpretations of Gen 1:26 that use *morphē* rather than *eikōn* as evidence that the same tradition is being cited when the alternative language is used (*Imago Dei*, 228).

141. *Eikōn* appears only six other times in the undisputed letters.

142. For example, Ralph Martin, citing the accumulation of adjectives as evidence, sees Paul citing a traditional formulation (*2 Corinthians*, WBC 40 [Waco: Word, 1986], 79), while Victor Furnish says this is not impossible (*II Corinthians: A New Translation with Introduction and Commentary*, AB 32A [Garden City, NY: Doubleday, 1984], 247-48). Jan Lambrecht, however, follows C. K. Barrett (*The Second Epistle to the Corinthians*, HNTC [New York: Harper & Row, 1973], 131) in seeing the multiple genitives as "Jewish Greek" (*Second Corinthians*, SP [Collegeville, MN: Liturgical Press, 1999], 65). Other commentators simply make no note of the possibility in their treatment of 2 Cor 4:4. For example, Mark A. Seifrid points broadly to

Margaret Thrall denies the presence of a prior liturgical tradition because the term *eikōn* appears in the New Testament only in the Pauline corpus. She sees it as Paul's combination of wisdom traditions and an Adamic Christology that sees Christ as the "prototype of the new humanity."[143] Given the uncertainty of interpreters and differing interpretations of the reasons for identifying it as a preformed piece, we will not attribute it to earlier tradition here. We should recognize, however, that the ideas represented by calling Christ "God's image" were widespread and prior to Paul's use of this expression.

Conclusion

The traditions we have seen Paul cite that involve the identity of Christ show that a complex and exalted Christology developed among believers earlier than and independent of the influence of Paul. These traditions show that church members called Jesus "Messiah" or "Christ" and identified him as the hoped-for descendant of David. The church also called Jesus "Lord" before Paul was in the church. The earliest church immediately identified Jesus as the one whom God raised. The absence of the resurrected one quickly led the church to summon his presence (either in conjunction with the Lord's Supper or as a plea for the parousia [or as a combination of the two in its origin]) with the expression *Maranatha*. This Aramaic phrase that designates Jesus as Lord was thus used in worship settings. Within the membership of the church that knew the Psalms, the acclamation of Jesus as Lord was quickly attached to Ps 110:1, as its exceedingly wide usage attests. This early claim of Jesus's exaltation to the right hand of God implied that Christ exercised God's power. This position implies that he has power over all other cosmic powers, an implication that Ps 8:6–7 was soon used to support. Exaltation to this position also suggested that veneration of this Lord was appropriate and would be required of all. The preformed liturgy of Phil 2:6–11 shows that this understanding of Jesus as Lord was already part of the church's beliefs about Jesus.[144]

Hellenistic Judaism as the source of this description (*The Second Letter to the Corinthians*, Pillar [Grand Rapids: Eerdmans, 2014], 196–98). Frank Matera identifies the wisdom tradition as its source (*II Corinthians: A Commentary*, NTL [Louisville: Westminster John Knox, 2013], 102).

143. Thrall, *Second Epistle to the Corinthians*, 1:309–10. Similarly see Dunn, *The Theology of Paul the Apostle*, 289–90.

144. How widespread the veneration of Christ was in the church may be seen in that depictions of worship of him appear in Phil 2:9–11; Rev 5:9–10; and Matt 28:17 (as identified by Bauckham, *Jesus and the God of Israel*, 25). The appearance of veneration in Matthew is

The church outside Paul's influence also identified Jesus as one sent from God. This may have originally meant no more than that he was commissioned by God for a particular task, just as the prophets and others were so commissioned. Before and beyond Paul's influence, the church also called Jesus "Son of God." While this could be understood as nothing more than calling a king the son of God, Jesus was set apart more distinctly because he has a soteriological function. It is through him that others are adopted into the family of God. The association the tradition of Rom 1:3–4 makes between the sonship of Jesus and the resurrection also suggests a distinctive and exalted understanding of this sonship. Finally, the tradition cited in 1 Cor 8:6 designates Christ as the mediator of creation. This attributes preexistence and participation in divine activity to Christ.

Importantly, all of these christological claims appear in traditions that Paul did not author and that derive from parts of the church that were not dominated by Paul's influence. All of these beliefs about Christ predate or develop outside Paul's influence. None of these descriptions of Jesus are attempts to convince readers to accept them; rather, Paul presupposes that the recipients of his letters already believe these things. He uses these assertions about the identity of Jesus to support arguments about other issues. They serve as effective warrants only if the readers already accept their truth. Paul does not make any argument to demonstrate that Christ holds any of these titles or positions; he simply assumes that all of his readers acknowledge these things about Christ. Dunn notes that there is no evidence that the church's exaltation of Christ to be judge and to rule over all things met with opposition from Jews who were not in the church. After all, before Jesus, other Jewish literature had accorded such roles to Elijah, Elisha, and Moses.[145]

Perhaps it is right to see Paul use the *Maranatha* cry as an attempt to maintain a connection between his predominantly gentile churches and the original Aramaic-speaking church in Jerusalem. It at least shows that his practice and teaching bring elements of that original church's worship into the worship of his gentile churches. The use of so much traditional material in Romans also shows that Paul expects there to be continuity between the confessions and liturgy of the earliest church and that of the Roman church. He expects them to recognize the cited traditions as elements of the faith that both he and they

---

important here because Wilson claims that this is the Gospel that comes from the "Jesus Movement" and opposes Paul's teaching (*How Jesus Became Christian*, 151). Even if we adopt Wilson's view, this Gospel's community has an understanding of Christ that allows Torah-observant Jews to offer him worship.

145. Dunn, "How Controversial Was Paul's Christology?" 162–63.

accept. Thus he can show his solidarity with their faith through demonstrating his conformity with the beliefs and confessions of the church that is outside his influence.

Before leaving the topic of Christology, we need to give attention to one other text, Rom 9:5. While it does not contain a citation of a preformed tradition, it may be a place where Paul calls Christ "God." Interpreters are deeply divided over whether the doxology at the end of the verse applies to God or to Christ. If it applies to Christ, it is the only place where Paul directly names Christ as God. The question comes down to whether the sentence ends after "Christ according to the flesh" or whether there is only a comma after that phrase. If the sentence ends, the doxology applies to God; if a comma is the correct punctuation, the doxology applies to Christ. Most interpreters recognize that there are difficulties with either reading. The reading that ends the sentence after "flesh" must explain the strange form of the doxology. Other doxologies begin with "blessed," but here this term appears as the sixth word. It also contains the anomaly of having the participle ōn ("being" or "is") within the construction that names God.[146] The view that sees the doxology addressed to Christ must explain why this unique attribution appears here. It is particularly problematic when viewed in conjunction with 1 Cor 15:24-28, where Christ is clearly subordinate to God.[147] In addition, the construction of Rom 9:5 has some significant parallels with the doxology of 2 Cor 11:31, where the "Lord Jesus" appears between "God and Father" and the doxology. This doxology also has the participle ōn following the article (ho, "the"). Some have found the choices so difficult that they suggest a textual emendation.[148]

It seems impossible to determine with certainty which option is correct. The virtue of being consistent with Pauline usage weighs heavily in favor of the doxology being directed toward God. But claiming that Christ is "over all" is not distinctive. We have seen that claim in Phil 2:10. Also in that tradition we hear that Christ is "in the form of God" (v. 6), he is given the "name above all names," and he is honored in ways that are appropriate only to God (vv. 10-11). So the step to using the term *theos* ("god") to refer to him may not be as much of a leap as it appears at first blush.[149] Thus even if Paul does call Christ God

---

146. See these and other arguments in Cranfield, *Romans*, 2:464-69; Jewett, *Romans*, 567-69; Fitzmyer, *Romans*, 548-49.

147. Dunn, *Romans 9-16*, 535-36. See below the treatment of this passage in ch. 5.

148. Recently, Ziesler is tempted to this option (*Romans*, 239). For a history of this solution see Cranfield, *Romans*, 2:465-66; Fitzmyer, *Romans*, 548-49.

149. This may especially be the case if we take into consideration how broad a meaning

here, as the majority of commentators conclude, he has not made a claim that moves significantly past what we have seen in the claims made about Jesus in the pre-Pauline traditions.

This investigation of Paul's use of christological traditions shows clearly that Paul is not a maverick who is creating new beliefs about the nature or work of Christ. Instead, he ties himself closely to the beliefs and confessions that the church proclaimed before he joined the movement and before he became an influential member of the community. He uses these traditions to address new problems and to arrive at conclusions about how the church should conduct its life. Sometimes his uses of the traditions make him quite different from many others in the church. But he builds his case for these positions (e.g., his view about how gentiles are related to the Torah) on the beliefs that he shares with those others in the church with whom he argues.

---

the term *theos* could have. See Marianne Meye Thompson, *The God of the Gospel of John* (Grand Rapids: Eerdmans, 2001), 17-54.

CHAPTER 4

"For Our Sins"
Understandings of Salvation

Those who argue that Paul was the inventor of Christianity often assert that Paul turned the church's teaching into a religion of otherworldly salvation. James Tabor says it was Paul who introduced the idea that Christ brings eternal life, while before Paul the church was just a community waiting for Jesus to return to establish an earthly kingdom.[1] Arguing for a similar view of the pre-Pauline church, Hyam Maccoby contends that Paul created the idea of a descending savior because of his "unsuccessful spiritual quest."[2] In this chapter we will examine Pauline texts that seem to cite earlier traditions that reveal something of the understanding of salvation that was in the church before Paul. We have already seen the ways the tradition before Paul interpreted the death of Jesus as salvific. Now we will see how the tradition describes that salvation and how it is accessed.

Romans 7:4 and 8:11

In Rom 7:4 Paul uses marriage as an analogy to argue that believers are free from the law and bound to Christ. He identifies this new state as being bound to "the one who was raised from the dead." This participial form with the

---

1. James D. Tabor, *Paul and Jesus: How the Apostle Transformed Christianity* (New York: Simon & Schuster, 2012), 25.
2. Hyam Maccoby, *The Mythmaker: Paul and the Invention of Christianity* (New York: Harper & Row, 1987), 184, 198.

inclusion of "from the dead" cites the same tradition we saw in the previous chapter that identifies Jesus as the one raised by God.[3] While the tradition is used to describe salvation as coming to those attached to Christ, the language that makes the soteriological claim is not part of the cited tradition. So even though the tradition is used in the service of an assertion about salvation, this passage does not show that this understanding of salvation is earlier than Paul.

Similarly, in Rom 8:11 Paul claims that the Spirit of Christ lives in the believer. The presence of this Spirit is the assurance that believers will be raised from the dead because it is the Spirit of "the one who raised Christ from the dead." This phrase repeats the same traditional identification of God that appears in Rom 7:4 and in the other passages we saw in the previous chapter.[4] The use of non-Pauline phrasing and formal style indicate that Paul is drawing on this tradition. But once again, the cited material speaks of God raising Christ, while it is only Paul's use of it that interprets that act as related to the salvation of believers.

1 Thessalonians 4:14

Several factors indicate that the same tradition appears in 1 Thess 4:14. The formal bipartite statement,[5] "Jesus died and was raised," is introduced with the *pistis* formula ("we believe") that has a recitative *hoti* ("that") to introduce the quotation.[6] Use of the name Jesus alone, particularly in relation to the resurrection, is unusual in Paul. The name Jesus without a title (Lord, Christ,

---

3. So James D. G. Dunn, *Romans 1-8*, WBC 38A (Waco: Word, 1988), 362; Dunn, *The Theology of Paul the Apostle* (Grand Rapids: Eerdmans, 1998), 175; Robert Jewett, *Romans: A Commentary*, Hermeneia (Minneapolis: Fortress, 2007), 435; Joseph A. Fitzmyer, *Romans: A New Translation with Introduction and Commentary*, AB 33 (New York: Doubleday, 1993), 459; Werner Kramer, *Christ, Lord, Son of God*, trans. Brian Hardy, SBT 1/50 (London: SCM, 1966), 22.

4. Among those who see Paul citing an earlier tradition here are Brendan Byrne, *Romans*, SP (Collegeville, MN: Liturgical Press, 1996), 161; Douglas Moo, *The Epistle to the Romans*, NICNT (Grand Rapids: Eerdmans, 1996), 505; Jewett, *Romans*, 477; C. E. B. Cranfield, *A Critical and Exegetical Commentary on the Epistle to the Romans*, 2 vols., ICC (Edinburgh: T. & T. Clark, 1975), 1:390-91; Dunn, *Romans 1-8*, 447; A. M. Hunter, *Paul and His Predecessors*, rev. ed. (London: SCM, 1961), 30; Kramer, *Christ, Lord, Son of God*, 22; Klaus Wengst, *Christologische Formeln und Lieder des Urchristentums*, SNT 7 (Gütersloh: Gütersloher Verlagshaus, 1972), 31.

5. Vernon H. Neufeld makes note of this feature (*The Earliest Christian Confessions*, NTTS 5 [Grand Rapids: Eerdmans, 1963], 46).

6. Kramer, *Christ, Lord, Son of God*, 29.

etc.) occurs only nine times in the undisputed letters outside 1 Thess 4:14. Of those nine, three are in other citations of traditions and refer to his resurrection or exaltation (Rom 8:11; 2 Cor 4:14; Phil 2:10).[7] The presence of the verb *anistēmi* ("to rise") also suggests that this verse quotes a tradition because it appears only when Paul is citing preformed material, with the possible exception of 1 Thess 4:16 (we will explore in ch. 5 whether this is also traditional material).[8] When Paul speaks of the resurrection of both Jesus and believers, his usual verb choice is *egeirō* ("raise"). The combination of these features indicates that this is the citation of a tradition.[9]

A number of interpreters find the description of the death and resurrection of Jesus in this verse very strange for the Hellenistic environment, so strange that it shows that the substance of this confession must go back to the Jerusalem church.[10] Paul goes on to associate believers with the resurrection of Christ in such a way that they are promised resurrection with him. While the short statement about the death and resurrection of Jesus almost certainly derives from a traditional formulation, the claim that his resurrection promises the resurrection of believers is not clearly a direct quotation. Thus we again cannot assign this understanding of salvation to the earlier tradition on the basis of this text. In the next chapter we will return to 1 Thess 4:14–17 in the discussion of citations of eschatological traditions.

Galatians 2:20

Multiple traditional elements appear in Gal 2:20, where Paul says he lives by faith "in the Son of God who loved me and gave himself for me." We have

---

7. The other uses are in Rom 3:26; 1 Cor 12:3; 2 Cor 4:10 (twice), 11; 11:4.

8. Abraham J. Malherbe observes that this verb appears in Paul only here and in v. 16 (*The Letters to the Thessalonians: A New Translation with Introduction and Commentary*, AB 32B [New York: Doubleday, 2000], 265). The other places it appears are in quotations of texts from the Hebrew Bible: Rom 15:12 and 1 Cor 10:7.

9. Those who see Paul citing a tradition here include M. Eugene Boring, *1 & 2 Thessalonians: A Commentary*, NTL (Louisville: Westminster John Knox, 2015), 161. A number of interpreters see the similar phrase "who died and was raised" in 2 Cor 5:15c as the citation of a similar formula (so Neufeld, *Earliest Christian Confessions*, 48; Kramer, *Christ, Lord, Son of God*, 29; Dunn, *Theology of Paul*, 175). But again the further theological claims in the passage are not part of the cited tradition.

10. Rudolf Bultmann, *Theology of the New Testament*, trans. Kendrick Grobel, 2 vols. (New York: Scribner's Sons, 1951–1955), 1:346; F. F. Bruce, *1 & 2 Thessalonians*, WBC 45 (Waco: Word, 1982), 97–98.

already seen the traditional use of "Son of God" and of *paradidōmi* ("to give") in other places. The two appear together in this passage. Both *paradidōmi* and the unusual *agapaō* ("to love") appear as participles. As we have seen, such uses of participles often appear in preexisting formulae. Further, identifying Jesus as "Son of God" and mentioning his love press a bit beyond what Paul needs to make his point here. We have also seen in chapter 2 that *hyper* ("for") in early formulae designates the recipients of the benefits of the death of Jesus. Paul has already cited this formula in Gal 1:4,[11] and now echoes it again in his summary of his basic argument against those who demand that gentiles observe Torah as Jews do.[12] We have already seen that Paul is familiar with the confession that Jesus was given over or that he gave himself (e.g., Rom 4:24-25; 8:32).[13] J. Louis Martyn reconstructs a complex tradition of the meaning and means of justification (or, in his language, rectification) in which this formula that says Jesus gave himself plays an important role. According to Martyn, this argument developed in a Jewish environment because it did not originally deal with the question of gentiles.[14] While his argument may stretch the evidence, he shows the way such a formula could be heard in the earliest days of the church as the death of Jesus was understood to bring forgiveness for transgressions of the covenant within a Jewish environment.

In Gal 2:20, Paul takes up the tradition that asserts that the death of Jesus provides forgiveness for violations of the covenant and alters it to fit his immediate argument. Thus the object of *hyper* ("for") is not "us" but "me." In the larger argument, Paul has identified himself with the death and resurrection of Christ, asserting that Christ lives in him—and by implication in all believers. The means of proper relationship with God is here the death of Christ. The

---

11. So e.g., Charles H. Cosgrove, *The Cross and the Spirit: A Study in the Argument and Theology of Galatians* (Leuven: Peeters, 1988), 35; James Dunn, *The Epistle to the Galatians*, BNTC (Peabody, MA: Hendrickson, 1993), 146-47.

12. Others who recognize the citation of a preformed tradition include Hans Dieter Betz, *Galatians: A Commentary on Paul's Letter to the Churches in Galatia*, Hermeneia (Philadelphia: Fortress, 1979), 125-26; Wengst, *Christologische Formeln*, 57, who identifies it as a variation on the "sending formula."

13. So F. F. Bruce, *The Epistle to the Galatians: A Commentary on the Greek Text*, NIGTC (Grand Rapids: Eerdmans, 1982), 145-46; Dunn, *Galatians*, 147. Reinhard Deichgräber identifies it as a preaching formula (*Gotteshymnus und Christushymnus in der frühen Christenheit: Untersuchungen zur Form, Sprache und Stil der frühchristlichen Hymnen*, SUNT [Göttingen: Vamdenhoeck & Ruprecht, 1967], 112); similarly Richard Horsley sees the "for you" element as a creedal formula or "homiletic slogan" (*1 Corinthians*, ANTC [Nashville: Abingdon, 1998], 161).

14. J. Louis Martyn, *Galatians: A New Translation with Introduction and Commentary*, AB 33A (New York: Doubleday, 1997), 264-68.

citation of the formula supports this point. The element of salvation that it supports most directly is that Christ now lives in the believer. But the claim of the indwelling is not part of the tradition Paul cites. While he makes a necessary connection between the two, this connection is part of his argument rather than part of the earlier tradition. It may be that some traditions make this connection, but they do not appear here. This passage does show that the tradition interpreted Jesus's death as vicarious, at least in the sense that it was beneficial for others.

We have now seen Paul use various traditional formulae to support his assertion of the shared identity or experience of the believer and Christ three times. But we have not seen the tradition assert that the believer is drawn into identity with Christ. The next passage, Gal 3:27-28, shows that the earlier tradition had indeed made that connection.

Galatians 3:27-28

Interpreters are nearly unanimous in identifying Gal 3:27-28 as a preexisting baptismal liturgy.[15] The fullest extant citation of the formula appears here. It proclaims a baptism in the name of Christ through which one becomes identified with Christ. It then announces the end of the significance of other identities, including some of the deepest social distinctions in the ancient world.

In addition to its presence in Gal 3, citations of this tradition appear in 1 Cor 12:13[16] and Col 3:11. Outside the Pauline corpus, Ignatius (*Smyrn.* 1.2)

---

15. Those who reject this identification include Troy Martin, "The Covenant of Circumcision (Gen 17:9-14) and the Situational Antithesis of Gal 3:28," *JBL* 122 (2003): 111-25. Dunn remains uncertain because it is such an extensive piece that he wonders whether it could have developed so quickly (*Galatians*, 201). Bernard C. Lategan has also argued that Paul composes this material ("Reconsidering the Origin and Function of Galatians 3:28," *Neot* 46 [2012]: 275-79), but he fails to take account of the cumulative nature of the evidence.

16. Among those who recognize that the same tradition is being cited are James Dunn, *Baptism in the Holy Spirit: A Re-examination of the New Testament Teaching on the Gift of the Spirit in Relation to Pentecostalism Today*, SBT 2/15 (Naperville, IL: Allenson, 1970), 109-13, 117-20, 127-31; Anthony C. Thiselton, *The First Epistle to the Corinthians: A Commentary on the Greek Text*, NIGTC (Grand Rapids: Eerdmans, 2000), 998; Anders Eriksson, *Traditions as Rhetorical Proof: Pauline Argumentation in 1 Corinthians*, ConBNT 29 (Stockholm: Almqvist & Wiksell, 1998), 127-29; Raymond F. Collins, *First Corinthians*, SP (Collegeville, MN: Liturgical Press, 1999), 462-63; Wolfgang Schrage, *Der erste Brief an die Korinther*, 4 vols., EKKNT 7.1-4 (Neukirchen-Vluyn: Neukirchener Verlag, 1991-2001), 3:207, who gives a succinct account of the evidence for identifying it as the same tradition.

"For Our Sins"

may echo the same formulation.[17] The clear parallels in the three citations within the Pauline corpus consist of simple pairs of opposites, references to baptism when baptism is not in the context, and references to putting on either Christ or the "new person."[18] Wayne Meeks notes that the simplicity of the pattern as well as the changes in the wording are common characteristics of early liturgies and kerygmatic formulae.[19] Beyond the references to baptism, these formulae also stand apart from their contexts. In the case of Galatians, this is seen in the inclusion of the male/female pair and the change in that pair to reflect the wording of Gen 1:27. There is also a change from first person plural to second person plural in the traditional material.[20] Since this change in person occurs at verse 26, it is possible that the formula shapes that verse as well.

Martyn identifies three possible backgrounds for this liturgy: (1) philosophical traditions that look to freedom from distractions that come from attention people give to such differences; (2) proto-gnostic thought that saw original humanity as androgynous; and (3) apocalyptic traditions that saw sexual differences disappearing at the resurrection. While he leans toward the third possibility, he is unwilling to rule out any of these contexts.[21] Hans Dieter Betz also leaves open multiple possibilities, but concludes that it is a preexisting non-Pauline formulation that Paul uses for his own purposes here.[22]

Some who contend that Paul invented Christianity would reject the evidence that this passage draws on a non-Pauline source. Tabor contends that Paul invented "Christian baptism" because the earlier apostles were not baptized in the name of Jesus and their practice of baptism was a continuation of the baptism of John the Baptist. The Acts account of those apostles baptizing in the name of Jesus is wrong because there is no account of the apostles themselves receiving this new baptism.[23] Thus if the formula includes a reference to being baptized into Jesus or Christ, it must reflect Pauline theology.

---

17. So Wayne A. Meeks, "Image of the Androgyne: Some Uses of a Symbol in Earliest Christianity," *HR* 13 (1974): 180.

18. See Robin Scroggs, "Paul and the Eschatological Woman," *JAAR* 40 (1972): 292; Meeks, "Image of the Androgyne," 180-81.

19. Meeks, "Image of the Androgyne," 181.

20. Meeks, "Image of the Androgyne," 181. David Hellholm cites several of these points as he concludes that this is the citation of a tradition ("The Impact of the Situational Contexts for Paul's Use of Baptismal Traditions in His Letters," in *Neotestamentica et Philonica: Studies in Honor of Peder Borgen*, ed. David E. Aune, Torrey Seland, and Jarl H. Ulrichsen, NovTSup 106 [Leiden: Brill, 2003], 152).

21. Martyn, *Galatians*, 379-80.

22. H. Betz, *Galatians*, 183-84.

23. Tabor, *Paul and Jesus*, 135-37.

Tabor writes as though it is shocking news to observe that the baptism of the church is different from that during Jesus's lifetime.[24] As noted in the introductory chapter, such a difference is not only *not* surprising—it is necessary for those who claim some attachment to the one they know to have been executed and raised from the dead. The church never just believed *with* Jesus; its membership was defined from the beginning as those who believed *in* the one God who raised Jesus from the dead.

The evidence of the Didache, which Tabor and Barrie Wilson say is not infected with Pauline theology but rather goes back to James and the church before Paul,[25] also demonstrates that a baptism that associated the believer with Christ was part of the church beyond and before the influence of Paul. The Didache's instructions on baptism tell the one baptizing to conduct the rite "in the name of the Father and the Son and the Holy Spirit" (7.1). This instruction is reiterated in 7.3. Then in its instructions about the Eucharist, it insists that only those "baptized in the Lord's name" be allowed to partake. That "the Lord" here means Jesus is made obvious by the immediately following citation of Matt 7:6 as a saying from this Lord (Did. 9.5). Clearly the Didache advocates a baptism that admits the person into the community that possesses salvation through Christ.[26] It is a baptism done "in the Lord's name."

It is difficult to identify the origin of the "in the name of" formula that appears in the Didache and various New Testament references to the church's baptism because it is very uncommon in Greek. Various hypotheses have been suggested, with few gaining much acceptance. The most probable seems to be that it is a literal translation of the Hebrew *ləšēm* or Aramaic *ləšûm*. The phrase "into someone's name" means in connection with or with regard to that person. A religious rite done in the name of a god would be one conducted with reference to that god rather than to another god.[27] Such a use means at least that the church's baptism is distinct from those of John or any others that might be known. Lars Hartman argues that such usage also meant that the one named was the "authority behind the rite, who conferred significance on the rite."[28]

---

24. See Tabor, *Paul and Jesus*, 137–38.

25. Tabor, *Paul and Jesus*, 46; Barrie Wilson, *How Jesus Became Christian* (New York: St. Martin's, 2008), 156–58.

26. See the remarks about salvation being through Christ in the prayers in Did. 10.2–3. Hellholm identifies the "name that was called over you" in Jas 2:7 as an allusion to this formula ("Impact of Situational Contexts," 151).

27. Lars Hartman, *"Into the Name of the Lord Jesus": Baptism in the Early Church*, SNTW (Edinburgh: T. & T. Clark, 1997), 40–43.

28. Hartman, *Into the Name*, 45.

Hartman maintains further that this origin shows that the formula developed within the earliest Aramaic-speaking church and then was adopted and translated literally into Greek.[29] Seeing the same origin for the formula, Robert Jewett interprets it as a rite that connects the believer with the lordship of Christ, perhaps even to a mystical union with Christ.[30]

If this hypothesis about the origin of the "in the name of" formula (of which the phrase "into Christ" is an abbreviation) is correct, then a fundamental element of this baptismal tradition is pre-Pauline. In addition, the lines describing the effect of baptism as identifying with Christ would have been early, even if open to a range of interpretations. Martyn makes a good case for seeing apocalyptic Judaism as the source for the elements of the formula that point to the elimination of the significance of, or even to the eradication of, the differences.[31] If that is correct, then more of the formula probably developed quickly because the church understood itself as an eschatological community from its beginning. It seems probable, however, that the fuller form that mentions the distinction between Jews and gentiles came into use only when it contributed something important. In that case, it became part of the formula sometime after the first gentiles were admitted into the church.

The tradition Paul cites in Gal 3:27-28 demonstrates that the church he is addressing already understands baptism as a rite that identifies believers with Christ and so gives them a share in the eschatological blessings that are mediated through him. The "in Christ" or "in the name of" formula shows that this understanding of baptism predates Paul's entrance into the leadership of the church, and probably his joining of the movement.

Romans 6:3

Romans 6:3 confirms the wider church's practice of baptism. Paul introduces the phrase "as many of us as have been baptized into Christ Jesus" with the rhetorical question "or do you not know?" This introductory remark shows that Paul expects the Roman church to be familiar with baptism as an initiatory rite and as one done in the name of Christ Jesus.[32] It is tempting to

---

29. Hartman, *Into the Name*, 43.
30. Jewett, *Romans*, 397. Robert C. Tannehill argues that the "into Christ" points to the baptized joining "an inclusive or corporate person" (*Dying and Rising with Christ: A Study in Pauline Theology*, BZNW 32 [Berlin: Töpelmann, 1967], 22-24).
31. Martyn, *Galatians*, 379-80.
32. So nearly all interpreters, including Dunn, *Romans 1-8*, 307, 311-12; Cranfield, *Romans*,

identify much of 6:3-5 as the citation of a formula because it echoes much that we have seen in various formulaic traditions. But only "baptized into Christ Jesus" appears in a wide enough group of texts for us to affirm that it repeats the form known throughout the church.[33] Interpreters are divided over how much interpretation Paul adds in the verses that follow. For our purposes it is enough to see that the church beyond Paul's sphere of influence understands baptism as a rite that brings one into the community of those who receive salvation through their relationship with Christ.

Galatians 2:16

Galatians 2:16 gives us further insight into what Paul shares with the predominantly Jewish church that preceded and continued while he established predominantly gentile congregations. The first assertion of this verse is that a person is not justified by "works of the law" but by "the faithfulness of [or faith in] Jesus Christ." The extended introduction to this citation demonstrates that Paul is saying something that he expects all the readers and participants in the debate to know and accept. In 2:15 he addresses "we who are Jews by nature." Given that this is a matter that is being discussed among church members, the people named here are Jews who are in the church. Paul explicitly distinguishes them from gentiles who are in the church. Paul then uses the more common introductory participle, "knowing," to introduce the citation. Finally, before beginning his presentation of the tradition, he inserts a recitative *hoti* that serves to introduce his quotation. What follows then changes the sentence from first person plural ("we") to third person ("a person"). While we do not find the kinds of grammatical forms that often appear in liturgical pieces, this extensive introduction indicates clearly that Paul is giving expression to something that all involved accept.[34] Thus it contains a theological affirmation

---

1:300-301; Fitzmyer, *Romans*, 433; Moo, *Romans*, 359; Jewett, *Romans*, 396; Leander Keck, *Romans*, ANTC (Nashville: Abingdon, 2005), 158; John Ziesler, *Paul's Letter to the Romans*, TPINTC (Philadelphia: Trinity Press International, 1989), 156.

33. Paul alludes to it in 1 Cor 1:13-15; and the fuller form, "into the name of Jesus Christ," appears in Acts 2:38; 8:16; 10:48; 19:5. We also see the yet more detailed form "into the name of the Father and the Son and the Holy Spirit" in Did. 7.1, 3 and Matt 28:19.

34. So nearly all recent commentators, including H. Betz, *Galatians*, 115-17; Richard Longenecker, *Galatians*, WBC 41 (Dallas: Word, 1990), 83; Sam K. Williams, *Galatians*, ANTC (Nashville: Abingdon, 1997), 65. Andrew Das names the apostles, the opponents, the Galatians, and the people of James among those who accept what appears in the first half of v. 16 ("An-

that Jewish members of the church outside Paul's sphere of influence know and believe.

The formulation of the church's message that appears in 2:16 shows that Paul is not the one to introduce justification, or even the language of justification, as something granted to believers in Jesus. Martyn has developed an outline of a "Jewish-Christian" justification tradition that he reconstructs from both Pauline texts and non–church-related Second Temple era texts.[35] The Qumran texts that he cites are particularly helpful in showing that there was a clear tradition of recognizing that human faithfulness to Torah observance was insufficient when one faced God's ultimate judgment. Among the texts he cites are 1QS 11:13-15; 11:12; 1QH 4:34-37. These texts all confess guilt and then express faith in God's grace to forgive and to grant right relationship (justification) on the basis of God's own righteousness (or in Martyn's language, "rectitude"). These texts, among many others, demonstrate that pious observant Jews saw the need for God to act in forgiveness to rectify the relationship between God and God's people.[36] Even if some elements of Martyn's reconstruction need more evidence, this point is firmly established. Importantly, this recognition of guilt and reliance on God's forgiveness did not imply that Torah observance was unnecessary, only that it was insufficient to maintain one's relationship with God. It would have been very unusual to find any observant Jews who thought that their relationship with God was secured by their observance. They recognized that they were granted their covenant relationship with God in advance of any observance. It is within this covenant relationship that they fail in their obligations and then look to God to forgive.[37]

---

other Look at *ean mē* in Galatians 2:16," *JBL* 119 [2000]: 536). Hanna Stettler follows Christoph Burchard ("Nicht aus Werken des Gesetzes gerecht, sondern Glauben an Jesus Christus—seit wann?" in *Frühes Christentum*, ed. Hermann Lichtenberger, vol. 3 of *Geschichte—Tradition—Reflexion: Festschrift für Martin Hengel zum 70. Geburtstag*, ed. Hubert Cancik, Hermann Lichtenberger, and Peter Schäfer [Tübingen: Mohr, 1996], 406-7) in seeing this tradition coming to Paul through the Hellenists who were in the church before Paul. She pushes it even further back, arguing that Peter also knew such traditions ("Did Paul Invent Justification by Faith?" *TynBul* 66 [2015]: 168-70). Her arguments for pushing the tradition's origin earlier, however, rely on attaching it to the Jesus tradition. In this study we are proceeding without making assumptions of such connections.

35. Martyn, *Galatians*, 264-68; Martyn, *Theological Issues in the Letters of Paul* (Nashville: Abingdon, 1997), 142-46.

36. See the many biblical and Second Temple texts that demonstrate this point in Williams, *Galatians*, 63-64.

37. Michael Bachmann argues that in Gal 2:16 God is the one who is active in justifying

The tradition Paul cites in Gal 2:16 identifies Jesus as the one through whom God grants the forgiveness that the Qumran texts attributed only to the character of God. This understanding of the medium of God's forgiveness set the earliest church apart from other observant Jews. As noted above, the introduction of this tradition assumes that all Jews who are in the church agree with it. This can be the case because this formulation of the kerygma is ambiguous.[38] The second half of the citation ("except [or: but] through the faithfulness of [or: faith in] Jesus Christ") may mean either that justification is granted through Christ as opposed to through the works of the law, or that works of the law are insufficient but still required of those justified through Christ.[39] Andrew Das finds this ambiguity to be the reason Paul can cite this tradition. It can be the starting point for Paul's argument because those on the other side accept its validity, but he can also use it to make his case that gentiles do not need the same Torah observance as Jews to be in right relationship with God.[40] However they may have heard the phrase in verse 16, Paul expects all Jews in the church to know and agree with this formulation of the church's message.

The central point for this study is that Paul expects all Jews in the church to accept this tradition's description of the means by which people are granted continual right relationship with God. It is important to recognize that Paul is not contrasting works and faith or doing and believing. Rather he contrasts two "soteriological mediums," the individual's Torah observance and the faithfulness of Christ (or faith in Christ).[41] As the Qumran references above show, church members were not the first to recognize the need for an act of grace beyond Torah observance to maintain justification in God's sight.[42] The move to identify the work of Christ as the means by which this grace is given was

---

by both "works of the law" and the faith of (or in) Christ ("Zwei Ebenen oder eher ein Niveau? Zur Entgegensetzung innerhalb von Gal 2, 16a," *BZ* 59 [2015]: 112–16).

38. See Charles H. Cosgrove, "Justification in Paul: A Linguistic and Theological Reflection," *JBL* 106 (1987): 661–62.

39. A running debate about which of these it means was sparked by James Dunn, "The New Perspective on Paul," *BJRL* 65 (1983): 95–122. Recent contributions to the discussion include Debbie Hunn, "*Ean mē* in Galatians 2:16: A Look at Greek Literature," *NovT* 49 (2007): 281–90; Das, "Another Look." But this issue was being debated as early as D. R. Goodwin, "*Ean mē* in Gal ii. 16," *JBL* (June 1886): 122–27.

40. Das, "Another Look," 539. Das even speculates that those on the other side of the debate may have used this expression to argue their case (538). Dunn thinks this is probable (*Galatians*, 133).

41. Cosgrove, "Justification in Paul," 661.

42. The Day of Atonement is much earlier and is very clear evidence of this recognition.

made before the inclusion of gentiles in the church because the formulation we see in Gal 2:16 did not originally suggest that Torah observance was unnecessary. The earliest church saw no tension between the act of grace seen in Christ's death and the continuing observance of the Torah, just as the Qumran covenanters saw no tension between the exercise of God's grace and strict Torah observance. The lack of tension between these elements, then, points to a time before the inclusion of gentiles in the church. Thus this combination of elements shows that Gal 2:16 is one of the formulae that Paul inherited from the earlier Jewish church.[43]

1 Corinthians 6:11

As part of his argument against believers taking one another to public court in 1 Cor 6, Paul includes a vice list and ends by saying that people who do such things will not inherit the kingdom of God (v. 10). To insist that the Corinthians distance themselves from such conduct, he then says that in the past some of them were those things, but now "you have been washed, you have been made holy, you have been justified in the name of the Lord Jesus Christ" (v. 11). Interpreters often find Paul drawing on the language of a baptismal tradition here. Fragments of the tradition are fairly obvious, especially the claim that these were done "in the name of. . . ." Since the name Jesus is seldom associated with baptism in the New Testament, this may point to its inclusion being drawn from the early tradition.[44] Reginald Fuller notes that the word Paul uses for "in" here (*en*) is not the preposition Paul would use if he were formulating it on his own. The usual preposition he uses in such contexts is *eis*.[45] We saw in connection with Gal 3:27-28 that identification with Christ is associated with baptism in the pre-Pauline tradition. The relationship between baptism and a cleansing from sin is made in Eph 5:26; Titus 3:5; and Heb 10:22. These multiple citations of this understanding suggest that it was earlier than and

---

43. So Martyn, *Galatians*, 249, 264; and following Reumann and Dahl, Cosgrove, "Justification in Paul," 669. H. Betz thinks that both earlier Jewish believers and Paul used this formula to oppose the theology of Pharisaic Judaism (*Galatians*, 115-18). But as we have seen, others within Judaism but outside the church look to an act of grace, not just Torah observance, as the basis for eschatological righteousness.

44. So Richard N. Longenecker, *The Christology of Early Jewish Christianity*, SBT 2/17 (Naperville, IL: Allenson, 1970), 44.

45. Reginald H. Fuller, "First Corinthians 6:1-11: An Exegetical Paper," *ExAud* 2 (1986): 102.

beyond Paul's influence.⁴⁶ In addition, the verb *apelousasthe* ("to be washed") appears only here in the Pauline corpus, indicating that Paul draws it from a source beyond his usage.⁴⁷ Further, that this verb appears in the passive may also indicate that it is part of the tradition.⁴⁸

If the substance of Paul's assertions about baptism here is drawn from earlier tradition, as seems probable, then baptism's associations with forgiveness of sins, with granting holiness, and perhaps with the coming of the Spirit are all part of the church's message before Paul wielded significant influence.⁴⁹ The Didache's use of baptism as the line of demarcation between those who may participate in the Eucharist and the "unholy dogs" also indicates that it sees baptism as the rite that cleanses and makes one holy (9.5). Even if we determine that the terminology of cleansing and making holy as they appear in 1 Cor 6:11 is not directly taken from earlier tradition, this passage in the Didache indicates that these understandings are part of the church's teaching before the time of Paul and outside his influence.

Romans 3:24-26

The vast majority of interpreters are convinced that Rom 3:24-26 contains preformed material that Paul employs here at the heart of the first major section of Romans. This identification of the material often relies on the arguments set out by Rudolf Bultmann and Ernst Käsemann, then strengthened and synthesized by John Reumann.⁵⁰ The reasons for identifying this passage as a tra-

---

46. So Schrage, *Erste Brief an die Korinther*, 1:427; Hans Conzelmann, *1 Corinthians: A Commentary on the First Epistle to the Corinthians*, trans. James W. Leitch, Hermeneia (Philadelphia: Fortress, 1975), 107.

47. R. Collins, *First Corinthians*, 237-38.

48. Conzelmann, *1 Corinthians*, 106-7. While many commentators are convinced that this material is drawn from tradition, Hartman finds it probable but not certain (*Into the Name*, 63n28). However, Hartman expresses much more confidence that this passage does rely on non-Pauline sources (83).

49. Hartman finds the reference to the Spirit as the piece of this passage that does not come from the tradition (*Into the Name*, 85).

50. See Bultmann, *Theology*, 1:46-47; Ernst Käsemann, "Zur Verständnis von Römer 3.24-26," *ZNW* 43 (1950/1951): 150-54; John Reumann, "The Gospel of the Righteousness of God: Pauline Reinterpretation in Romans 3:21-31," *Int* 20 (1966): 432-52. See 432n2 for a review of the discussion up to 1965. A lot of the evidence provided in the next three paragraphs for understanding this text as the citation of a tradition derive from Reumann's account of that evidence (435-38), much of which he draws from Käsemann.

"For Our Sins"

dition are legion. The beginning of verse 24 takes an unexpected grammatical turn. Rather than affirming with a declarative statement (an indicative) that all are declared righteous by God's grace, the verse has a participle, one of those features that often dominate in preformed material. Then verse 25 begins with a relative pronoun (*hon*, "whom"), followed by two relative clauses.[51] So the syntactical construction of verse 23 is never really completed. The piling up of genitive constructions and prepositional phrases present in these verses is also a characteristic of liturgical material.

In addition, several words, particularly in verse 25, appear only here or rarely in Paul's writings. The term *apolytrōsis* ("redemption") in verse 24 appears only here and in Rom 8:23 and 1 Cor 1:30 in the undisputed letters. Notably, a number of interpreters find a citation of traditional material in 1 Cor 1:30 as well.[52] The term *hilastērion* (which Cranfield translates as "propitiatory sacrifice") appears only here and in Hebrews in the New Testament, and *paresis* ("letting go") appears only here in the New Testament. The term *endeixis* ("indication" or "demonstration") is found twice in this passage (once each in vv. 25 and 26), and only two other times in Paul (Phil 1:28; 2 Cor 8:24). *Anochē* ("forbearance") in Rom 3:26 occurs in the New Testament only here and in 2:4, and the verb *protithēmi* ("put forward") is found only two other times in the New Testament, once in Paul (Rom 1:13, where it means "plan"; perhaps its presence there was influenced by Paul's intention to cite the tradition in Rom 3) and once in Eph 1:9.

Beyond these terms that are rare, this is one of the few places that Paul uses the plural *sins*. The plural appears only in quoted material except for its use in 1 Cor 6:18, where he speaks of the many kinds of sins one could commit. It is also unusual for Paul to refer to the blood of Jesus. All the other references to it appear in passages that many also identify as preformed traditions (Rom 5:9; 1 Cor 10:16; 11:25, 27).[53] Finally, Reumann notes that Paul rarely uses *dia* ("through") with an accusative as he does in verse 25, "through the forbearance."[54]

---

51. Reumann, "Gospel," 435. Keck sees a series of three parallel clauses in vv. 22, 24, and 25 (*Romans*, 103).

52. For example, R. Collins, *First Corinthians*, 112; I. Howard Marshall, "The Development of the Concept of Redemption in the New Testament," in *Reconciliation and Hope: New Testament Essays on Atonement and Eschatology Presented to L. L. Morris on His 60th Birthday*, ed. Robert Banks (Grand Rapids: Eerdmans, 1974), 164.

53. We will deal with the 1 Corinthians texts in ch. 6 below on the Lord's Supper. A number of interpreters also identify Rom 5:9 as the citation of a tradition; e.g., Bultmann, *Theology*, 1:295-96; Herman Ridderbos, "The Earliest Confession of the Atonement in Paul," in *Reconciliation and Hope*, ed. Banks, 80; Jewett, *Romans*, 363; Ziesler, *Romans*, 141. Others find that unlikely, e.g., Keck, *Romans*, 140.

54. Reumann, "Gospel," 437.

Despite the many anomalies of this passage, a few interpreters remain unconvinced. Douglas Moo notes that scholars disagree about what elements Paul has added to the tradition, showing that uncertainty about what could be traditional remains.[55] Indeed, interpreters do disagree about the extent of the citation. Some begin it in verse 24, others in verse 25; most see Pauline insertions such as "through faith" in verse 25. For example, Jewett begins the citation at verse 25 and finds "as a demonstration of his righteousness" to be a Pauline insertion.[56] Alternatively, Bultmann and I. Howard Marshall think the citation begins in verse 24.[57] Käsemann argues that Paul cites the tradition that includes what Jewett would see as an insertion and offers a corrective to that tradition in verse 26b.[58] In response to attempts such as those of Käsemann to solve difficulties of interpretation by finding a tradition with Pauline insertions, Cranfield argues that it is unlikely that Paul would place a tradition that he must correct at such a central place in his argument. Thus this material is more likely simply composed by Paul.[59]

The questions raised about the extent of the tradition cited and the way Paul interacts with it are important, but the many irregularities when compared to the rest of the Pauline writings indicate that Paul is drawing on material that he did not author and that he thinks the Roman believers accept as an uncontroversial part of the faith. He may put these beliefs to a new use, but he does not have to argue for their validity. Perhaps the best way forward is to recognize that Paul is combining more than one preformed expression that describe the salvation that the work of Christ effects. Combining such traditions while adding his own emphases can account for the tensions present in the multiple images in these verses.

---

55. Moo, *Romans*, 227, 233n69; Douglas A. Campbell, *The Rhetoric of Righteousness in Romans 3:21–26*, JSNTSup 65 (Sheffield: JSOT Press, 1992), 37–57.

56. Jewett, *Romans*, 288–89. Martyn (*Theological Issues*, 142–43) and Thomas H. Tobin also see the beginning of the citation in v. 25 ("The Use of Christological Traditions in Paul: The Case of Rom 3:21–26," in *Portraits of Jesus: Studies in Christology*, ed. Susan E. Myers, WUNT 321 [Tübingen: Mohr Siebeck, 2012], 229). J. William Johnston allows that it is possible that vv. 25–26 contain traditional material, while being convinced that v. 24 does not ("Which 'All' Sinned? Rom 3:23–24 Reconsidered," *NovT* 53 [2011]: 156).

57. Bultmann, *Theology*, 1:46, 293; Marshall, "Development," 164. So also Ernst Käsemann, *Commentary on Romans*, trans. Geoffrey W. Bromiley (Grand Rapids: Eerdmans, 1980), 95–96; Hunter, *Paul and His Predecessors*, 120–22; Kramer, *Christ, Lord, Son of God*, 24; Longenecker, *Christology of Early Jewish Christianity*, 103.

58. Käsemann, "Zur Verständnis," 152–53. For example, he sees v. 26b as a correction of the proposed two eras of God's dealing with people in vv. 25–26a.

59. Cranfield, *Romans*, 1:200–201.

"For Our Sins"

We noted above how rare the compound term *apolytrōsis* is in Paul. It appears only ten times in the entire New Testament, but those occurrences are spread across a range of texts: two in Hebrews, one in Luke, and four in the disputed Paulines. The simple noun (*lytron*) and verb (*lytroomai*) on which the compound is built are also fairly rare in the New Testament. *Lytron* is used only in the Son of Man sayings in Mark 10:45 and Matt 20:28. The verb occurs in Luke 24:21; Titus 2:14; and 1 Pet 1:18. This constitutes a rather broad range of the branches of the church that use this rare word group. The cognate noun *lytrōsis* appears in Luke 1:68; 2:38; and Heb 9:12. Use of this image across this wide spectrum of the church is due to its derivation from images in the Hebrew Bible. While *apolytrōsis* appears only once in the Septuagint (Dan 4:32),[60] *lytron* and *lytroō* appear with some frequency. Outside the Septuagint, these terms refer to attaining freedom for captives, but they also appear in cultic contexts where a gift is given to a deity in exchange for a life, an exchange that emphasizes the graciousness of the god.[61] In the Septuagint there is particular emphasis on identifying God as the redeemer of Israel, especially from slavery in Egypt. Exodus 6:6 uses this image and terminology for God's saving acts in the freeing of the Israelite slaves.[62] Among the places this language is picked up are Deut 7:8; 9:26; 13:5; Pss 24:22 (LXX); 25:11 (LXX); Isa 41:14; and 43:1, 14. So it is a well-known image that appears in various parts of the Hebrew Bible.

The more frequent metaphorical employment of this word group in the Septuagint suggests that its use in the church arises in a community that knows this image from the Hebrew Bible.[63] Its distribution across so many New Testament sources indicates that its use began early. Since the use of this image is drawn from the biblical texts, its use in the church to interpret the death of Jesus probably began with Jewish believers because they are the people who would be more familiar with the biblical texts. Its rarity in Paul combined with its breadth of use indicates that its use developed outside his sphere of

---

60. The appearance of the compound form in Daniel is probably due to its being composed in the Hellenistic era when compounds gained more popularity. The verb *apolytroō* appears only in Exod 21:8 and Zech 3:1.

61. See F. Büchsel, "*lytron*," *TDNT* 4:340-41. He cites Lucian, *Dial. d.* 4.2 (210), and Aeschylus, *Choephori* (*Libation Carriers*) 48. In Lucian the ransom is a sheep, in Aeschylus it is a ransom of blood. See also the discussions of *lytron* in G. H. R. Horsley, *NewDocs* 2 (1982): 90, no. 58; 3 (1983): 72-75, no. 46.

62. See also the example in which the firstborn is redeemed with a sacrifice, Exod 13:13, 15.

63. Dunn says it is "almost impossible to doubt" that it comes from these early biblical uses (*Romans 1-8*, 169). Fitzmyer also recognizes "through the righteousness in Christ Jesus" as a pre-Pauline formulation (*Romans*, 348).

influence. This is further supported by his expectation that the Roman church will know and accept this interpretation.

The combination of the rare expressions *hilastērion* ("mercy seat," "place of propitiation") and "in his blood" seems to come from the earlier tradition. As noted, Paul almost never refers to the blood of Jesus except when adopting the language of an existing tradition.[64] *Hilastērion* is used often in the Septuagint for the seat on the top of the ark of the covenant in the temple where the presence of God was seen to dwell. It was on this seat that blood was sprinkled to cleanse the temple and the priests so they could offer sacrifices on the Day of Atonement. Jewett argues that this use of blood must be understood apart from the sacrifices for atonement of sins that followed. The function of this sprinkling is purification, not forgiveness.[65] Jewett makes an important distinction here, but the use of *hilastērios* in 4 Macc 17:22 implies that the connection between purification and forgiveness is sometimes closer than what he allows. As 4 Maccabees interprets the death of the martyrs, it says that they purify the homeland, are a ransom for the nation, and through their blood they are an atoning sacrifice (17:21–22). This understanding of the martyrs has significant parallels with the tradition cited in Rom 3:25, most notably bringing together propitiation and shedding of blood.

This passage from 4 Maccabees shows that the way of understanding Jesus's death that we see in Rom 3:25 was a known and accepted way of understanding martyrs' deaths within Hellenistic Judaism. Jewett follows Wolfgang Kraus in asserting that the tradition in Romans has done to the death of Jesus exactly what 4 Maccabees did with the deaths of its martyrs.[66] Jewett, however, observes that what is said of Jesus differs from what 4 Maccabees envisions because in 4 Maccabees the atonement is only for the nation of Israel, while the atonement that comes through Jesus is for the whole world.[67] As Dunn notes, the new use of the language of the mercy seat and blood does not insinuate that the connection to the temple ceremony has been lost.[68] It is effective as an image in part because of the known associations with those services. The image's use in 4 Maccabees shows that Hellenistic Jews knew these associa-

---

64. Despite the unusual vocabulary, Fitzmyer asserts that Paul adds this phrase to the formula (*Romans*, 348).

65. Jewett, *Romans*, 284–86.

66. Jewett, *Romans*, 286. Wolfgang Kraus, *Der Tod Jesu als Heiligtumsweihe. Eine Untersuchung zum Umfeld der Sühnevorstellung in Römer 3,25-26a*, WMANT 66 (Neukirchen-Vluyn: Neukirchener Verlag, 1991), 41.

67. Jewett, *Romans*, 286-87.

68. Dunn, *Romans 1–8*, 171.

tions. Importantly, such an understanding of the deaths of martyrs did not suggest that those who held that view rejected temple worship. Knowledge and recognition of these associations without an explicit reminder of them make the Hellenistic Jewish church a probable place of origin for this tradition in Romans. They know the terminology from the Septuagint and know its use to interpret the deaths of martyrs.

The mention of blood in this connection also seems to point us to ceremonies of covenant initiation and renewal. We will see such a connection in the tradition Paul cites in 1 Cor 11. (We will take up the question of whether this is a tradition and deal with its meaning in ch. 6.) The shedding of blood to initiate a covenant is implied in the service recorded in Gen 15:8-11, 17-21, in which God makes a covenant with Abraham. Similarly, when Jacob and Laban make a covenant, Jacob offers a sacrifice (Gen 31:50-54). Most importantly, the sprinkling of the blood on the altar and on the people at the initiation of the Mosaic covenant (Exod 24:4-8) shows the connection between blood and covenant. This connection is renewed with the sprinkling of blood on the *hilastērion* each year. Käsemann argues that the images of both redemption and propitiation derive from Hellenistic Jewish believers because they hark back to the experience of the renewal of the covenant in the wake of sin.[69]

The meaning of what seems to be a dividing of eras between the time before the crucifixion and the time after, and how Paul deals with that distinction, does not need to detain us here. Our concern at present is to identify the origins of the doctrines and images of salvation that appear in this passage. Clarity about the meaning of God passing over sins will not contribute substantively to that. We note only that this distinction of eras suggests that the death of Jesus has an eschatological significance.

In this setting in which so many unusual words for Paul surface, the appearance of *endeixin* ("demonstration") suggests that the phrase, "a demonstration of his [God's] righteousness," is also part of the traditions Paul uses here.[70] The same phrase appears in verses 25 and 26. Its repetition may indicate that it is important or, as Reumann suggests, that Paul sees a need to comment on it.[71] If it is part of the preformed material, then the tradition before Paul used the metaphor of justification to interpret the results of the death and resurrection of Jesus. In this case, it is not bestowing righteousness (however that

---

69. Käsemann, "Zur Verständnis," 153-54.
70. Contra Jewett, who identifies it as a Pauline addition (*Romans*, 288-89). It would be surprising, however, to find Paul using *endeixis* twice here if it is not part of the citation.
71. Reumann, "Gospel," 435.

is understood) on the believer. Rather, the death and resurrection of Jesus are a demonstration of God's own righteousness, which here includes taking sin seriously and acting graciously toward the sinner. If it is part of the cited tradition, it demonstrates that what some see as Paul's signature image for salvation derived from the church's teaching before Paul had significant influence. This possibility will remain less than certain because this phrase gives expression to perhaps the central assertion of Romans, that the gospel is a demonstration of the righteousness of God (1:16-17). Given the centrality of this claim for the whole letter, Paul may be the one to formulate this phrase even though it would mean that he does so with very unusual terms.

Despite the difficulty interpreters have in trying to reconstruct a single, complex, traditional confession from Rom 3:24-26, we have seen that several elements within these verses have a non-Pauline and earlier origin. He seems to have brought together multiple existing liturgical or kerygmatic formulae to express a major theological point of the letter, that the death and resurrection of Christ rectify the problems created by the sins people commit. That Paul is willing to piece together multiple traditions is not surprising. We regularly see him use this technique in his citations of texts from the Hebrew Bible (e.g., in the immediately preceding paragraph, 3:10-18). By citing and identifying his teaching with these traditions that the Roman church knows, "Paul has created a firm bond between himself and the various congregations in Rome, establishing a persuasive basis for a jointly sponsored mission in behalf of the impartial righteousness of God."[72]

1 Thessalonians 1:9b-10

Many interpreters identify 1 Thess 1:9b-10 as a citation of a tradition of the early Jewish church's preaching to gentiles. Hooker traces this identification as far back as Harnack.[73] The description of the Thessalonians becoming members of the church contains a number of terms that are uncommon in Paul. These include *epistrephō* ("turned") to describe the conversion of these gentiles.[74] Paul

---

72. Jewett, *Romans*, 293.

73. Morna D. Hooker, "1 Thessalonians 1.9-10: A Nutshell—But What Kind of a Nut?" in *Frühes Christentum*, ed. Hermann Lichtenberger, 435, vol. 3 of *Geschichte—Tradition—Reflexion*, ed. Cancik, Lichtenberger, and Schäfer, 3:435, where she cites Adolf Harnack, *Mission and Expansion of Christianity*, trans. and ed. James Moffatt, 2 vols. (New York: Putnam's Sons, 1908), 1:89.

74. So, e.g., Gerhard Friedrich, "Ein Taufleid hellenistischer Judenchristen: 1. Thess. 1,9f.," *TZ* 21 (1965): 506.

usually speaks of people coming to believe in Christ rather than turning from idols. Paul does use this verb in 2 Cor 3:16 and Gal 4:9. In the former it is in a citation of Exod 34:34, and in the latter it is used to describe people turning away from God.[75] These uses are, then, rather different from the use of the verb in 1 Thessalonians. Paul uses *alēthinos* ("true") only here; he otherwise uses the cognate *alēthēs*. Further, Paul usually uses *dechomai* to speak of waiting for the parousia, but here employs *anamenō*, a New Testament hapax legomenon. This is also one of the few places in Paul that the name Jesus appears without an accompanying title (e.g., Lord or Christ).

When Paul speaks of salvation, he usually uses words related to *sōzō*, but here he uses *rhyomai* ("rescue"). The latter appears five other times in the undisputed letters, but not with a clear reference to eschatological salvation, as it has here.[76] One of those other usages is Rom 11:26, where it appears in a citation of Isa 59:20. There Isaiah says that a rescuer will come out of Zion. Christoph Burchard argues that the participle *rhyomenon* in 1 Thess 1:10 should also be translated as "Rescuer" rather than as an adjective describing what Jesus does.[77]

Some have seen the absence of any reference to the death of Jesus in these verses as evidence of the non-Pauline content of the passage. Some of these interpreters think this absence links the tradition with some of the theology in the Q community.[78] We should also add that outside Romans, where it appears most often in chapters 1–5, Paul uses *orgē* ("wrath") only in 1 Thessalonians. It does appear, however, as a way to speak of God's coming judgment in Q (Matt 3:7; Luke 3:7), John, the disputed Paulines, Hebrews, and Revelation.

Most are convinced that the constellation of these unusual terms is good evidence that this passage contains a traditional confession or the preformed content of the church's preaching to gentiles.[79] Kramer argues that the passage

---

75. Hooker notes that both do, however, point to a "wholesale turning" of the person's orientation ("1 Thessalonians 1.9–10," 437).

76. It occurs in Rom 7:24; 11:26; 15:31; 2 Cor 1:10 (twice). In Rom 7:24 it appears in the question, "Who will rescue me from this body of death?" This is certainly asking about salvation, but does not name the parousia as the moment of rescue.

77. Christoph Burchard, "Satzbau und Übersetzung von 1 Thess 1,10," *ZNW* 96 (2005): 272–73.

78. See Earl Richard, *First and Second Thessalonians*, SP (Collegeville, MN: Liturgical Press, 1995), 75.

79. So, e.g., Ernest Best, *A Commentary on the First and Second Epistles to the Thessalonians*, BNTC (London: Black, 1972), 85–87 (and the resources he lists on 87); Richard, *First and Second Thessalonians*, 74–76; Bruce, *1 & 2 Thessalonians*, 17–18; Gerd Lüdemann, *Paul, Apostle to the Gentiles: Studies in Chronology*, trans. F. Stanley Jones (Philadelphia: Fortress, 1984), 219; Boring, *1 & 2 Thessalonians*, 69.

can be traced back to the Aramaic church because its Christology relates only to the parousia and calls Jesus "God's Son" in relation to his role in the eschaton.[80] He also notes that the idea of rescue from wrath can be traced to the Q material and so points to the Aramaic church.[81] Morna Hooker and Charles Wanamaker have argued at length against finding the presence of preformed material here, working to show the weakness of the individual elements that make up the cumulative case.[82] While they show that it is too much to claim that 1 Thess 1:9b-10 contains a single preset formula that formed the kerygma of preaching to gentiles, there do seem to be traditional elements embedded in this text, as the large number of unusual terms suggests. We have already seen how the title *Son* came to be used in the tradition and how the expression "raised from the dead" seems to rely on non-Pauline sources. Romans 1-5 shows clearly that Paul can envision salvation as rescue from divine wrath. Since Paul seldom uses *rhyomai* to speak of this rescue, this passage seems to show that understanding salvation as rescue from God's wrath did not originate with Paul.

Abraham Malherbe shows that the idea that God's eschatological wrath was coming upon gentiles and any unrepentant person was widely known in Jewish writings outside the church.[83] Given the strength of this idea throughout apocalyptic Judaism, it may have been drawn upon first by either Paul or the Jewish church beyond his influence. The use of a term that Paul seldom uses to describe the rescue from the wrath suggests, however, that this expression was formulated by someone other than Paul. Gerd Lüdemann says the consensus position traces the tradition in 1 Thess 1:9-10 to

---

80. Kramer, *Christ, Lord, Son of God*, 124, 126. Günther Bornkamm also sees "Son of God" as a pre-Pauline title of Jesus ("The Revelation of Christ to Paul on the Damascus Road and Paul's Doctrine of Justification and Reconciliation: A Study in Galatians 1," in *Reconciliation and Hope*, ed. Banks, 100).

81. Kramer, *Christ, Lord, Son of God*, 124-25. Claus Bussmann also finds all but "who raised him from the dead, Jesus," as the citation of earlier tradition (*Themen der paulinischen Missionspredigt aus dem Hintergrund des spätjüdisch-hellenistischen Missionsliteratur*, EHS series 23, Theologie 3 [Frankfort: Lang, 1971], 38-56).

82. Hooker, "1 Thessalonians 1.9-10," 435-43; Charles A. Wanamaker, *The Epistles to the Thessalonians: A Commentary on the Greek Text*, NIGTC (Grand Rapids: Eerdmans, 1990), 84-89. Malherbe is convinced by Wanamaker that these verses do not preserve pre-Pauline traditions (*Letters to the Thessalonians*, 118-19).

83. Malherbe, *Letters to the Thessalonians*, 122. His citations are from Sib. Or. 3.545-72; 5.75-89; 12.110-12. For a sample of the range of Second Temple texts that speak of God's wrath, see Erik Sjöberg and Gustav Stählin, "The Wrath of God in Later Judaism," TDNT 5:412-16.

"For Our Sins"

Hellenistic Jewish believers.[84] Thus before Paul's influence the church held to belief in eschatological salvation with Jesus as the one who rescued believers from wrath.

Other Possible Citations

In addition to the more certain appearances of preformed material about salvation in Paul, a number of other passages may contain traditional material on this topic. While these passages do not have a sufficient number of indicators to use with certainty, the evidence is sufficient for them to warrant attention.

In a number of places Paul comments on the suffering of believers as an experience of sharing Christ's suffering that will lead to salvation. John Kloppenborg identifies Rom 8:17c as a variation of the "he died/was raised" formula.[85] The clause "since we suffer with him so that we might be glorified with him" uses vocabulary that is unusual for Paul. He seldom uses *paschō* for suffering[86] and uses the compound verb *sympaschō* ("suffer with") only here and in 1 Cor 12:26. In addition, the verb *syndoxazō* ("to glorify with") appears only here in the New Testament. Beyond unusual vocabulary, the insertion of this phrase that ties suffering to glory exceeds the needs of the context.[87] This evidence, however, has proven too little to convince commentators that Paul is citing a tradition here. Even when it is seen as a citation, it is usually viewed as a significant Pauline variation on the tradition. If it is a citation and if it retains the basic claim of that formula, then the tradition includes identifying believers with Christ in the present and in a future that includes life with God after death.

Some interpreters see Paul's identification of Jesus as the Passover lamb in 1 Cor 5:7 as the citation of an earlier tradition. Paul switches from second person plural ("you") to first person plural ("our") as he identifies Christ in

---

84. Lüdemann comments, "There is no need for us to demonstrate again that Paul is citing tradition in 1 Thess. 1:9–10" (*Paul, Apostle*, 253n95). He cites Friedrich, "Tauflied hellenistischer Judenchristen."

85. John Kloppenborg, "An Analysis of the Pre-Pauline Formula 1 Cor 15:3b–5 in Light of Some Recent Literature," *CBQ* 40 (1978): 363.

86. It appears only five times in the undisputed letters, and the noun cognate appears only in 1 Cor 5:7, which is probably the citation of a tradition.

87. Fitzmyer comments on its surprising insertion here (*Romans*, 502). Still, the following paragraph takes up the topic of the suffering of believers, but it uses the terminology Paul usually uses (*pathēma*) to speak of them.

this way. This is unusual language for Paul; indeed, it is the only reference in Paul to Christ as a lamb or as the Passover lamb. This imagery does appear in 1 Pet 1:19; Rev 5:6, 9, 12 (and multiple other places in Revelation); and John 1:29, 36.[88] In addition, Acts 8:32 applies Isa 53:7, which speaks of the slaughter of a lamb, to Jesus. Further, Paul assumes that this designation of Christ will be uncontroversial because he uses it as a central part of his argument that requires the church to expel the man who is sleeping with his stepmother. He argues that the church must be a holy community, just as a Jewish household was to be pure of yeast at the time of Passover. The analogy works because it identifies Christ as the lamb sacrificed at Passover.

The evidence that Paul is citing a tradition is strong, but the parallels drawn to other uses of the imagery are not as precise as one might hope because Paul does not use any of the terms for "lamb" that the other texts use to identify Christ as a lamb.[89] Moreover, the references to Jesus as the sacrificed lamb in John clearly refer to the sacrifice of the Day of Atonement because he is the one who takes away sin. So it seems that the evidence for calling Jesus the Passover lamb may be more limited than it first appeared. Still the imagery of Jesus as a sacrificed lamb is found across a significant number of branches of the church. This indicates that while the image of Jesus as a sacrificed lamb was widely used, it was given various interpretations. The association of the death of Jesus and the Last Supper with the Passover may be evidence that Jesus's death was understood by others, aside from Paul, to be a Passover sacrifice. The best evidence for this is John's timing of Jesus's death to coincide with the sacrifice of the Passover lamb. There is no other clear evidence that he was identified specifically as the Passover lamb outside the Pauline tradition by this date.

One may conclude, then, that the pre-Pauline and non-Pauline church had begun to refer to Jesus as a sacrificial lamb before the time of 1 Corinthians. One cannot determine what claim they made about the effect of that sacrifice on the basis of 1 Cor 5:7 or the non-Pauline citations of this tradition, with the exception of John 1:29. This verse demonstrates that within the Johannine church the death of Jesus was envisioned as the sacrifice of the Day of Atonement and thus as the death of the lamb that removed sin. Similarly, Acts' citation of Isa 53 includes the removal of judgment through the lamb's

---

88. So Schrage, *Der erste Brief an die Korinther*, 1:382–83; Conzelmann, *1 Corinthians*, 98–99; Joachim Jeremias, "*pascha*," *TDNT* 5:900–901.

89. Revelation consistently uses *arnion*, while John 1:29 and 36 use *amnon*. The citation of Isa 53:7 in Acts 8:32 uses *amnon* and *probation*. Paul uses *pascha* rather than a general word for lamb or sheep.

"For Our Sins"

death. But, as we just saw, John also identifies Jesus with the Passover lamb. Similarly, as 1 Cor 5:7 shows, the imagery signaled various meanings in different texts and traditions.

In Rom 9:32-33 Paul is interpreting the rejection of his gospel by so many of his fellow Jews. These verses may also contain the citation of a traditional formulation. Verse 32b echoes a number of passages of the Hebrew Bible that speak of Israel stumbling.[90] Verse 33 contains a conflation of Isa 28:16 and 8:14 that also appears in 1 Pet 2:6. Paul seems to have altered some of the language of the citation to suit the context of his argument. While the beginnings and ends of the conflated citation are nearly identical, their middle differs. The 1 Peter citation follows the language of Isa 28:16 ("a chosen and precious cornerstone"), while Paul's citation has the language of Isa 8:14 ("stone of stumbling and rock [of stumbling]"). Brendan Byrne, Douglas Moo, and Robert Jewett think there is sufficient evidence to suppose that Paul and 1 Peter have access to an early anthology of biblical citations that the church had already compiled.[91]

These verses also contain language that is rare in Paul. He uses the verb *proskoptō* ("to stumble") only one other time (Rom 14:21). Beyond its two appearances in 9:32-33, the term *proskomma* ("something that causes one to stumble") appears only three times in his letters (Rom 14:13, 20; 1 Cor 8:9). The two usages in Romans may have been provoked by its appearance in the citation. Even *lithos* ("stone") is unusual in Paul, appearing only two times outside Rom 9:32-33 (1 Cor 3:12; 2 Cor 3:7), and he uses it to refer to Jesus only in this Romans text. While the quotation in Rom 9:33 is introduced with a citation formula, Paul identifies it as a passage of Scripture ("as it is written") rather than a tradition. Thus this formula does not help us in determining whether the combination of these texts and their identification of Christ as a stumbling stone is a pre-Pauline tradition.

While the combination of these Isaiah passages and their identification of Jesus as a stumbling stone is significant evidence that this is traditional material, it is not as solid as other passages we have seen. If it is from the tradition, it is the church's interpretation of the rejection of their message by most of their fellow Jews. On balance it seems more likely to have come from the predominantly Jewish church than to have been a formulation of predominantly gentile churches, who would have been less concerned to in-

---

90. Jewett mentions Deut 28:25; Exod 23:33; Isa 29:21; Ps 91:12 (*Romans*, 611).

91. Byrne, *Romans*, 314; Moo, *Romans*, 628-29; Jewett, *Romans*, 612. Keck, however, thinks Paul combined these Isaiah texts (*Romans*, 244).

terpret the rejection of their message by most Jews. The citation also assumes a familiarity with the Hebrew Bible and perhaps a need to reinterpret the "stone" passages.

This citation identifies Jesus as the one through whom God grants salvation. Its concern is not to assert how that is accomplished, only to make Jesus central to it. If this conflation of Isaiah texts is pre-Pauline, it indicates that the predominantly Jewish church already saw Christ as the means of relationship with God. They made this so central that they needed to interpret his rejection by many of their fellow Jews through Scripture.

Conclusion

We have seen in this chapter that a number of ideas about salvation in the Pauline letters appear in pre-Pauline traditions. In places Paul clearly relies on formulations that are earlier than their incorporation into the letters. These prior formulations include some of the central soteriological ideas that we find in Paul.

This study of Gal 2:20 and Rom 3:24–26 demonstrates that the church outside Paul's sphere of influence understood the death of Jesus as the means through which transgressions of the covenant and more generally sin are forgiven. This idea could easily develop within Jewish theological categories, as the similar interpretation of the deaths of martyrs in 4 Maccabees shows. Similarly, Gal 2:16 shows that Jewish believers saw Christ as the one through whom sins were forgiven and saw no conflict between this claim and the demand for careful Torah observance.

Interpretations of salvation in addition to forgiveness are also present in the traditions Paul cites. The idea of eschatological salvation that involves avoiding wrath appears in the traditions behind 1 Thess 1:9–10. The metaphor of redemption also appears in the tradition Paul uses in Rom 3:24–26. Again, it draws on theological categories that were already part of Jewish thought, thought that has deep roots in the Hebrew Bible. So no move beyond the predominantly Jewish church is required for this idea to develop. More surprising, and perhaps more importantly, if Paul is right in expecting all Jewish believers in Christ to acknowledge what he says in Gal 2:16, Paul was not the originator of the use of justification language to speak of salvation. It is part of the tradition he cites that all of his fellow Jewish church members recognize.[92] So even

---

92. This may strengthen the case for the subjective genitive reading of *pistis Christou*

what many see as Paul's signature doctrine was part of the church's teaching before Paul used it so extensively in Galatians and Romans. It is even possible that the idea that the gospel is a demonstration of God's righteousness is part of the tradition Paul cites in Rom 3:24–26. But this remains uncertain. Even though the unusual vocabulary suggests this, the centrality of the assertion to the argument of Romans requires one to admit some uncertainty.

Preformed traditions also show that baptism was an initiation rite that associated one with Christ and salvation before Paul was a leader in the church. The baptismal liturgy in Gal 3:26–28 shows that the church understood baptism as a rite that identified believers with Christ and granted them admission into the eschatological sphere of existence. These blessings are mediated through being identified with Christ. The formula "into the name of" or its shortened form "into Christ" also acknowledges the lordship of Jesus, and some (e.g., Jewett) would say that it implies a mystical union with him. Further, the tradition in Rom 6:3 identifies believers with Jesus.[93] Finally, 1 Cor 6:11 shows that baptism was widely understood to be the act indicating that one receives forgiveness of sins through Jesus. The silence of Acts about the apostles' baptism cannot outweigh this evidence for these meanings of baptism.

The understandings of salvation seen in the pre-Pauline and non-Pauline traditions he cites in his letters demonstrate that Paul's teachings are compatible with those of the wider church. Whatever his innovations, he was not the first to proclaim that Jesus was the means of receiving forgiveness of sins and redemption by God. Neither was he the first to understand identification with Christ as the way to participate in the blessings of the eschaton.

---

because it may suggest that it was Christ's faithful Torah/covenant observance that allows him to share that obedience with those who identify with him.

93. Jewett (*Romans*, 397–98) follows A. J. M. Wedderburn (*Baptism and Resurrection: Studies in Pauline Theology against Its Graeco-Roman Background*, WUNT 44 [Tübingen: Mohr Siebeck, 1987], 54–60) in arguing that the symbolism of baptism included the dying of the baptizands and so links them to the death of Jesus.

CHAPTER 5

"The Coming of the Lord"
Envisioning the Kingdom

Among the arguments given to support the idea that Paul is the inventor of Christianity is that he, apparently single-handedly, changed the church's eschatology from an expectation of an earthly messianic kingdom to an otherworldly hope for life in heaven.[1] So Paul replaced expectations about the defeat of the Romans that one finds in Jesus and the Jerusalem "Jesus movement" with a scheme in which Jesus reigns over all things from heaven. Again, supporters of this idea say that the truth of what Jesus and his earliest and faithful followers said about such things can be found in the Didache and the materials we have from the Ebionites. Barrie Wilson adds Matthew and James as sources that retain the beliefs of that earlier group.[2]

The early church's discussion of eschatology involved more than just talk about the future decisive act of God. It seems most likely that Jesus understood himself to be an eschatological figure. If he did not, all who believed in his resurrection did—as even those who say Paul invented Christianity acknowledge.[3] All members of the earliest church believed that the resurrection of Jesus was an eschatological event. Whatever else was in dispute, all agreed that the resurrection of Jesus meant that God's intervention had begun and would continue soon.

1. Hyam Maccoby, *The Mythmaker: Paul and the Invention of Christianity* (New York: Harper & Row, 1987), 125; James D. Tabor, *Paul and Jesus: How the Apostle Transformed Christianity* (New York: Simon & Schuster, 2012), 12–13; Barrie Wilson, *How Jesus Became Christian* (New York: St. Martin's, 2008), 92, 95–103.
2. Wilson, *How Jesus Became Christian*, 151–54.
3. See, e.g., Tabor, *Paul and Jesus*, 25.

"The Coming of the Lord"

In this chapter we will examine some pre-Pauline and non-Pauline traditions in Paul's letters that involve eschatology or that have eschatological implications. We will also look at some passages in documents that those who accuse Paul of perverting the church's outlook say contain the earlier views of Jesus's followers. We will give renewed attention to a number of passages we have already identified as traditions. Even though we dealt with those texts under different topics, their content is also relevant to seeing what elements of Paul's eschatology were present in the church before he wrote and what elements developed outside his influence.

1 Corinthians 16:22

In chapter 3 we saw that one of the earliest confessions of the church was the acclamation of Jesus as Lord. One of the evidences of its early use is the expression *Maranatha*. It appears not only in 1 Cor 16:22 but also in Did. 10.6. *Maranatha* is an Aramaic expression that has been transliterated into Greek. It is thus evidence that this Aramaic expression had become an element of the church's worship before Paul exerted any influence. Some interpreters think that the phrase invoked the risen Lord to be present at the Lord's Supper. In the Didache it is said at the conclusion of the prayer either at the end of the meal (probably before the Lord's Supper proper; see ch. 6) or before what might have been a second cup, though there is no indication in the text that there was a second cup. But even the Didache's use of *Maranatha* in association with the Eucharist also asks for the eschatological intervention of God.[4] The request that appears just two lines above it is that the world might end. Even if we do not connect the *Maranatha* formula to that request, the call for the presence of the risen Lord at the supper sets this phrase in an eschatological context. It assumes that Jesus has assumed an exalted position and a role in God's eschatological plans.[5]

John Fotopoulos argues that it shows more than this about Christ. He interprets the use of *Maranatha* as part of the curse that immediately precedes it. He identifies it as an example of using *voces mysticae* ("mystical names") in a curse formula.[6] If he is correct, it means that Paul invokes Christ as the

---

4. For further support of seeing the expression as eschatological, see John Fotopoulos, "Paul's Curse of Corinthians: Restraining Rivals with Fear and *Voces Mysticae* (1 Cor 16:22)," *NovT* 56 (2014): 279n16.

5. See the discussion in ch. 3.

6. Fotopoulos, "Paul's Curse of Corinthians," 304–7. See the examples there of other Aramaic-derived similar expressions used in curses.

deity who is to carry out the curse on those who do not heed the letter.[7] This assumes an identity that is at least closer to divinity than simply the one who is God's agent.

Paul's use of the term in 1 Corinthians is certainly a call for Christ to return and so to bring the close of the present age. It is notable that his predominantly gentile church knows this Aramaic formula.[8] This suggests something about the importance this expression had in its original setting and about its use throughout the church. It encapsulates important beliefs concerning both Jesus's identity and the church's eschatology. It demonstrates that the church looks to Jesus as the agent of God's eschatological act. Its use in 1 Corinthians may also suggest that Paul works to maintain ties with the Jerusalem church and its traditions. Obviously he would have had to translate this phrase and explain its significant to the Corinthian congregations, which had very few (perhaps no) speakers of Aramaic. So it took some effort to make this phrase meaningful, even if the Corinthians hear it only as something of an incantation. Clearly its meaning was a call for the return of Christ with an attendant, dramatic saving act of God.[9]

This passage establishes that the earliest Jerusalem believers saw Christ as the exalted Lord (see the discussion in ch. 3 about its connection with Ps 110). As Raymond Collins affirms, its presence in 1 Corinthians "is an indication not only of Paul's reliance upon early Christian traditions in his composition of the letter but also of the generally conservative character of liturgical and prayer formulae."[10] It does not indicate what kind of intervention the return of Christ will bring to the world, only that it will be accomplished at his return. We have to look to other passages for an indication of what God does at that moment.

---

7. Fotopoulos, "Paul's Curse of Corinthians," 306.

8. Fotopoulos acknowledges this as a possibility while also suggesting that Paul may not translate it so that it remains a foreign term and thus seems to convey mystical power ("Paul's Curse of Corinthians," 307). Other uses of the phrase (as in the Didache) or its translation (Rev 22:20) suggest that they do know what it means. Chris Tilling contends that it is a passionate expression of covenant love when Paul uses it (*Paul's Divine Christology* [2012; repr. Grand Rapids: Eerdmans, 2015], 192–93). Even if true for Paul, this is probably not the frame within which the gentile Corinthians hear it.

9. Raymond Collins comments that the presence of this formula "confirms the eschatological expectations of the Corinthian Christians" (*First Corinthians*, SP [Collegeville, MN: Liturgical Press, 1999], 614).

10. R. Collins, *First Corinthians*, 614. He cites the *abba* formula of Rom 8:15 and Gal 4:6 as further evidence of this point.

Galatians 3:27–28 and 1 Corinthians 12:13

In chapter 4 we saw the extensive evidence for identifying Gal 3:27–28 and 1 Cor 12:13 as citations of a preformed baptismal liturgy. That evidence includes its pairs of opposites, the insertion of baptism into the context, and the change from first person plural ("we") to second person plural ("you"). These all indicate that (at least) Gal 3:27–28 is a set piece that Paul inserts into his argument. This formula provides evidence for an early partially realized eschatology. In this formula, those baptized are brought "into Christ" and have "been clothed with Christ." This identification with Christ brings the baptized into the realm that is determined by Christ's identity. The eschatological nature of this claim is evident in the return to oneness. This is nowhere more clear than in the allusion to Gen 1:27. The obvious change in the pattern of the opposed pairs in the formula shows that the oneness in Christ that the liturgy proclaims is a return to the primordial or Edenic ideal state.[11] It is a common feature of apocalyptic Judaism to see the coming age as a return to the ideal original state of creation. This formula draws on that understanding in its allusion to Gen 1:27. The formula also proclaims that this state of existence is a present reality for the baptized.

Given that the formula claims that Jews and Greeks are one, it developed within the wing of the church that admitted gentiles. In addition, Paul assumes that citing this formula will help him make his case against believers who want gentiles to be circumcised. So he expects that it will be accepted by his readers and will be useful in their debates with those he is opposing. It seems, then, to be a widely recognized liturgy, even if some gave it a different interpretation than Paul does here. This suggests that the vast majority of New Testament scholars are correct in identifying this as a pre-Pauline formula. Thus it demonstrates that there was a mission to gentiles before Paul was influential and that the church already had an eschatology that was more complex than simply waiting for the Messiah to free Israel from Roman domination. This eschatology assumes the necessity of identifying oneself with Christ and that this act brings one into a realm in which the eschatological state has begun to exist. The reunification of humanity from the divisions of ethnicity, social status, and gender is an act that reaches beyond the borders of Israel. Such a claim sees the future eschatological act of God as an event that has at least worldwide effects. These effects involve more than the status of the nation of Israel.

---

11. See Wayne A. Meeks, "Image of the Androgyne: Some Uses of a Symbol in Earliest Christianity," *HR* 13 (1974): 165–208.

Philippians 2:6-11

Philippians 2:6-11 is one of the most widely recognized and extensive preformed liturgical pieces in Paul's letters. As noted in the discussion of Christology (ch. 3), its elevated style, parallel clauses, opening with the pronoun "who" (*ho*), and separation from the surrounding text clearly set it off as a preformed piece. We observed in chapter 3 that most interpreters see its origin in the Hellenistic church, but an arm of that church that is also influenced by Jewish thought. We also maintained that it is not possible to claim definitively that it was composed outside the Pauline sphere of influence, even though it has non-Pauline elements.[12] Still some elements of the beliefs expressed in this liturgy clearly echo traditions of the wider and earlier church. The claim that Jesus is Lord is among the church's earliest claims about Jesus. We have also noted that this claim was associated with the wide use of Ps 110:1 to assert the exaltation of Jesus to God's right hand, where he rules over all things. The wide spectrum of early texts in which this assertion of Jesus's place is found shows that it was part of the church's teaching before Paul was influential.[13]

The liturgy in Phil 2:6-11 ties an eschatological element to the claim of the lordship of Jesus. The exaltation of Jesus by God has its completion in the eschatological defeat of all beings in the cosmos (above, on, and below the earth) who oppose God's will (vv. 10-11). As we saw in Gal 3:26-28, this passage also has a type of realized eschatology. The exaltation of Jesus has begun, but its fullness will not be manifest until all powers are subjected to him.

If this lengthy liturgy is produced within the Pauline sphere, it shows that the present exaltation and eschatological completion of that exaltation are accepted as true in Paul's churches. If it is from the non-Pauline Hellenistic church, it shows that the wider church claims a cosmic lordship for Jesus.

1 Thessalonians 1:9b-10

In chapter 4 above we identified 1 Thess 1:9b-10 as a citation of a traditional formula. Its accumulation of words that are unusual in Paul convinces most interpreters that he is borrowing this description of conversion from a prior

---

12. For example, rather than referring to the resurrection as God's response to Jesus's death, this liturgy speaks of Jesus's exaltation.

13. Richard Bauckham notes that this assertion is made in Matt 11:27; Luke 10:22; John 3:35; 13:3; 16:15; Acts 10:36; 1 Cor 15:27-28; Eph 1:22; Phil 3:21; Heb 1:2; 2:8 (*Jesus and the God of Israel* [Grand Rapids: Eerdmans, 2008], 23n45).

"*The Coming of the Lord*"

formulation. We may add that the full statement of verse 10 interrupts the description of the Thessalonians' reception of Paul and his gospel. He resumes that disrupted flow of thought with a repeat of "entrance" (*eisodon*) in 2:1. Among the important terms that appear in 1:10b are "rescue" (*ton rhyomenon*) and "wrath" (*orgē*). The verb "rescue" occurs only five other times in the undisputed letters. One of those uses appears in a quotation of Isa 59:20 in Rom 11:26. Three of them refer to Paul being rescued, quite literally, from people who are seeking to do him harm in the present (Rom 15:31; 2 Cor 1:10, where it appears twice). The only place Paul uses the verb in a less literal sense outside a quotation is Rom 7:24, where he asks, "Who will rescue me from this body of death?" So he does not use it to describe eschatological salvation any place other than in this citation of a tradition in 1 Thess 1:10.[14]

"Wrath" (*orgē*) is also a relatively uncommon word in Paul. Beyond its three uses in 1 Thessalonians (one of which many interpreters identify as an interpolation, 2:16), he uses it only in Romans, where it appears often but mostly in chapters 1–5. This term does, however, appear in many other early writers as a description of God's coming judgment. In Matt 3:7 and Luke 3:7 it is part of Q's description of the preaching of John the Baptist. He speaks of "the coming wrath" (*tēs mellousēs orgēs*). Elsewhere in the New Testament it appears with the sense of God's eschatological judgment (John 3:36; Eph 5:6; Col 3:6; Rev 6:16, 17; 11:18; 14:10; 16:19; 19:15). This sense also occurs in Ignatius (*Eph.* 10.1). So while this language is known and used across various branches of the church, Paul seldom uses it. Furthermore, the idea of the "coming wrath" and being rescued from it are also found in non-church-related Second Temple Jewish texts.[15] Gerhard Friedrich has observed that the theme of coming wrath is characteristic of earlier biblical thought, so that the origins of the whole of 1 Thess 1:9–10 are to be located in the Hebrew Bible and Jewish thought.[16] The only place Paul uses *orgē* to refer to God's judgment outside this place in 1 Thessalonians is in the letter to the church he did not found. His

---

14. Jacob W. Elias also notes that Paul's other uses of *rhyomai* are to deliverance in the present (" 'Jesus Who Delivers Us from the Wrath to Come' (1 Thess 1:10): Apocalyptic and Peace in the Thessalonian Correspondence," in *Society of Biblical Literature 1992 Seminar Papers*, SBLSP 31 [Atlanta: Scholars Press, 1992], 123).

15. Claus Bussmann cites Let. Aris. 254; Sib. Or. 3.309, 556, 632; Wis 16:6-7; 18:20-21 as examples of coming wrath, and Sib. Or. 3.561 as an example of being rescued from it (*Themen der paulinischen Missionspredigt auf dem Hintergrund der spätjüdisch-hellenistischen Missionsliteratur*, EHS series 23, Theologie 3 [Frankfurt: Lang, 1971], 55).

16. Gerhard Friedrich, "Ein Tauflied hellenistischer Judenchristen: 1. Thess. 1,9f.," *TZ* 21 (1965): 511.

use of it there seems to assume that the Roman church members are familiar with this language.

All of this indicates that Paul is probably citing a tradition that comes from a wing of the church that he does not dominate. Bussmann identifies it specifically as a Hellenistic Jewish mission tradition that predates Paul.[17] The use of "awaiting" (*anamenein*) may provide some support for this view. It appears only here in the New Testament but is used in the Septuagint for waiting for the eschatological acts of God (Jer 13:16; Isa 59:11; Sir 2:6-8).[18] Thus it has some currency among Greek-speaking Jews. Given the biblical precedents for elements of this passage, Friedrich finds its origin in Jewish Christian mission preaching.[19] Whether we can be that specific or not, this passage indicates that identifying Jesus as the one who saves believers in eschatological judgment arises in the church before and outside Paul's influence.

2 Corinthians 4:14

In his defense of his manner of apostleship, Paul supports his confidence in the presence of God's power living in him by citing a tradition about the resurrection. He begins 2 Cor 4:14 with an introductory formula, "knowing that." This formula is followed by the substantive participle *egeiras* ("the one who raised") and names the one raised as "the Lord Jesus." This is clearly a citation of the well-known raising formula that we have seen in a number of places (see ch. 3).[20] But this passage seems to cite a longer confession, which continues, "and

---

17. Bussmann, *Themen der paulinischen Missionspredigt*, 56.
18. Abraham J. Malherbe, *The Letters to the Thessalonians: A New Translation with Introduction and Commentary*, AB 32B (New York: Doubleday, 2000), 121. He is followed by Pieter G. R. de Villiers, "In the Presence of God: The Eschatology of 1 Thessalonians," in *Eschatology of the New Testament and Some Related Documents*, ed. Jan G. van der Watt, WUNT 2/315 (Tübingen: Mohr Siebeck, 2011), 316n38.
19. Friedrich, "Taufleid hellenistischer Judenchristen," 510-12. He also asserts that the teleological, salvation-historical eschatology of the passage is a product of Jewish Christianity.
20. Among interpreters who recognize this tradition are Rudolf Bultmann, *The Second Letter to the Corinthians*, ed. Erich Dinkler, trans. Roy A. Harrisville (Minneapolis: Augsburg, 1985), 122; Margaret E. Thrall, *A Critical and Exegetical Commentary on the Second Epistle to the Corinthians*, 2 vols., ICC (Edinburgh: T. & T. Clark, 1994-2000), 1:342; Ralph Martin, *2 Corinthians*, WBC 40 (Waco: Word, 1986), 89; Paul Barnett, *The Second Epistle to the Corinthians*, NICNT (Grand Rapids: Eerdmans, 1997), 242n17; Klaus Wengst, *Christologische Formeln und Lieder des Urchristentums*, SNT 7 (Gütersloh: Gütersloher Verlagshaus, 1972), 46; Werner Kramer, *Christ, Lord, Son of God*, trans. Brian Hardy, SBT 1/50 (London: SCM, 1966), 24.

will raise us with him." A very similar citation of this extended form appears in 1 Cor 6:14 and in a bit different form in Rom 8:11. Victor Furnish notes that this same tradition appears in Ignatius (*Trall.* 9.2) and Polycarp (*Phil.* 2.2).[21] While the passage in Ignatius is a significant expansion of the formula, the citation in Polycarp differs only in having the pronoun "him" rather than "Lord Jesus" and in lacking the phrase "with Jesus." Beyond these other appearances of the tradition, its form takes Paul away from his immediate point so that he has to add commentary that fits its final phrase to his argument. The tradition affirms the resurrection of "us." In the context, Paul has been using the first person plural to refer to apostles in distinction from the Corinthians. So he immediately includes the Corinthians in this "us" who are raised by adding, "and will bring [us] with you."

Klaus Wengst identifies this inclusion of believers as the incorporation of ideas from mystery cults. He contends that identifying believers with the fate of the god was drawn from those cults.[22] But this is not the only source from which the church might have drawn this idea. The concept of corporate personality was well known within Judaism. The church could just as easily have attached believers' eschatological fate to Christ's through this concept. Further, we have already seen that in non-Pauline traditions (e.g., Gal 3:27-28) baptism was understood to transfer the believer into the sphere of identity with Jesus. Moreover, the absence of "with Jesus" in some citations of this formula demonstrates that it does not rely on identification with the fate of a god. While the earliest versions of the tradition may have lacked "with Jesus," they still point to a common exercise of the power of God for both Jesus and those who believe in him. Thus their eschatological fate is revealed in God's resurrection of Jesus. The addition of "with him/Jesus" may simply have been making that idea explicit. It would not take long, one expects, for the ideas of being one with Christ and that of being raised like him to come together. And as the incongruence with the context of 2 Corinthians suggests, it had become part of the formula before Paul cites it there.[23] As noted in chapter 3, the confession that names God as the one who raised Jesus comes from the earliest Palestinian church. Since the belief that the resurrection of Jesus ini-

---

21. So Victor P. Furnish, *II Corinthians: A New Translation with Introduction and Commentary*, AB 32A (Garden City, NY: Doubleday, 1984), 258.

22. Wengst, *Christologische Formeln*, 46.

23. While William R. Schoedel identifies "one who raised Jesus" as a Pauline formula (*Ignatius of Antioch: A Commentary on the Letters of Ignatius of Antioch*, Hermeneia [Philadelphia: Fortress, 1985], 154), we have already seen evidence of its pre-Pauline origins. See the discussion of Rom 8:11 and related passages in ch. 3.

tiated the resurrection of the eschaton also emerges from the church's earliest days, the confession that mentions both may have had its origin in that early time as well.

The citation in 2 Cor 4:14, then, indicates that some relationship between the resurrection of Jesus and that of believers was posited in some of the church's earliest confessions. Even the addition of "with Jesus" fits with the earliest baptismal liturgies that identify the baptized with Christ. So the confession in 2 Cor 4:14 shows that before Paul influenced the beliefs of the church, it held that God would act for believers as God had acted for Jesus and that their resurrection would be "with him."

1 Thessalonians 4:13-18

The issue Paul addresses in 1 Thess 4:13-18 involves whether or how believers who have died will participate in the resurrection. The Thessalonians seem to think either that those who die before the parousia will miss out completely on resurrection existence or that they will in some way be disadvantaged in comparison with those who live until the parousia. This problem is particularly vexing because this community is experiencing persecution.[24] They must be weighing whether it is worth enduring the persecution if there is a good possibility that they will die and so receive no response from God for their faithfulness or at least that they will be excluded from some things that others will enjoy. Paul's response assures them that the dead will participate fully in the parousia.

In chapter 4 we saw that 1 Thess 4:14 recites the creedal formula, "Jesus died and was raised." This statement is introduced with the *pistis* formula ("we believe") and then uses the verb *anistēmi* ("raised") and the name Jesus with no qualifiers, both of which are unusual in Paul. Ernest Best and Charles Wanamaker argue that such a reference to Jesus without a title shows that this creedal statement goes back to a time before it was "customary" to call Jesus "Lord" or "Christ." Thus it must go back to the Palestinian church.[25]

---

24. See J. M. G. Barclay's discussion of how this crisis might develop and of the dangers of speculating about what Paul might have preached during his inaugural visit to Thessalonica (" 'That You May Not Grieve, like the Rest Who Have No Hope' [1 Thess 4:13]: Death and Early Christian Identity," in *Not in the Word Alone: The First Epistle to the Thessalonians*, ed. Morna D. Hooker, Monograph Series of Benedictina [Rome: St. Paul's Abbey, 2003], 135-38).

25. Ernest Best, *A Commentary on the First and Second Epistles to the Thessalonians*, BNTC (London: Black, 1972), 187; Charles A. Wanamaker, *The Epistles to the Thessalonians: A*

"The Coming of the Lord"

We can now note that verse 14b also reflects the tradition we identified in connection with 2 Cor 4:14. While only the first part of the Corinthian text is clearly a direct citation of a set formula, the idea that the general resurrection of the dead was connected with and would coincide with the return of Christ was part of a set formulation before Paul wrote 1 Thessalonians. What follows in 1 Thess 4:15-17 confirms this position.

In verse 15 Paul identifies what he is about to say as a "word of the Lord." Interpreters have understood this "word of the Lord" to refer to either a saying of the earthly Jesus or a saying of the exalted Lord that was received by a prophet.[26] Abraham Malherbe and Earl Richard are among those who identify Paul as the prophet who received this "word."[27] Some who see Paul referring to a saying of the earthly Jesus contend that it is an agraphon, a saying not recorded in any extant source. Others identify it with a particular passage from the Gospels. Wanamaker, for example, connects it with Matt 24:29-31.[28] Alternatively, Robert Gundry contends that it is an elaboration of John 11:25-26.[29] Less specifically, F. F. Bruce follows Bultmann in identifying it as a tradition from the Jerusalem church.[30]

Ulrich Müller compares this statement to the ways prophets in the Hebrew Bible introduce their messages, noting that both the John of Revelation and Paul use the form.[31] He concludes that prophetic formulae such as this were used in early Christianity to introduce eschatological prophecies.[32] Citing

---

Commentary on the Greek Text, NIGTC (Grand Rapids: Eerdmans, 1990), 168. Rudolf Bultmann also traces this tradition, with its talk of "resurrection of the dead," back to "Jewish-Christian tradition," saying it would sound "strange to Hellenistic ears" (*Theology of the New Testament*, trans. Kendrick Grobel, 2 vols. [New York: Scribner's Sons, 1951-1955], 1:346).

26. For example, Best, *Epistles to the Thessalonians*, 192.

27. Malherbe, *Letters to the Thessalonians*, 268-70; and Earl Richard, *First and Second Thessalonians*, SP (Collegeville, MN: Liturgical Press, 1995), 226.

28. Wanamaker, *Epistles to the Thessalonians*, 171. He says that it may be a midrash on this tradition.

29. Cited in J. Ramsey Michaels, "Everything That Rises Must Converge: Paul's Word from the Lord," in *To Tell the Mystery: Essays on New Testament Eschatology in Honor of Robert H. Gundry*, ed. Thomas E. Schmidt and Moisés Silva, JSNTSup 100 (Sheffield: JSOT Press, 1994), 183.

30. F. F. Bruce, *1 & 2 Thessalonians*, WBC 45 (Waco: Word, 1982), 98; Bultmann, *Theology*, 1:188-89. Bruce also leaves open the possibility that it came from a prophet (*1 & 2 Thessalonians*, 99).

31. Ulrich B. Müller, *Prophetie und Predigt im Neuen Testament: Formgeschichtliche Untersuchungen zur urchristlichen Prophetie*, SNT 10 (Gütersloher: Gütersloher Verlagshaus, 1975), 44-46.

32. Müller, *Prophetie und Predigt*, 165.

the grammatical form of verses 15–17, he identifies this statement as a tradition of the Hellenistic church that fits the form of prophetic speech in the Gospels. So when Paul says it is a "word of the Lord," Paul thinks it is a saying of Jesus, but it is really an element in the tradition of the Hellenistic church.[33] Michael Pahl rejects this line of thought by surveying the ways "word of the Lord" is used in early Christian literature. He observes that it is never used to refer to a saying of Jesus. Furthermore, given Paul's need to encourage the Thessalonians not to dismiss prophecy (5:20), it is unlikely that he is referring to a prophetic oracle. Therefore, it must be a reference to the whole of the gospel message about the death and resurrection of Jesus.[34]

Given the difficulty interpreters have in determining the meaning of this introductory phrase, it seems best not to invest our understanding of what follows too deeply in its meaning. We turn, then, to whether one can identify the content of verses 15b–17 with earlier tradition. The introductory phrase identifying something in the context as a "word of the Lord" (whatever that means) indicates that some kind of citation is involved. The following recitative *hoti* (a "that" which introduces a quotation) identifies the material cited. A *hoti* appears immediately after the identification of the material as a "word of the Lord" in verse 15b, and another is found at the beginning of verse 16. Either or both may serve to introduce cited material, so they are not decisive in determining where the citation begins.

The three parallel clauses of verse 16 that begin with the preposition *en* ("in") suggest a formal pattern that is characteristic of liturgical or recited material. Thus they lend support to identifying at least verses 16–17 as preformed material. The strongest evidence for identifying this material as a citation of a preformed tradition is its vocabulary. Only in these verses (once each in v. 15 and v. 17) does the word *perileipomai* ("left") appear in the New Testament. Likewise, *keleusma* ("command," v. 16) occurs only here in the New Testament, and *archangelos* ("archangel," v. 16) is only here and in Jude 9. Only in this passage does *apantēsis* ("meeting," v. 17) appear in Paul, and it refers to an eschatological meeting only here in all of the New Testament. The verb *harpazō* (v. 17) means to be snatched up at the eschaton only here in the New Testament, but does refer to being taken up in a visionary experience in 2 Cor 12:2 and 4. *Salpinx* ("trumpet," v. 16) is used by Paul only here and in 1 Cor 14:8; 15:52; but it occurs elsewhere in the New Testament (Matt 24:31; Heb 12:19; Rev

---

33. Müller, *Prophetie und Predigt*, 165–77, 222–24.
34. Michael Pahl, *Discerning the "Word of the Lord": The "Word of the Lord" in 1 Thessalonians 4:15*, LNTS 389 (Edinburgh: T. & T. Clark, 2009), 120–22, 153, 166–69.

1:10; 4:1; 8:2, 6, 13; 9:14). Paul seldom employs the verb *anistēmi* ("to raise") to mean the resurrection of the dead, but uses it twice here (vv. 14 and 16). His other two uses are in quotations of passages from the Hebrew Bible (Rom 15:12; 1 Cor 10:7). We will note below the places in the New Testament where this verb does refer to resurrection. Finally, Paul uses the term *parousia* only one time outside 1 Thess 2–5 to speak of the second coming of Christ (1 Cor 15:23). As with *anistēmi* ("to raise"), we will return to this term's use in other New Testament writings.

The constellation of language not used by Paul or other New Testament authors, words not used by Paul but only by other New Testament authors, and terms used in ways that are unusual for Paul demonstrate that Paul is here citing material rather than composing on his own. It remains difficult to determine where the citation begins. Both *perileipomai* ("to leave," "who are left") and *parousia* are present in verse 15b,[35] but the change in style seems more evident beginning in verse 16.[36] In addition, the content of verse 15b addresses the issue at hand directly, while what follows in verse 16 adds description that serves as proof for Paul's response to the more specific problem. The use of unusual terminology in verse 15 may be due to conforming that response to the tradition that provides the proof. Gerd Lüdemann notes further that verses 16–17 are in the third person, while verse 15 is still in the first person, which is typical for epistolary style.[37] So we are on firmer ground starting the citation with verse 16.[38]

The appearance of both *parousia* and *anistēmi* ("to raise") points to an early and non-Pauline origin for the content of this tradition. These terms occur in other New Testament writings with the eschatological meanings that they have here but that are so unusual for Paul. While the verb *anistēmi* appears with the meaning of resurrection only in this passage in Paul, it connotes resurrection in Matt 17:9; Mark 12:25; Luke 16:31; 24:46; John 11:23, 24; and Acts 17:3. So it is language known and used in Matthew's church, the churches of the other

---

35. Bruce is among those who argue that the citation begins with v. 15b (*1 & 2 Thessalonians*, 98).

36. Among those who begin the citation at v. 16 are Best, *Epistles to the Thessalonians*, 193–94; Richard, *First and Second Thessalonians*, 244.

37. Gerd Lüdemann, *Paul, Apostle to the Gentiles: Studies in Chronology*, trans. F. Stanley Jones (Philadelphia: Fortress, 1984), 221. He gives a detailed argument for identifying vv. 16–17 as traditional material and provides a reconstruction of the underlying tradition (222–27). M. Eugene Boring sees the citation as vv. 16–17a (*1 & 2 Thessalonians: A Commentary*, NTL [Louisville: Westminster John Knox, 2015], 166).

38. We should not, however, rule out the possibility that v. 15b is part of the preformed tradition. Müller also remains uncertain about whether v. 15b is part of the citation (*Prophetie und Predigt*, 224).

Synoptic authors, and that of John. As noted above, Paul uses *parousia* only one time outside 1 Thess 2–5 to refer to the return of the risen Christ, though he uses it often to refer to the arrival of other people at a particular location. It has the meaning of the end-time return of the Son of Man four times in the eschatological discourse of Matthew (24:3, 27, 37, 39). Then in James (twice, 5:7, 8) and in 2 Peter (3:4, 12, and perhaps also 1:16) it is a technical term for the return of Christ. Since James and Matthew are not influenced by Pauline theology, according to Wilson, the use of this language in those works demonstrates that it was used in pre-Pauline churches and in churches outside his sphere of influence. Thus the tradition reveals that the earliest church looked for the return of Christ and connected it with the resurrection of the dead.

Raymond Collins reconstructs the tradition that lies behind verses 16–17 as follows:

ho kyrios
  en keleusmati
    en phōnē archangelou kai en salpingi theou
katabēsetai ap' ouranou
kai hoi nekroi en kyriō anastēsontai
hoi perileipomenoi hama syn autois harpagēsontai
  en nephelais
    eis apantēsin tou kyriou eis aera

The Lord
  with a shout
    with the voice of the archangel and the trumpet of God,
will come down from heaven,
and the dead in the Lord will be raised.
Then those who are left will be snatched up with them
  in the clouds
    in order to meet the Lord in the air.[39]

This reconstruction seems to fit the evidence quite well. Lüdemann reconstructs this preexistent tradition in a nearly identical way.[40] This reconstruction

---

39. Raymond F. Collins, "Tradition, Redaction and Exhortation in 1 Thess 4,13–5,11," in *Studies on the First Letter to the Thessalonians*, BETL 66 (Leuven: Leuven University Press, 1984), 161. The translation here is mine.

40. Lüdemann identifies the tradition as: "The Lord will descend from heaven with a cry of command, with the archangel's call, and with the sound of the trumpet of God. And the

allows that Paul has added some elements to fit the tradition into the argument he is making, but has maintained much of it intact. By this account, in line 5 Paul changes *kyriō* ("Lord") to *Christō* ("Christ") and adds *prōton* ("first"). Then in line 6 he changes "*they* will be snatched up" to "*we* will be snatched up."[41] These changes do not alter the basic scenario that the tradition proposes. Even if this reconstruction overreaches the evidence, the basic sequence and structure do seem secure when one takes account of the non-Pauline elements of verses 16–17.

Some have argued that Paul is the one who first postulates the connection between the return of Christ and the end-time resurrection. Joost Holleman concludes that Paul brings these traditions together in response to issues raised in Thessalonica and Corinth.[42] Others argue that this connection was made by Paul through ideas taken from mystery cults, particularly identifying the experience of the believer with that of the god, as we saw above in connection with 2 Cor 4:14.[43] But the evidence that much of 1 Thess 4:16–17 comes from an author other than Paul is overwhelming.[44] This tradition shows that these elements were already joined before Paul needed to address questions about the resurrection in 1 Thessalonians. Thus the earliest communities and those that remained outside Paul's dominant influence looked to the return of Christ as the moment of the resurrection of the dead.

Some interpreters also assert that Paul is the one who shifted the focus of the church from an earthly kingdom to a heavenly one. A number have seen this passage as evidence for the belief in an earthly kingdom because it envisions Christ "coming down from heaven" and it uses the term *apantēsis* to describe believers "meeting" him in the sky. This term is used in some

---

dead will rise. Those who are left will be caught up into the clouds to meet the Lord in the air" (*Paul, Apostle to the Gentiles*, 225).

41. Lüdemann, *Paul, Apostle*, 224.

42. Joost Holleman, *Resurrection and Parousia: A Traditio-Historical Study of 1 Corinthians 15*, NovTSup 84 (Leiden: Brill, 1996), 71. Still, he acknowledges that this connection could have been made before Paul (124), even as he attributes it to Paul. Richard Ascough seems to discuss these verses as a Pauline composition but leaves open the possibility that they were pre-Pauline ("A Question of Death: Paul's Community-Building Language in 1 Thessalonians 4:13–18," *JBL* 123 [2004]: 526n82). His argument focuses on how the Thessalonians would have heard these verses given the ways associations dealt with the deaths of their members. That background, however, gives no help in determining whether the material is preformed.

43. For example, Wengst, *Christologische Formeln*, 46.

44. Christopher M. Tuckett also arrives at this conclusion, as he identifies it as a saying of another early church prophet ("Synoptic Tradition in 1 Thessalonians?" in *Thessalonian Correspondence*, ed. Collins, 179–82).

contemporaneous literature to describe the response of a city to the coming of a dignitary. A company of people would go out to meet the dignitary and accompany her or him into town.[45] Some interpreters contend that this image indicates that Christ continues with this entourage and comes to earth, where he reigns. Michael Cosby has argued, however, that the similarities between the use of *apantēsis* in 1 Thessalonians and its use to describe the procession that accompanies a dignitary have been overdrawn.[46] Furthermore, even if the use of *apantēsis* has this event in view, it is an overly wooden reading of the image to assert that it must include the entry of the dignitary into the city of those who greet her or him. Additionally, this passage says nothing about escorting Jesus or returning to earth. The purpose here is to be gathered to the Lord, not to escort him.[47] Indeed, rather than going to meet Jesus, believers are passive—they are given no active role here. The purpose of being taken up here is not to return, but, as Peter de Villiers notes, to be given a new and heavenly mode of existence.[48]

Neither do we need to look to mystery cults or other sources outside Judaism to find precedents for belief in a resurrection that gives recipients a nonearthly and heavenly existence. Albert Hogeterp has demonstrated clearly that even the nonsectarian Qumran materials show that Jews had expectations of an eschatological resurrection to a heavenly realm as early as the second century BCE.[49] He notes that the Hodayot, particularly 1QH^a 12:22–37, point to belief in a bodily resurrection. Resurrection language is also found in sources ranging from 1 En. 106:19 (4Q204) to the text of Isaiah in 1QIsa^a. This reflects

---

45. This understanding of *apantēsis* goes back at least to Erik Peterson, "Die Einholung des Kyrios," *ZST* 1 (1930): 682–702. See the review of this position in Michael R. Cosby, "Hellenistic Formal Receptions and Paul's Use of *apantēsis* in 1 Thessalonians 4:17," *BBR* 4 (1994): 15–33. For a defense of this view in response to Cosby see Robert H. Gundry, "A Brief Note on 'Hellenistic Formal Receptions and Paul's Use of *apantēsis* in 1 Thessalonians 4:17,'" *BBR* 6 (1996): 39–41.

46. Cosby, "Hellenistic Formal Receptions," 20–33.

47. Malherbe, *Letters to the Thessalonians*, 277.

48. De Villiers, "In the Presence of God," 322–23. He suggests further that being snatched up into the air is "functionally equivalent" to being "changed" in 1 Cor 15:51–52.

49. Albert L. A. Hogeterp, *Expectations of the End: A Comparative Traditio-Historical Study of Eschatological, Apocalyptic and Messianic Ideas in the Dead Sea Scrolls and the New Testament*, STDJ 83 (Leiden: Brill, 2009), 247–334; see esp. the summary on 326–34. See also Hermann Lichtenberger, "Aufstehung in den Qumranfunden," in *Auferstehung—Resurrection*, ed. Friedrich Avemarie and Hermann Lichtenberger, WUNT 135 (Tübingen: Mohr Siebeck, 2001), 79–91. Lichtenberger comes to the clear conclusion that the Qumran covenanters looked forward to individual salvation after death (90–91).

a tradition that was developing as early as Dan 12:1-3 and remained current (see 1 En. 104:2, 4, 6, which envision some kind of an angelic existence). Even being caught up into the heavens is found in 1 En. 70-71. The idea of believers being taken up into the clouds also seems to draw on understandings found in rabbinic traditions.[50] These are in addition to the Pharisees' well-known belief in a resurrection (Acts 23:6-8).

Thus the evidence for the presence of traditional material in 1 Thess 4:16-17a is overwhelming.[51] This prophetic word, whether it echoes a saying of Jesus or not, employs so much non-Pauline vocabulary that its formulation cannot be attributed to Paul. Its language and ideas do appear in a wide range of traditions, which suggests that its basic content and perhaps even its form were set quite early. Importantly, this pre-Pauline, or at least non-Pauline, tradition asserts a nonearthly resurrection for believers. The church had already begun to posit a nonearthly (or better, transearthly) kingdom as the realm in which Christ would reign and in which resurrected believers would live. The tradition gives Jesus the role of eschatological savior. If the phrase "in Christ" (v. 16) is part of the tradition rather than a Pauline insertion,[52] then this tradition also indicates that there was a very early association of the identity of the resurrection of believers with that of Christ. They are raised as those who are in Christ. Given that the tradition speaks only of the resurrection of believers, it is certainly plausible that "in Christ" belongs to it.

Verse 15b may be a Pauline innovation. As we have seen, a number of interpreters argue that the citation of the tradition begins after the *hoti* ("that") of verse 16. In that case, the presence of unusual vocabulary in verse 15b is an echo of the tradition Paul is about to cite. The Thessalonians are clearly worried about the fate of those who die before the parousia. As noted above, they seem to think either that those who die completely miss it or that they are at some disadvantage. Tracy Howard cites 4 Ezra 13:22-24 as an example of a text that recounts how those who die before the end are indeed disadvantaged.[53] Whichever view some Thessalonians hold, Paul asserts that those who have

---

50. Candida R. Moss and Joel S. Baden, "1 Thessalonians 4.13-18 in Rabbinic Perspective," *NTS* 58 (2012): 199-212.

51. Andreas Lindemann limits the tradition to v. 16, with the possibility that it extends into v. 17a ("Paulus und die korinthische Eschatologie: Zur These von einer 'Entwicklung' im paulinischen Denken," *NTS* 37 [1991]: 378-79). It does seem likely that Paul adds the final sentence of v. 17.

52. Lindemann argues that Paul did add "in Christ" here ("Paulus und die korinthische Eschatologie," 379).

53. Tracy L. Howard, "The Literary Unity of 1 Thessalonians 4:13-5:11," *GTJ* 9 (1988): 168.

died are not disadvantaged. De Villiers cites Paul's assertion of the "preferential status" of the dead as an innovation to the church's teaching. If this is the case, Paul might have added "first" to the wording of the tradition at the end of verse 16.[54] Such a shift in understanding of the participation of the dead in the parousia does not change the basic understanding of the kingdom or its location. It would, however, be a demonstration of a way Paul used existing beliefs and traditions to address questions his churches raise.[55] It would seem strange, on the other hand, to find that the question of the place of the dead had not troubled other churches, whether Pauline, pre-Pauline, or non-Pauline, until nearly twenty years after the death of Jesus. So even if verse 15b is Paul's elaboration and explication of it, the tradition may have already asserted the priority of the dead at the second coming. Either way, Paul assumes that the readers of this letter affirm that Jesus would return from heaven in the role of savior and give believers life in another realm.[56]

1 Corinthians 15:20–28

A number of interpreters find Paul citing or relying on traditional formulations in 1 Cor 15:20–28, especially in verses 24–28. Paul is here responding to some in Corinth who claim there is no resurrection of the dead. Having reminded the readers of their belief in the resurrection of Christ (15:1–11), Paul turns to speak of its implications for believers. He begins with the assertion that "Christ has been raised from the dead" (v. 20). We saw in chapter 3 that this assertion rests on a very early tradition. But Paul is not quoting it here. The assessment of R. Collins seems correct that Paul is here reprising that tradition.[57] Paul adds to this assertion that in the resurrection Christ is the "firstfruits of those who have fallen asleep." Paul uses the term "firstfruits" (*aparchē*) only six times, three in 1 Cor 15–16 and three times in Romans. Even though Paul seldom uses the term, he uses it in multiple and varying ways. It can refer to the first converts from a place (Rom 16:5; 1 Cor 16:15), to the ancestors of Israel (Rom 11:16), and to the Spirit (Rom 8:23). Since this term so clearly belongs to Paul's

---

54. So R. Collins, "Tradition, Redaction and Exhortation," 161. Collins also thinks Paul added the reference to Christ in this line and the phrase "Then we who are living" that begins v. 17.

55. Richard sees this as an instance in which Paul fit a tradition to his understanding (*First and Second Thessalonians*, 244).

56. Richard, *First and Second Thessalonians*, 244.

57. R. Collins, *First Corinthians*, 550.

active vocabulary, it cannot serve as evidence that he is citing a tradition. So his use of "firstfruits" to describe the relationship between Christ's resurrection and that of believers may be an innovation.

In 1 Cor 15:21-22 Paul sets out a typology that relates Adam and Christ. Paul uses the fall story to identify Adam as the one responsible for bringing death into the world and then makes Adam represent a realm in which all humans must experience death. Correspondingly, Christ is the one through whom resurrection enters the world, and he represents the realm in which humans are given life. This typology appears only a few times in Paul, and only within Romans and 1 Corinthians. But in these five appearances, Adam always represents the beginning of an era or life within it (Rom 5:14 [twice]; 1 Cor 15:22, 45 [twice]). The parallel structure of each pair within the typology in 1 Cor 15:21-22 may suggest that this reflects a preformed piece.[58] Furthermore, there is a change to the third person plural ("they") at verse 20. This may also indicate that Paul is citing a formula here because it fits awkwardly with the point he wants to make. As he argues that *dead believers* are raised, his Adam/Christ typology instead includes all *humans* in the realms Adam and Christ constitute. But then verse 22 says that "*they* all die" and "*they* all are given life." Translations and interpreters leave the shift to the third person invisible. While the point of the typology concerns all of humanity, the preceding verse 21 has those who have died as its topic. Then, in the following verse (v. 23), it seems that the people included in the resurrection are only those who are "of Christ." So while this typology makes a vital contribution to the argument, its form does not fit well in the flow of thought. Wolfgang Schrage adds that this inclusion of "all" in the resurrection does not fit what Paul says elsewhere about it. Thus he concludes that the "all" must be part of the tradition Paul is citing.[59]

Lindemann's review of positions taken on the origin of the Adam typology notes that Ulrich Wilckens and Georg Strecker identify it as a pre-Pauline tradition. Others, however, identify it as a tradition that Paul takes over from rabbinic Judaism (e.g., W. D. Davies and Otto Betz), and still others trace its pre-Pauline use to Philo (Gerhard Sellin). Lindemann argues that the image comes from apocalyptic Judaism.[60] Anthony Thiselton, on the other hand,

58. Richard Horsley also notes the schematic and formulaic character of these verses (*1 Corinthians*, ANTC [Nashville: Abingdon, 1998], 204).

59. Wolfgang Schrage, *Der erste Brief an die Korinther*, 4 vols., EKKNT 7.1-4 (Neukirchen-Vluyn: Neukirchener Verlag, 1991-2001), 4:162, 166.

60. Andreas Lindemann, "Die Auferstehung der Toten: Adam und Christus nach 1.Kor 15," in *Eschatologie und Schöpfung: Festschrift für Erich Grässer zum siebzigsten Geburtstag*, ed. Martin Evang, Helmut Merklein, and Michael Wolter, BZNW 89 (Berlin: de Gruyter, 1997),

seems to have Paul be the one who makes this connection between Adam and Christ.[61] James Dunn, who has written extensively on this typology, sees it as central to Paul's theology. He regularly speaks of how Paul uses it, often in somewhat cryptic ways.[62] But he does not find it to be Paul's invention. Rather, after noting the various ways this interpretation builds on Ps 8:4-6 and its use elsewhere in the New Testament (esp. Heb 2:5-9), Dunn comments, "There does seem to have been abroad in the first generation of Christianity an already quite sophisticated Adam christology."[63] If Dunn is correct in seeing the church's use of Ps 8 as an element of an Adam Christology, it seems Paul is quoting a tradition here. Even if that Adam Christology is less developed and pervasive in the church and in Paul than Dunn envisions, it seems likely that Paul is citing at least the content of a theological idea that is widely held in the early church, including those branches that were outside his influence.

This tradition identifies Jesus as an eschatological figure, one whose presence and work mark the change to a new era. We have seen other traditions identify Jesus as God's eschatological agent. This tradition adds that Jesus is now a representative of humanity and has an identity and function that change the course of history, a function that has a cosmic effect. It is in Christ that God reclaims the cosmos from the effects of Adam's sin. While this clearly has importance for the earliest church's soteriology, its central assertion is here eschatological and perhaps christological. Although this expression of the way believers are identified with Christ adds little to what we have seen in passages such as Gal 3:27-28, it does indicate how broadly these ideas were held throughout the earliest church. It also highlights the cosmic dimensions of the eschatology, Christology, and soteriology of the church from very early times and outside Paul's influence.

155-57. To those who argue that Paul develops this view through his Jewish background, we may add Robin Scroggs, *The Last Adam: A Study in Pauline Anthropology* (Philadelphia: Fortress, 1966). See further his argument against relating Paul's thought about Adam to Philo's (115-22).

61. Anthony C. Thiselton, *The First Epistle to the Corinthians: A Commentary on the Greek Text*, NIGTC (Grand Rapids: Eerdmans, 2000), 1225.

62. For example, James Dunn, "1 Corinthians 15:45—Last Adam, Life-Giving Spirit," in *Christ and the Spirit in the New Testament: Studies in Honour of Charles Francis Digby Moule*, ed. Barnabas Lindars and Stephen S. Smalley (Cambridge: Cambridge University Press, 1973), 127-41; Dunn, *The Theology of Paul the Apostle* (Grand Rapids: Eerdmans, 1998), 199-204, 210-11.

63. Dunn, *Theology of Paul*, 203. A. M. Hunter also identifies this typology as pre-Pauline (*Paul and His Predecessors*, rev. ed. [London: SCM, 1961], 123).

"The Coming of the Lord"

At 1 Cor 15:23 Paul returns to his main point, that the resurrection of Christ assures believers of the certainty and the nature of their resurrection.[64] Only the rare use of *parousia* to refer to the return of Christ would suggest that Paul is here citing a tradition. That is too little evidence to identify it as such. Some, however, contend that the sequence of events in verses 23-24 indicates that there is a time between the parousia and "the end." L. Joseph Krietzer finds this to be the most likely reading of the passage. He locates the roots of this view in various Jewish apocalyptic works that posit a temporary kingdom between God's initial eschatological act and the final event.[65] If this passage does posit such a kingdom, it is in conflict with all of Paul's other descriptions of the end. Thus it might suggest that Paul is drawing on a tradition, at least in the scheme that these verses set out. Most interpreters, however, do not think that these verses imagine a temporary kingdom of that sort. Instead of rendering the *eita* ("then") at the beginning of verse 24 as chronological, they see it as explanatory.[66] If read in this way, which seems more likely, it does not contradict Paul's other descriptions of the second coming, and so the sequence of events Paul sets out is not evidence that Paul is citing a tradition.

Many identify much of what appears in verses 24-28 as elements of preformed tradition. Lindemann, followed by others, including Thiselton,[67] calls the content of these verses a "little apocalyptic drama."[68] A number of features of these verses indicate that they derive in part from traditional formulae. First, they stand out from the context because they are not directly about the resurrection of the dead but about the events of the eschaton and the broader

---

64. Martinus de Boer calls vv. 23-28 a "soteriological application" of the affirmation of the resurrection of Christ (*The Defeat of Death: Apocalyptic Eschatology in 1 Corinthians 15 and Romans 5*, JSNTSup 22 [Sheffield: JSOT Press, 1988], 123).

65. L. Joseph Kreitzer, *Jesus and God in Paul's Eschatology*, JSNTSup 19 (Sheffield: JSOT Press, 1987), 90, 147. The works in which this interregnum appears are 1 Enoch, 2 Baruch, and 4 Ezra. This is very clear in 2 Bar. 29-31. The eight-thousand-year era of 1 En. 91:9-14 also seems to be an example of an interim kingdom in which the righteous are blessed and there is great abundance, as in Eden.

66. So Thiselton, *First Epistle to the Corinthians*, 1230-31; Schrage identifies the *interregnum Christi* as the time between Christ's resurrection and the parousia (*Erste Brief an die Korinther*, 4:170-71). R. Collins agrees and cites the argument of Charles E. Hill, "Paul's Understanding of Christ's Kingdom in I Corinthians 15:20-28," *NovT* 30 (1988): 297-32, as decisive (*First Corinthians*, 552). So also Andrew Chester, "Resurrection and Transformation," in *Auferstehung—Resurrection*, ed. Avemarie and Lichtenberger, 74.

67. Thiselton, *First Epistle to the Corinthians*, 1230. This is notable because he seldom accepts the conclusion that Paul is citing a tradition.

68. Lindemann, "Paulus und die korinthische Eschatologie," 383. He labels it "ein kleines apokalyptisches Drama."

events connected to it.[69] The subject of the place of humans in those events returns only when Paul notes that death is destroyed (v. 26), and then in the resumption of the discussion of the resurrection after this section in verse 29.

A second indication that this material comes from a tradition is the reference to Christ turning the kingdom over to God. Paul uses the term "kingdom" (*basileia*) only eight times. In four of those instances he says that those who behave in sinful ways "will not inherit the kingdom" (1 Cor 6:9, 10; Gal 5:21; Eph 5:5). A fifth time he says that "flesh and blood" cannot inherit it (1 Cor 15:50, a passage that may also contain a traditional formula; see below). The two remaining references indicate that the kingdom is already in existence because he identifies characteristics of living in it (Rom 14:17; 1 Cor 4:20). These uses show that Paul is familiar with this language and occasionally uses it. But the image of Christ handing the kingdom over to God is absent from Paul and is perhaps, as Walter Schmithals contends, "entirely non-Pauline."[70] While using different terminology, verse 28b returns to the idea of Christ handing over power. In this verse, "the Son himself will be subject" to God. Given its coherence with the idea of handing over the kingdom, this phrase may also come from a tradition.

Beyond this extraordinary reference to Christ transferring his reign to God, the passage has a number of internal tensions and places where Paul seems to qualify what he has just written. This suggests that he says something that he thinks needs an interpretation. One tension is in the treatment that the "powers" receive. In verses 24b and 26a they are destroyed, but in the citations of the Pss 110 and 8 and in verse 27b they are made subject to Christ. The language of subjection clearly comes from Pss 110:1 and 8:7. We have already seen that these psalms were widely used in the early church outside Paul's influence. Paul interprets the assertion of their submission to mean that the powers are destroyed in order to fit the language of these psalms to the needs of his argument. He identifies death as one of the powers that is subjected and then asserts that it is among those who are destroyed. Since the language of destruction appears in verse 24b as part of Christ's ceding the kingdom to God, it is possible that the tradition itself introduced this tension.[71]

---

69. So Walter Schmithals, "The Pre-Pauline Tradition in 1 Corinthians 15:20-28," *PRSt* 20 (1993): 361-62; Martinus de Boer, "Paul's Use of a Resurrection Tradition in 1 Cor 15,20-28," in *The Corinthian Correspondence*, ed. R. Bieringer, BETL 125 (Leuven: Leuven University Press, 1996), 639.

70. Schmithals, "Pre-Pauline Tradition," 371.

71. Schmithals contends that all of the language of destruction is from Paul ("Pre-Pauline Tradition," 372). Hans Conzelmann does not seem to see a tension between subjection and annihilation; the annihilation seems to be the form that the subjection takes (*1 Corinthians: A*

Another tension is the shift in the active party in the eschatological drama. In other uses of these psalms, God remains the one who places all things under Christ's feet. But here Christ is the one who subjects the powers and places them under his own feet.[72] The immediate qualification of "all things" that are subjected in verses 27–28 makes clear that Christ is the one who subjects the powers. The phrase with which Paul introduces this interpretation in verse 27, "when it says," shows that he expects his readers to recognize it as a citation.[73] Paul qualifies the "all" in verse 28 by excluding God. He makes clear that God is the one who subjects all things to Christ, which is Paul's usual view (e.g., in Phil 2:9–11).[74] It is interesting that this tension is created by the insertion of "all" into Ps 110. The "all" is present in Ps 8, but Paul or the tradition inserts it in this citation of Ps 110. If Paul inserts it, he does so to include death among "all enemies." But the problem the "all" creates for Paul seems to make it more probable that it was already in the tradition he is citing.

The change in tense between the psalm in verse 27 and its interpretation in verse 28 also points to Paul interpreting a tradition the readers know. The psalm is in the aorist (past) tense, but the interpretation is in the perfect tense. While the psalm asserts that all has been placed under Christ's feet, the following interpretation fits Paul's argument because it admits that there are still enemies (particularly death) who must be defeated in the future.[75]

Martinus de Boer notes that the citation of Pss 110 and 8 together further suggests that Paul is citing a tradition. They appear together in Eph 1:20–23; 1 Pet 3:21b–22; and Heb 1:3, 13; 2:8, passages that all have a connection to the resurrection of Jesus. Furthermore, they all also enumerate the powers that had been subjected.[76] The Ephesians text also has the phrase "all in all," which appears at the end of 1 Cor 15:28. These parallels and the tensions we have seen within verses 24–28 indicate that Paul is at least alluding to known traditions in verses 24–28.[77] Schmithals reconstructs an eight-line "instructional text"

Commentary on the First Epistle to the Corinthians, trans. James W. Leitch, Hermeneia [Philadelphia: Fortress, 1975], 273).

72. So Conzelmann, *1 Corinthians*, 273. R. Collins (*First Corinthians*, 553–54) cites Jan Lambrecht, "Paul's Christological Use of Scripture in 1 Cor. 15.20–28," in *Pauline Studies: Collected Essays*, BETL 115 (Leuven: Leuven University Press, 1994), 134–40, as the article that presents the decisive argument for this reading.

73. M. de Boer, "Paul's Use," 640.

74. We may also note that God is the one who raises the dead at the second coming in 1 Thess 4:14.

75. M. de Boer, "Paul's Use," 649.

76. M. de Boer, "Paul's Use," 649.

77. Felipe de Jesús Legarreta-Castillo sees Paul as the one who puts these psalms together here

that he finds cited not only here but also in Eph 1:20–23; 1 Pet 3:21b–22; and Pol. *Phil.* 2.1.[78] If we follow his lead but limit ourselves to the evidence of 1 Corinthians, the tradition Paul cites seems to include:

Paradōsein tēn basileian tō theō
dei auton katargein
pasan archēn kai exousias kai dynameōs. (v. 24b)
Dei auton basileuein (v. 25a)
achri hou thē tous echthrous hypo tous podas autou. (v. 25b)
Hotan de hypotagē autō ta panta (v. 28a)
tote kai autos ho huios hypotagēsetai (v. 28b)
(hina ē ho theos panta en pasin). (v. 28c)

Who will hand the kingdom over to God
he must destroy
all rulers and authorities and powers. (v. 24b)
He must reign
until he puts his enemies under his feet. (v. 25b)
And when he subjects all things (v. 28a)
then also the Son himself will be subject (v. 28b)
(so that God may be all in all). (v. 28c)

This reconstruction incorporates elements that are clearly held in many branches of the church very early. It also has the virtue of clarifying the confusion of subjects that appears in the citation of the psalms. That virtue, however, also means that this is the lone tradition that makes Christ rather than God the

---

(*The Figure of Adam in Romans 5 and 1 Corinthians 15: The New Creation and Its Ethical and Social Reconfiguration* [Minneapolis: Fortress, 2014], 134n46). In this he asserts he is following Lambrecht, "Paul's Christological Use of Scripture." But even as he sees Paul using these psalms in his own argument, Lambrecht acknowledges that the psalms were probably already together in the tradition.

78. His reconstruction reads:

pisteuomen (homologoumen)
eis ton egeiranta 'Iēsoun ek nekrōn.
kai kathisanta auton en dexia autou
hyperanō archēs kai exousias kai dynameōs. (v. 24b)
Dei auton basileuein (v. 25a)
achri hou thē tous echthrous hypo tous podas autou. (v. 25b)
Hotan de hypotagē autō ta panta (v. 28a)
tote kai autos ho huios hypotagēsetai (v. 28b)
hina ē ho theos panta en pasin. (v. 28c)

one who is the actor in the subjection of the enemies. It is difficult to determine whether the language of "handing the kingdom over to God," which is unique in Paul, is part of the tradition or an attempt by Paul to interpret the tradition so that it better fits within his theological outlook.

Even if we cannot be certain about all the content and the extent of the tradition, there are some elements that Paul does clearly draw from tradition.[79] We have already seen that the citations of the psalms with God as the one who subjects the enemies reside firmly within the earliest traditions of the church.[80] The idea of all things being subject to Christ and of Christ turning over control of the kingdom to God also seems to be an element of the tradition, as is seen by the vocabulary and the attention to subjection and its limits in verses 27–28. Perhaps it is also correct that "he must reign" is a line from the tradition. Given that the connections between these elements of tradition are unclear, it may be that Paul combines more than one known tradition as he composes this passage.

If these elements are from preformed traditions, they make assertions that Paul does not. If the tradition includes the act of Christ giving the kingdom to God, it may have a less theocentric focus than Paul. While he constantly has God as the actor in exalting Christ, this tradition makes Christ's reigning dependent on his own power. The reading of the psalms that makes Christ the one who acts to subdue the powers grants Christ power that is God's in other places in Paul and so suggests that Paul is citing a tradition. Paul's need to interpret the expression "all things will be subjected" also seems to indicate that he is dealing with material that comes to him from elsewhere. Were the correction already part of the traditional material, as Schmithals proposes,[81] Paul would not have needed to add the disclaimer in verse 27a before he continued with the explication of the unfolding of events. Both the elements of tradition and Paul's additions and applications accord Christ a leading role in a transearthly kingdom. The enumeration of the powers that is part of the tradition that cites the two psalms[82] demonstrates clearly that the wider church envisioned a kingdom that was more than an earthly reign.

---

79. R. Collins allows that there "may be some truth" to Schmithals's reconstruction (*First Corinthians*, 549).

80. M. de Boer identifies the citation of Ps 8:7 in v. 27a as "part of a christological credo known to the Corinthians as to Paul" (*Defeat of Death*, 125). Hill also sees the combination of Pss 110:1 and 8:7 as pre-Pauline (*Paul and the Trinity*, 123–24).

81. Schmithals argues that in the Hellenistic synagogue it was intended to prevent the development of ditheism ("Pre-Pauline Tradition," 378–79).

82. Even though the Polycarp citation (*Phil.* 2.1) does not list the powers, it does say that all things in the heavens and on earth are subjected.

A number of interpreters have also seen the end of verse 28 as an element of tradition and as evidence that it comes from the Hellenistic church because it echoes Stoic understandings of God.[83] But in this eschatological context, the assertion that God will be "all in all" is not about the nature of God but about God's sovereignty.[84] Whether it is formulated by Paul or is part of the tradition, it is an affirmation of the theocentric goal of eschatology for Paul and perhaps for the wider church.

The presence of some tradition in 1 Cor 15:24–28 is clear, particularly the citations of the psalms and probably in the idea of Christ handing the kingdom over to God. This tradition is evidence that the church beyond Paul's influence envisioned the return of Christ as more than the establishment of an earthly kingdom. And if the strand of tradition known in Corinth made Christ the one who subjects the powers, as seems to be the case, it has exalted him by giving him a task that Paul and most other traditional material reserve for God.[85] The presence of the mention of the powers who are defeated at the eschaton also shows that the extra-Pauline church thinks of the kingdom as transearthly. If it is correct that the Adam/Christ typology is part of the church's theology and tradition before Paul makes use of it, it is also witness to the cosmic nature of the earliest church's understanding of the work of Christ. It makes him the agent through whom God reverses the effects of the fall. If this Christology is as important to Paul as Dunn envisions, its use demonstrates Paul's extensive dependence on the pre-Pauline tradition. It would make him dependent on prior tradition for an important way that he understands the person and work of Christ.

1 Thessalonians 5:2–3, 6–8

Paul begins a new phase of his discussion of eschatological matters in 1 Thessalonians at 5:1–3. He marks this new beginning with the phrase "now concerning," with a direct address of the readers, and with the comment that he does not really need to address this topic. Most commentators think Paul is responding to a question the Thessalonians have raised about the timing of the

---

83. See the citations of Stoic material in Conzelmann, *1 Corinthians*, 275n112.

84. So, e.g., M. de Boer, *Defeat of Death*, 125–26; Schrage, *Erste Brief an die Korinther*, 4:186–87, 225–26. R. Collins translates the phrase, "so that God might be everything to everybody" (*First Corinthians*, 547, 555).

85. Hill acknowledges the asymmetric relationship between God and Christ, but also asserts that there is a mutuality (*Paul and the Trinity*, 133–34).

"The Coming of the Lord"

parousia.⁸⁶ A number of elements of verses 2–3 lead interpreters to see the material there as drawn from non-Pauline tradition. The term *asphaleia* ("safety") appears only here in Paul but is used in Luke 1:4 and Acts 5:23, though not in a discussion about the eschaton. The word *aiphnidios* ("suddenly") occurs only here in Paul. Its only other New Testament use is in Luke's eschatological discourse (21:34). *Ephistēmi* ("come," "come near") also appears only here in Paul, but is used often in Luke and Acts. In addition, Paul usually uses the term *eirēnē* ("peace") in a religious sense, but here uses it as a parallel with "safety."⁸⁷ Paul also seldom uses the third person plural "they say" without having some specific people in mind, but he uses it here. Similar use of "they say" in Luke 17:26 and the parallel in Matt 24:37–39 convinces Béda Rigaux that this impersonal use of the third person is a characteristic of apocalyptic.⁸⁸ Notably, this Matthew text is commonly identified as part of Q. Finally, Paul uses *ōdin* ("pain") only here in verse 3, but it also appears with a similar use in the apocalyptic discourse in Mark 13:8 and Matt 24:8. Its only other New Testament occurrence is Acts 2:24. Paul makes this pain the pain of being in labor. This is the only place Paul uses that image to describe the times before the eschaton.⁸⁹ The image of labor for the coming of the end is found, however, in 2 Esd 16:37–39.

In addition to these individual terms, Paul uses the image of the parousia coming as a "thief in the night" only here in verses 2 and 4. It is also used in more parabolic form to urge watchfulness for the unpredictable coming of

---

86. R. Collins is the exception to this generalization. He says that it is not clear that Paul is responding to a question, even though this is a new topic in the letter ("Tradition, Redaction and Exhortation," 163).

87. Wanamaker, *Epistles to the Thessalonians*, 180. Joel R. White suggests, however, that in this place Paul has used "peace" to allude to the Roman claim of bringing peace and "security" as an allusion to the promise of cities to provide it. Alluding to both claims, Paul asserts that neither offers safety at the parousia ("'Peace' and 'Security' [1 Thess 5.3]: Roman Ideology and Greek Aspiration," NTS 60 [2014]: 499–510). Of course, if Paul could make this distinction and expect readers to pick it up, so could another person who could have composed the assertion. See further White's rejection of the view that "peace and security" was a Roman slogan in "'Peace and Security' (1 Thessalonians 5.3): Is It Really a Roman Slogan?" NTS 59 (2013): 382–96.

88. Béda Rigaux, "Tradition et rédaction dans 1 Th. V.1–10," NTS 21 (1975): 325. Wanamaker notes this without committing himself to Rigaux's conclusion (*Epistles to the Thessalonians*, 180). R. Collins agrees with Rigaux's conclusion about this ("Tradition, Redaction and Exhortation," 165).

89. R. Collins, "Tradition, Redaction and Exhortation," 165. While they do not mention labor, the Synoptics all say "woe to those who are pregnant" in their descriptions of the difficulties of the end (Matt 24:19; Mark 13:17; Luke 21:23).

the end in Matt 24:43 and Luke 12:39, but in 2 Pet 3:10; Rev 3:3; and 16:15 it is used directly of the coming of Christ. So it is a well-known image across multiple branches of the church, including Matthew's church. The presence of this metaphor across so many texts is made all the more significant by Best's observation that it is not used in Jewish apocalyptic before its presence in these texts.[90]

Malherbe notes that 1 Thess 5:2 is the only place in the New Testament where "in the night" is part of the image. He comments further that this full expression is rather "infelicitous" here because Paul also uses the expression "day of the Lord." Thus the text says that the day comes in the night.[91] The presence of this phrase leads René Kieffer to see the fuller expression as the original on which the shorter references to the end coming "as a thief" rely.[92] While some find the origin of this image in Q, Malherbe and Best are uncertain.[93] More ambiguously, Richard says it is "the community's proverbial" motif.[94]

Whatever the origin of the thief image, the accumulation of so much non-Pauline language in verses 2–3 suggests that Paul is citing a tradition formulated by someone else.[95] Richard argues that the "themes, vocabulary, and sequence of ideas" suggest a connection between these verses and Luke 21:34–36.[96] Malherbe similarly concludes that the parallels between these two passages are so close that they must both be dependent upon the same tradition.[97]

This passage suggests that the church had already begun to shift its focus from the imminence of the second coming to its suddenness, from the expectation that it will happen immediately to the need to be prepared always. Paul may think it is coming within his lifetime, but his adoption of this tradition

---

90. Best, *Epistles to the Thessalonians*, 205.

91. Malherbe, *Letters to the Thessalonians*, 290.

92. René Kieffer, "L'eschatologie en 1 Thessaloniciens dans une perspective rhétorique," in *Thessalonian Correspondence*, ed. R. Collins, 206–19.

93. Malherbe, *Letters to the Thessalonians*, 290; Best, *Epistles to the Thessalonians*, 205. Both think it is uncertain whether the metaphor begins with Paul or in Q.

94. Richard, *First and Second Thessalonians*, 249. Similarly, Wanamaker identifies it as a "traditional metaphor" (*Epistles to the Thessalonians*, 177).

95. Best is among the few to think that Paul is the one who takes a "known truism" and applies it to the eschaton (*Epistles to the Thessalonians*, 207).

96. Richard, *First and Second Thessalonians*, 250.

97. Malherbe, *Letters to the Thessalonians*, 292. Richard N. Longenecker goes so far as to argue that Paul has the eschatological teaching of Jesus in mind in 1 Thess 5:1–11 ("The Nature of Paul's Early Eschatology," *NTS* 31 [1985]: 91).

"The Coming of the Lord"

indicates that he already agrees that its coming is unpredictable. In this shift in emphasis, he is preceded by the tradition he cites here.[98]

The accumulation of non-Pauline vocabulary in 1 Thess 5:6-8 also leads some to find it dependent on a preformed tradition. *Nēphō* ("be sober") appears in Paul only here in verses 6 and 8. The verb *grēgoreō* ("be alert") is in Paul only here, again in verse 10 (see below), and in the final exhortations of 1 Cor 16:13. It is, however, a common verb in the Synoptic eschatological discourses (Matt 24:42, 43; 25:13; Mark 13:34, 35, 37; Luke 12:37, 39). It is also used as an eschatological exhortation in Rev 3:2, 3; 16:15. Paul uses *katheudō* ("to sleep") three times, all here in 1 Thess 5. In verses 6 and 7 it is the opposite of being ready for Christ's return; in verse 10 it is a circumlocution for being literally dead. The fourth verb that occurs only here in Paul is *methyskō* ("to be drunk"). It is used in Eph 5:18 and Luke 12:45. In the latter it appears in a parable that calls readers to be prepared for Christ's return as judge.[99] These vocabulary peculiarities lead R. Collins to contend that Paul is borrowing a tradition, even if he shapes it for his own purposes.[100] Müller thinks that the exhortations to take up a new life in verse 8 show that the tradition was part of a set of baptismal exhortations.[101] Indeed, he contends that this passage, along with Rom 13:12b-14, shows that the combination of the proclamation of the coming of the end and paraenesis originated in baptismal paraenesis.[102]

The collection of unusual terms suggests that Paul is using material originally composed by someone else, but any more specific identification of its origin seems to go beyond the evidence. Still we should note that it uses language that the communities that read the Synoptics also found in eschatological texts. The exhortation to be ready through living a proper life adds nothing to our understanding of the early church's eschatology. We cannot tell how soon those who used these exhortations expected the end to come. Neither can we tell what sort of kingdom it would bring or where it would be.

---

98. However, Ben Witherington III follows Fitzmyer's reading of this image in Luke and so contends that it does not suggest any delay in the coming, only that the coming will be unexpected (*Jesus, Paul, and the End of the World: A Comparative Study in New Testament Eschatology* [Downers Grove, IL: InterVarsity Press, 1992], 46). In this passage in Paul, however, it does seem to help the readers deal with the delay in that coming.

99. The second word Paul uses for "getting drunk" here (*methyō*) is also rare in Paul, but he does use it one other time, to chide the Corinthians for their practices at the Lord's Supper (1 Cor 11:21).

100. R. Collins, "Tradition, Redaction and Exhortation," 167.
101. Müller, *Prophetie und Predigt*, 165.
102. Müller, *Prophetie und Predigt*, 165.

Other Possible Citations

Interpreters commonly acknowledge that Rom 14:9 contains an altered form of the "Christ died and was raised" formula that we already encountered in chapter 3.[103] Paul has substituted "lives" for "raised" to suit his context and argument. We saw in chapter 3 that this confession took many forms, beginning with "God raised Jesus." Paul has already quoted this confession in Rom 10:9. He now alters the tradition to reflect his contention that all of life is to be determined by the believer's relationship with God. He makes the point emphatically by saying that if we die, we die "to the Lord"; and if we live, we live "to the Lord," concluding the sentence by asserting that believers belong to the Lord (10:8). Then he alludes to this tradition: "Christ died and he lives." The statement stands apart from what precedes it by changing the subject from "the Lord" to "Christ" and by inserting a reference to the death and resurrection of Jesus. This short allusion has fewer characteristics than is usually required to identify a phrase with a tradition, but the ubiquity of this confession in its various forms leaves little doubt that Paul is referring to it to bolster his argument.

Fewer interpreters have recognized that the latter half of verse 9 may also allude to a preformed tradition. The unexpressed subject of this phrase, which is drawn from the first half of the verse, is Christ. Paul has made the content of verse 9 the basis for his assertion that allegiance to the Lord should determine all of life. He now identifies the Lord as Christ. More than any unusualness of the individual words, verse 9b echoes a formula that is found across a wide range of early sources. Commenting on 1 Pet 4:5, Hans Windisch identifies the phrase "to judge the living and the dead" (*krinai zōntas kai nekrous*) as a set formula because it appears in such a cross-section of writings.[104] Forms of this expression with *krinō* ("to judge") as either an infinitive or a participle appear in Acts 10:42; 2 Tim 4:1; Ep. Barn. 7.2; and 2 Clem. 2.1. Citing this evidence, A. M. Hunter comments that this "phrasing is surely not accidental."[105]

Romans 14:9 is not a direct quotation of this formula. It has a finite verb

---

103. So, e.g., Robert Jewett, *Romans: A Commentary*, Hermeneia (Minneapolis: Fortress, 2007), 849; James D. G. Dunn, *Romans 9–16*, WBC 38B (Waco: Word, 1988), 808; Dunn, *The Theology of Paul the Apostle*, 175n72; Douglas Moo, *The Epistle to the Romans*, NICNT (Grand Rapids: Eerdmans, 1996), 845; Wengst, *Christologische Formeln und Lieder des Urchristentums*, 45; Kramer, *Christ, Lord, Son of God*, 29–30.

104. Hans Windisch, "Der erste Petrusbrief," in *Die katholischen Briefe*, HNT 4.2 (Tübingen: Mohr Siebeck, 1911), 72.

105. Hunter, *Paul and His Predecessors*, 107n1.

"The Coming of the Lord"

and it reverses the order of the living and the dead, perhaps to conform to the order of the preceding confession about Christ ("he died and he lives," v. 9a). The verb is even different; Paul asserts that Christ "rules over" (*kyrieusē*) both the living and the dead. This statement supports Paul's claim that each believer is most centrally responsible to his or her Lord. But the matter at hand involves judgment. The immediately following question is, "Why do you judge your brother?" (v. 10). While Paul is clearly not quoting the formula that names Christ as the judge of the living and the dead, he may be alluding to it generally. Even if Paul does not have this traditional formula in mind, the evidence for its early existence is solid. Its appearance in other literature shows that believers outside the Pauline sphere saw Jesus as the eschatological judge in the early years of the church.

A number of interpreters identify parts of 1 Cor 15:50-52 as material drawn from preexisting traditions. Conzelmann argues that the phrases "flesh and blood" and "inherit the kingdom of God," along with the style of the passage, indicate that Paul found this material "ready to hand."[106] We noted above how rarely Paul mentions the kingdom of God, but when he does, he often (in four of the eight times he uses it) refers to whether or how one inherits it. In the three other places Paul speaks of inheriting the kingdom, he asserts that those who behave immorally will not inherit it. Here it is not one's moral behavior but the material of which one is composed that prohibits the inheritance.[107] Beyond the use of "kingdom," verse 50 also begins with an introductory formula. But this formula ("I say this") suggests that this is Paul's formulation rather than a quotation. Thus while it seems that Paul falls back on a known expression when he speaks of the kingdom of God, he is not quoting anything more extensive in verse 50.

More interpreters look to parts of verses 51-52 as those that contain traditional material. Some identify the clause "I tell you a mystery" as the introduction of an authoritative saying that is parallel to the clause "I have a word of the Lord" in 1 Thess 4:15.[108] In addition, it is only here and in 1 Thess 4:16 (which we identified as a citation of a tradition) that Paul refers to an endtime trumpet.[109] Further, the term *atomos* ("instant") appears only here in

---

106. Conzelmann, *1 Corinthians*, 289.

107. Cf. R. Collins, *First Corinthians*, 579-80.

108. See Helmut Merklein, "Der Theologe als Prophet: Zur Function prophetischen Redens im theologischen Diskurs des Paulus," *NTS* 38 (1992): 402-29; Lindemann, "Paulus und die korinthische Eschatologie," 391; Michaels, "Everything That Rises Must Converge," 184-85; R. Collins, *First Corinthians*, 580.

109. He does use the image of a trumpet one other time, in 1 Cor 14:8.

the New Testament. All but one of Paul's uses of *aphtharsia* ("immortality") are clustered in 1 Cor 15:42–54.[110] Its cognate *aphthartos* ("immortal"), which Paul uses in verse 52, appears only two other times in Paul (Rom 1:23; 1 Cor 9:25). The opposite of these cognates is equally rare in Paul, occurring in only two places outside these verses (Rom 1:23; 1 Cor 9:25, here as the opposite of *aphthartos* ["immortal"] that we just noted).[111] Further he uses *allassō* ("to change") only four times (two of them here in vv. 51–52), and only here in an eschatological sense.[112]

A number of questions surround this passage and what it says about the resurrection. These include whether Paul thinks he will still be alive at the parousia and whether he envisions the resurrection of all people or only the resurrection of "all" believers. The problems are complicated by the manuscript tradition, particularly the question of whether the "not" (*ou*) should be in the last phrase of verse 51 rather than in the penultimate phrase. If it belongs with the last phrase, the verse would read, "we will all die, but we will not all be changed."[113] Most interpreters, however, remain convinced that the usual reading is correct. Despite these issues, these verses can shed light on our investigation.

Paul clearly "reprise[s] the motifs" of the eschatological drama in verses 51–52,[114] making use of known eschatological terms and phrases. He seems to draw on the same tradition we saw him use in 1 Thess 4:15–17. But it seems impossible to isolate how much of these verses comes from the tradition and how much Paul has shaped them. The traditional elements seem to include the mention of the resurrection and the change of those who have not died, as the tradition in 1 Thess 4:15–17 does. If so, 1 Cor 15:51–52 is more evidence that before Paul and outside his influence the church was looking for a transearthly kingdom, whether the resurrection includes all or only believers. If, as it seems most likely, Paul wrote 1 Thessalonians before 1 Corinthians, he obviously had knowledge of the tradition that included belief in a transearthly existence with

---

110. His only other use of the term is in Rom 2:7.

111. The term also appears in 1 Tim 1:17 to describe God, notably calling God the one who reigns (*basileuō*). Outside the wider Pauline corpus, this term is also used to describe eschatological existence in 1 Pet 1:4, 23.

112. The other uses are Rom 1:23 and Gal 4:20.

113. See Sebastian Schneider, "1 Kor 15,51-52: Ein neuer Lösungsvorschlag zu einer alten Schwierigkeit," in *The Corinthian Correspondence*, ed. R. Bieringer, BETL 125 (Leuven: Leuven University Press, 1996), 661–69, who argues that there was originally a "not" in both phrases. Most interpreters have not been convinced of his argument.

114. R. Collins, *First Corinthians*, 581.

"The Coming of the Lord"

God as a result of the parousia. Given that, it may be that he uses this tradition to argue for the need of a body and of its transformation into a different kind of body. If only the terminology of trumpets and unexpected arrival are from the tradition, they serve as confirmation of the eschatological orientation of the earliest church.

Following his citation of confessional material in 1 Thess 5:2-3 and 6-8, Paul may also continue to rely on preformed material in verses 9-10. We have noted before that Paul seldom uses the term "wrath" (*orgē*) outside Romans, except when quoting preexisting material. In addition to finding this unusual term in verse 9, the same verse also contains the noun *peripoiēsis* ("obtaining"), which appears only here in Paul's undisputed letters. It does appear in Eph 1:14; 2 Thess 2:14; Heb 10:39; and 1 Pet 2:9. In all of these uses except 1 Pet 2:9, where it is part of the list of identities taken from Exod 19:6 and Isa 43:20-21, it refers to obtaining salvation. We noted above that Paul uses the verb *grēgoreō* ("be alert") only once outside 1 Thess 5:6-8, here in verse 10. Further, Paul uses *katheudō* ("to sleep") only within the same verses. Some interpreters see the use of *tithēmi* to mean "appoint" as evidence of a traditional formulation because it is regularly found in the Septuagint and in some New Testament quotations of the Hebrew Bible. Abraham Malherbe, however, observes that, in eight of Paul's thirteen uses of the verb, God is the subject.[115] Thus it is not strong evidence that Paul is continuing his use of preformed material. Some do, however, find enough evidence here to claim that Paul's use of confessional material is continuing.[116] The unusual vocabulary is a strong indication that this is composed by someone other than Paul. But the evidence is less compelling than in other places because the reuse of some of these unusual terms may be echoes of the confessions cited in the previous verses.

The substantive evidence for identifying 1 Thess 5:9-10 as preformed material seems to fall just short of the kind of certainty we have been requiring in this study. If it is traditional material, it adds to what we have already noted in relation to 1 Thess 5:2-3 and 6-8 only that the tradition expects those who have died to participate in the second coming. Of course, we have already seen that point in other traditional material.

---

115. Malherbe, *Letters to the Thessalonians*, 298.
116. For example, Rigaux, "Tradition et rédaction dans 1 Th. V.1-10," 333; Wolfgang Harnisch, *Eschatologische Existenz: Ein exegetischer Beitrag zum Sachanliegen von 1. Thessalonicher 4,13-5,11*, FRLANT 110 (Göttingen: Vandenhoeck & Ruprecht, 1973), 123-24.

Conclusion

In this chapter we have seen Paul rely extensively on earlier traditions for his eschatology. We saw from 1 Cor 16:22 that his view of Jesus as the exalted Lord is taken directly from the Aramaic-speaking church. The call for Jesus to return shows that the church sees Jesus as God's eschatological agent. The church's understanding of Jesus's exaltation soon included the idea that the powers would be subject to Christ. This view came about through the church's interpretations of Pss 110 and 8. This understanding of the return of Christ is explicit in Phil 2:6–11, but this liturgy may be from the Pauline sphere. If the tradition incorporated into 1 Cor 15:20–28 makes Christ the active one in subduing the powers, it accords Christ a higher role in that work than what we see elsewhere in Paul. In other places, it is God who subjects the powers to Christ. Having the powers be subject to Jesus may have quickly followed his identification as Son of Man. Daniel 7:13–14 already has the Son of Man reigning over the earth. The rulers that the traditions in 1 Cor 15 and Phil 2 have in mind are more cosmic than the kings of the earth, so the church has already begun to see a kingdom that is more than the restoration or establishment of an earthly kingdom. Already there was thought of a transearthly kingdom outside Paul's influence.

The tradition reflected in Rom 14:9 shows that the church before Paul envisioned Jesus as the eschatological judge. In addition, the church identifies Jesus as the one who saves believers in the final judgment. This is evident in the traditions in 1 Thess 1:9–10 and 4:14–17. Thus the church before Paul sees Christ as the agent who exercises God's judgment and who mediates eschatological salvation.

The traditions Paul cites in 1 Thess 4:14–17 and 1 Cor 15:50–52 are clear evidence of a transearthly understanding of the eschaton. They envision believers being taken up into another realm and having to be transformed to participate in it. Even if those who think 1 Thess 4 envisions a return to earth are correct, it is with a transformed body and so not simply the establishment of a kingdom like others, only more powerful. The eschaton brings Christ and the transformation of believers into a new type of existence. The element that Paul may contribute here is that he gives the faithful dead an advantaged position rather than allowing that they are disadvantaged, as some other apocalyptic visions held.

Some of the traditions envision this salvation coming through an identification of the believer with Christ. In the tradition Paul cites in 2 Cor 4:14, the resurrection of believers is "with Jesus." Thus God's act of raising believers is done in conjunction with the resurrection of Jesus. This tradition shows that Paul was not the person who first saw the resurrection of Jesus as the

"The Coming of the Lord"

inauguration of the eschatological resurrection.[117] The tradition quoted in Gal 3:27–28 and 1 Cor 12:13 more directly identifies believers with Christ. They put on his identity and in doing so overcome consequences of the sin in Eden. The unification of humanity implied in the allusion to Gen 1:27 demonstrates that the church already thought of this identification with Christ in terms that go beyond the restoration of the nation of Israel.

If those who think that an Adam Christology was in the church before Paul are correct, then the work of Christ was given a cosmic dimension before Paul took up this metaphor. The identification of Christ as a second Adam makes at least part of what he accomplishes be a reversal of the fall. This goes far beyond thinking of Jesus as an earthly ruler.

The tradition Paul refers to in 1 Thess 5:2–3 indicates that the church before Paul had begun to rethink its position on the timing of the second coming. The emphasis has already shifted from simply imminence to its unpredictability. The widespread use of the image of the thief indicates that this image gained fairly quick currency as the final resurrection did not occur as soon as the earliest church expected. That widespread use also indicates that Paul is not the originator of the metaphor. Paul's citation of this tradition may also suggest that he is less sure in 1 Thessalonians than is often supposed that he will survive until the end.

As noted at the beginning of this chapter, those who assert that Paul invented Christianity say that Paul turned the church from hoping for an earthly messianic kingdom to hoping for a heavenly existence. We also noted that they commonly see the Didache and Matthew as texts that have escaped Paul's influence. So we will briefly look to those texts to see what eschatological views they espouse.

The Didache has some statements that could point to a hope for either an earthly kingdom or a transearthly kingdom. Some consider the discussion of the two ways at the beginning of the Didache a good indication of the distance between it and Paul. Yet in the middle of setting out the way that believers should live, it speaks of believers as those who share in immortality (4.8). It mentions this in passing as a warrant for the command to help the needy. Since it needs no support, this is a belief the author thinks he shares with the readers. Kurt Niederwimmer interprets this as a reference to "eternal, heavenly good."[118] This mention of immortality suggests that the eschatology

---

117. Contra Holleman, *Resurrection and Parousia*, 137.

118. Kurt Niederwimmer, *The Didache: A Commentary*, trans. Linda M. Maloney, Hermeneia (Minneapolis: Fortress, 1998), 109.

of the Didache includes belief in something beyond an earthly kingdom. It minimally demonstrates that its eschatology is more complex than belief in the establishment of a kingdom of the sort that is already known in the world. Its author and the tradition he relies on believe they will have life after death.

In Did 9.4, the prayer for the bread at the Eucharist asks God to gather the church from across the world into God's kingdom. This indicates that the author has in mind something other than the restoration of the nation of Israel.[119] Other statements in this section help clarify how the Didache does understand this kingdom. We get some hint from 10.2, where the author thanks God for the gifts of "knowledge and faith and immortality."[120] Here the prayer looks beyond the earthly realm to life with God. This immortality is made known to us through Jesus. In the next paragraph a similar expectation for life beyond an earthly kingdom is apparent. There the author instructs those who pray at the Eucharist to give thanks for the spiritual food and drink and the eternal life[121] (*zōēn aiōnion*) that comes through Christ (10.3). Finally, immediately following the prayer is the request that "this world" (*ho kosmos houtos*) would pass away (10.6). This language cannot reasonably be interpreted as referring only to a major change in the way that the governance of the world is structured. If it had spoken of a coming "age" (*aiōn*), that might be a possible interpretation, but the use of *kosmos* precludes this.[122] Many trace this liturgy back to the earliest Aramaic-speaking church.[123] This means that a transworldly kingdom was part of the church's theology clearly outside Paul's influence and probably before he was in the church.

Looking to Matthew's Gospel, we likewise find clear indications that he also envisions a kingdom that is transearthly. In passages from Q, Matthew connects

---

119. Niederwimmer says it describes the "eschatological gathering of the church" (*Didache*, 149).

120. The term used here is *athanasia*. That term appears in Paul only in 1 Cor 15:53 and 54. Given that this follows immediately what we have identified as a reference to traditional material, it could be that even here Paul is borrowing language from his predecessors.

121. Strangely, Kirsopp Lake translated this phrase "eternal light" (*Apostolic Fathers*, 2 vols., LCL [Cambridge: Harvard University Press, 1912], 1:325). Bart Ehrman's translation corrects this (*Apostolic Fathers*, 2 vols., LCL [Cambridge: Harvard University Press, 2003], 1:433). Niederwimmer notes that this sacramental food is said to convey "more than earthly life" (*Didache*, 158).

122. Niederwimmer sees it as the plea for "the coming of a future world" (*Didache*, 162).

123. For example, Johannes Betz, "The Eucharist in the Didache," in *The Didache in Modern Research*, ed. Jonathan A. Draper, AGJU 37 (Leiden: Brill, 1996), 253; Niederwimmer, *Didache*, 149-50. Enrico Mazza even dates the composition of Did. 9-10 to before the Jerusalem conference ("Didache 9-10: Elements of a Eucharistic Interpretation," in *Didache in Modern Research*, ed. Draper, 283).

the eschatological resurrection and final judgment (Matt 12:38–42/Luke 11:29–32 and Matt 11:21–23/Luke 10:13–15). This connection is clearly present in the church outside Paul's sphere of influence and before he is in the church.[124] This event is also connected to the return of Christ, which Matthew calls the *parousia*. Paul uses this term only once outside 1 Thessalonians to refer to the second coming of Christ. In 1 Thessalonians it occurs in the traditional material he cites and in places close to it. Matthew uses it in the eschatological discourse of chapter 24 (vv. 3, 27, 37, 39). While use of this term to refer to the second coming is uncommon in the New Testament, it also appears in Jas 5:7. So in both writings that Wilson proclaims untainted by Paul, this language for the end is used, and these uses clearly point to Jesus's coming as God's eschatological agent.

The parable of the talents and of the judgment of the nations in Matt 25 also point to a judgment and the establishment of a kingdom that is more than a restored Israel. At the conclusion of the talents parable the offender is cast into outer darkness, where there is weeping and gnashing of teeth (25:30). More explicitly transearthly is the conclusion of the judgment of the nations parable. There the offenders are sent to eternal punishment and the righteous are given eternal life.

On six occasions Matthew speaks of the result of judgment being that the wicked are sent to a place of outer darkness and gnashing of teeth. That this refers to transearthly eschatological judgment is clear from the expression's use in his interpretation of the parable of the weeds among the wheat (13:24–30, 36–43). Matthew's interpretation has the harvest occur at the "end of the age," when eschatological judgment is pronounced. The evil are removed from "his kingdom," which some could interpret as the reconstitution of Israel, and are sent to the place of weeping and gnashing of teeth. But if Matthew envisions a literal earthly kingdom in verse 41, in verse 43 he clearly has a different and transearthly kingdom in view. Here the righteous are taken to the "kingdom of the Father," where they shine like the sun. The expression "shine like the sun" may be taken from Dan 12:3, where a transearthly final end of the righteous is in view. Thus it seems likely that all six of Matthew's use of the teeth-gnashing image point to belief in a transearthly judgment and kingdom.

These references to a transearthly judgment and kingdom in Matthew and the Didache demonstrate that Paul did not introduce this idea to the church. It was common currency before him and outside the sphere of his influence. The church looked for eschatological salvation that was more cosmic than

---

124. Holleman argues that this view would have been present among the followers of Jesus during his lifetime (*Resurrection and Parousia*, 90–92).

the restoration of Israel from very early times. There are clear precedents for such beliefs in apocalyptic Judaism, so it is not surprising that they were part of the church's teaching from very early. If it is correct that Jesus proclaimed the coming of the kingdom, and so was an apocalyptic prophet, then it is not surprising to find an understanding of that kingdom as a transearthly realm in the wake of his death and resurrection. Since calls for his return began within the Aramaic-speaking church (as seen by the *Maranatha* plea), it is most likely that this expanded understanding of the kingdom developed there. This is confirmed by the presence in Q of sayings that connect not only the judgment and the end, but also those in which Jesus is seen as coming judge (e.g., Matt 10:32/Luke 12:8; Matt 23:39/Luke 13:35; Matt 19:28/Luke 22:29–30; and multiple times in Matt 24).

A careful look at even the evidence in the writings that clearly fall outside the influence of Paul shows that the beliefs about eschatology that are sometimes called Paul's inventions were present in the church before Paul joined the movement and in branches of the movement that had little contact with Paul and were certainly not determined by him. Paul took up the traditions that were already current and used them in his churches. At times, his letters simply allude to them without needing to explain them (e.g., *Maranatha*). At other times he relied on those traditions for the points he needed to make (e.g., 1 Thess 5:6–8). At other times, they served as a starting point for his reasoning. For example, he may be the one who first said explicitly that the dead were not disadvantaged at the second coming. If so, he may have relied on some martyr theologies that gave martyrs an advantage over others who had died.[125] Since the martyr theologies were available to him, they were also available to others in the church, so he may not even have been the first to use them for this point. Thus while Paul may have drawn out new implications of the claims the church made about the eschaton, its nature, location, and the place of Christ in it, he was not the first to see it as a cosmic event that brought a transearthly kingdom into fullness. These ideas came from earlier teachers, some from the Aramaic-speaking earliest church that had members who may have known the earthly Jesus. Further, these beliefs were not part of the single branch of the church whether led by Paul or someone else; they were elements of the beliefs of the church across its various communities. Paul's explications of these beliefs remained consonant with most of them, and his views were often dependent on them.

---

125. See e.g., Rev 6:9–11 where martyrs are already in heaven before other believers who have died. See Jerry L. Sumney, "The Resurrection of the Body in Paul," *HBT* 31 (2009): 12–26.

CHAPTER 6

"In Remembrance of Me"
The Lord's Supper

The Lord's Supper or Eucharist is among the practices Paul is sometimes accused of inventing. James Tabor contends that Paul's introductory statement, "I received from the Lord," in 1 Cor 11:23 means that Paul did not get the following account of the institution of the Lord's Supper from the tradition of the church. Instead, it indicates that Paul received it through what he claimed was a revelation. After all, Paul says in Gal 1:11–12 that he did not get his gospel from humans. The combination of this Galatians text with 1 Cor 11:23 signals, Tabor asserts, that the 1 Corinthians account of the supper comes "from Paul and Paul alone."[1] Further, he says the absence of an account of the institution of the supper in John shows that the author of that Gospel rejected its historicity.[2] Tabor claims that this reconstruction is confirmed by the account of the supper in Did. 9–10. Since it is not influenced by Paul, but rather comes from the Q community and James, it does not contain the words of the institution of the supper.[3] Barrie Wilson adds that the Didache does not connect Jesus's death and resurrection to the Lord's Supper.[4]

The most detailed argument for the Pauline origin of the Lord's Supper tradition found in the New Testament documents comes from Hyam Maccoby.

---

1. James Tabor, *Paul and Jesus: How the Apostle Transformed Christianity* (New York: Simon & Schuster, 2012), 146. Similarly, Hyam Maccoby says, "Paul and no one else was the creator of the Eucharist" (*The Mythmaker: Paul and the Invention of Christianity* [New York: Harper & Row, 1987], 118).
2. Tabor, *Paul and Jesus*, 147.
3. Tabor, *Paul and Jesus*, 148.
4. Barrie Wilson, *How Jesus Became God* (New York: St. Martin's, 2008), 159.

He contends that the Gospels contain accounts of its institution only because they were forced to include it under the influence of Paul. The differences in the accounts of the supper in the Gospels demonstrate for him that there was no set Jerusalem tradition about it.[5]

Like Wilson and Tabor, Maccoby looks to the Didache for evidence of an account of the Eucharist that has no connection to the death of Jesus or to the Last Supper. It is a Eucharist that he says is earlier than the Pauline tradition and authentically comes from the earlier church community. The account of the meal in Did. 10 concludes with a welcome call to those who are holy to come and the *Maranatha* prayer. He argues that the meal described here in the Didache is not an agape meal that precedes the Eucharist (as most think) because the account of the Eucharist in Justin's *First Apology* includes this invitation to the holy and the *Maranatha* prayer. He further argues that the Jerusalem church could not have celebrated any sacred meal outside the temple because that would constitute a repudiation of both the temple and Judaism.[6] He contends that the Eucharist began as an annual remembrance of Jesus's celebration of the Passover with his disciples. It was transmuted into a sacred rite related to Jesus's death only after Paul has a vision that leads him to make it such.[7]

Before looking in detail at the tradition about the Lord's Supper that appears in 1 Cor 11:23-26, we need to examine two of the more general claims about the celebration of the Eucharist that Maccoby and others make. Maccoby asserts that Justin's *1 Apol.* 66 demonstrates that the meal described in Did. 10 is the Eucharist (not an agape meal) because it, like the Didache, contains the call for the holy people to come and the *Maranatha* plea. The *First Apology*, however, contains neither of these statements. In neither the accepted text nor in any significant textual variants do we find either a call for holy people to come or the expression *Maranatha*.[8] It is simply not there. So one of the most significant supports for Maccoby's identification of the Didache meal with the Eucharist rests upon a false premise.

Second, the claim that Jews could not partake of any cultic meals outside

---

5. Hyam Maccoby, "Paul and Eucharist," *NTS* 37 (1991): 249-50. Paul Bradshaw and Maxwell Johnson have also argued that Paul is the one who associated these words with the supper and interpreted them to refer to the death of Jesus (*The Eucharistic Liturgies: Their Evolution and Interpretation* [Collegeville, MN: Liturgical Press, 2012], 23).

6. Maccoby, "Paul and Eucharist," 251-53, 251n9.

7. Maccoby, "Paul and Eucharist," 262-63.

8. See the recent critical edition, *Justin, Philosopher and Martyr: Apologies*, ed. Denis Minns and Paul Parvis, Oxford Early Christian Texts (Oxford: Oxford University Press, 2009).

the temple without repudiating it and all of Judaism is shown to be false by the evidence of Qumran. Hubertus van de Sandt notes that the Qumran community regarded their communal meals as ritually holy. They excluded members for moral failings and allowed only members of the community to participate, and then only after ritual washings.[9] The Qumran covenanters were among the many Jews of the first century who applied purity rules to communal meal practices without rejecting temple worship.[10] Van de Sandt argues that this expansion of ritual holiness outside the temple was a way that various groups within Judaism (including the Didache community) were able to "maintain a viable religious life and experience the divine, in particular, in the communal meal itself," with or without the temple.[11] Meeting for a cultic meal outside the temple clearly does not presuppose rejecting the temple or leaving Judaism.

Maccoby, Wilson, and Tabor all identify the meal whose prayers are described in Did. 9–10 as the Eucharist. The prima facie evidence for this is that it is called the Eucharist in 9.1. The question, of course, is whether this term *eucharist*, which simply means "thanksgiving," had taken on the narrow liturgical sense that it has in later times of referring to the central ritual meal of the church's worship. As early as 1976, Willy Rordorf could assert that it was the common view among interpreters of the Didache that the prayers described in these chapters refer to a common meal rather than to the Lord's Supper and that this meal preceded the celebration of the Lord's Supper proper.[12] Further, the flow of prayers and eating follows that of Jewish meals that included guests, and the content of the prayers in Did. 10 follows that of the blessings of Jewish prayers said at the conclusion of festive meals.[13] It seems likely that the deviations of these prayers from the *Birkat Ha-Mazon* are intentionally constructed

---

9. Hubertus Waltherus Maria van de Sandt, "Why Does the Didache Conceive of the Eucharist as a Holy Meal?" *VC* 65 (2011): 19–20.

10. Van de Sandt, "Holy Meal," 11–15.

11. Van de Sandt, "Holy Meal," 20.

12. See Willy Rordorf, "The Didache," in *The Eucharist of the Early Christians*, by Rordorf et al., trans. Matthew J. O'Connell (New York: Pueblo, 1978), 6 (French original published in 1976). The rare exception to this trend seems to be Johannes Betz, "The Eucharist in the *Didache*," in *The Didache in Modern Research*, ed. Jonathan A. Draper, AGJU 37 (Leiden: Brill, 1996), 244–75. He finds sacramental meanings in various aspects of the prayers in these chapters.

13. Rordorf, "Didache," 8–10; Michelle Slee, *The Church in Antioch in the First Century CE: Communion and Conflict*, JSNTSup 244 (Sheffield: Sheffield Academic Press, 2003), 95–97. Kurt Niederwimmer is among those who identify the model for these prayers as the *Birkat Ha-Mazon* (*The Didache: A Commentary*, trans. Linda M. Maloney, Hermeneia [Minneapolis: Fortress, 1998], 155).

to distinguish the church's meals from those of other Jews.[14] Charles Bobertz sees Did. 7–10 as a text that describes the ritual movement of gentiles into the church: through teaching, then baptism, then meal. This meal signifies that they are now part of the new community. If he is correct, this full integration of gentiles prepares them for participation in the community's Lord's Supper.[15]

Seeing these prayers as part of the meal that preceded the more focused Lord's Supper helps explain why they have "eucharistic overtones" without actually being part of the remembrance of the last meal or the passion.[16] Niederwimmer and Rordorf contend that 10.6 is decisive in identifying the prayers of chapters 9–10 as preceding the Lord's Supper. This verse, which concludes the description of the prayers around the meal, contains an invitation for people to participate in a meal and the *Maranatha* prayer that they see as a request for the presence of Christ at the supper.[17] The nature of the meal envisioned in these chapters is also revealed in 10.1. This verse begins by saying that the following prayers are to be given after the people have had their fill of food.[18] It clearly envisions the completion of a full meal. This makes the invitation to come inexplicable unless the people are being invited to something after the satiating meal. We will explore below how it would make good sense to move from a community meal to a ritual or to worship as we look at the parallels between ancient banquets and church gatherings.

Even if these chapters do include the more sacramental part of the Lord's Supper, they are perhaps not without reference to the death of Jesus, as some claim. Enrico Mazza sees the reference to the spiritual food given through "your servant [*pais*]" as an allusion to the Last Supper.[19] Rordorf further finds

---

14. So Niederwimmer, *Didache*, 158; Enrico Mazza, *The Origins of the Eucharistic Prayer* (Collegeville, MN: Liturgical Press, 1995), 14, 25.

15. Charles A. Bobertz, "Ritual Eucharist within Narrative: A Comparison of Didache 9–10 with Mark 6:31-44; 8:1–9," in *Ascetica, Liturgica, Orientalia, Critica et Philologica, First Two Centuries*, ed. J. Baun, A. Cameron, M. Edwards, and M. Vinzent, StPatr 45 (Leuven: Peeters, 2010), 93–95. Mazza also sees Did. 9–10 describing rituals connected with initiation into the community (*Origins of the Eucharistic Prayer*, 13–14).

16. Rordorf, "Didache," 6–7.

17. Niederwimmer, *Didache*, 143; Rordorf, "Didache," 8. So also Otfried Hofius, "The Lord's Supper and the Lord's Supper Tradition: Reflections on 1 Corinthians 11:23b-25," in *One Loaf, One Cup: Ecumenical Studies of 1 Cor. 11 and Other Eucharistic Texts*, ed. Ben F. Meyer, NGS 6 (Macon, GA: Mercer University Press, 1993), 103.

18. Mazza notes that the verb used here (*emplēsthē*) is the same verb used in Deut 8:10, the text that is the basis the rabbis give for the *Birkat ha-Mazon* (*Origins of the Eucharistic Prayer*, 16–17).

19. Enrico Mazza, "Didache 9–10: Elements of a Eucharistic Interpretation," in *Didache in Modern Research*, ed. Draper, 299.

an allusion to the passion in the mention of the "vine of David" in the prayer recited over the first cup of the meal (9.2).[20] As we have seen, these possible allusions probably point toward the more explicit memorial of Jesus that follows the meal of chapters 9-10, but if that is incorrect there is still attention given to the passion even in these chapters.

If the majority of interpreters are correct about the nature of the meal envisioned in Did. 9-10, and the evidence we have just seen supports that view,[21] it is no wonder that those chapters contain no references to the words of institution or any explicit reference to the passion. The reason is not that the church of the Didache assigned them no significance, but that the meal celebrated here precedes the rite in which those things would be the focus of attention. Given what we have seen, Did. 9-10 reveals nothing about the origin of the traditions about the Lord's Supper.

1 Corinthians 11:23-25

Our next task is to determine whether the text in 1 Cor 11:23-25 is preformed and non-Pauline material. Those who argue that Paul created the Lord's Supper tradition may acknowledge that it is preformed, but argue that it still comes from Paul or from his influence. We may note first that it is clearly a self-contained unit. The telling of this narrative stands apart from the context of Paul's direct response to the conduct of the Corinthian church while celebrating the Lord's Supper. It serves as a basis for his rejection of their practice.

One of the criteria for identifying preformed material is that the author identifies it as a tradition. Paul introduces this account of the Last Supper using *paralambō* ("to receive") and *paradidōmi* ("pass on"). As is widely recognized, the Hebrew equivalents of these terms are used among the rabbis as technical terms for receiving and passing on traditions.[22] As Wolfgang Schrage acknowl-

---

20. Rordorf, "Didache," 9.
21. Niederwimmer and Rordorf give more attention to other specifics within these chapters that support their understanding of these prayers as part of a communal meal that comes before the more sacramental supper.
22. For example, Joachim Jeremias, *The Eucharistic Words of Jesus*, trans. Norman Perrin (1966; repr. Philadelphia: Fortress, 1977), 101; Hans Conzelmann, *1 Corinthians: A Commentary on the First Epistle to the Corinthians*, trans. James W. Leitch, Hermeneia (Philadelphia: Fortress, 1975), 195-96; Gordon Fee, *The First Epistle to the Corinthians*, NICNT (Grand Rapids: Eerdmans, 1987), 548; Anthony C. Thiselton, *The First Epistle to the Corinthians: A Commentary on the Greek Text*, NIGTC [Grand Rapids: Eerdmans, 2000], 867; Wolfgang Schrage, *Der*

edges, these rabbinic parallels are all from later writings.[23] Still, their use for this purpose in the first century seems certain.[24] These terms were used in other Hellenistic sources for passing on traditions, including religious traditions.[25] Indeed, we have already seen Paul use it in 1 Corinthians to introduce material that was clearly a preformed tradition (15:3).[26] Furthermore, following use of these words denoting the passing on of tradition, a recitative *hoti* (which sets off what follows as a quotation) introduces the story of the supper.[27] The change from first person ("memory of me") in verse 25 to third person ("the Lord's death") in verse 26 indicates that the preformed tradition has come to an end because Jesus is no longer the speaker and Paul is now addressing the Corinthians directly.[28]

These clear indications that the content of verses 23b-25 is traditional material are complicated by Paul citing its source. He says he received it "from the Lord" (v. 23). Beyond those mentioned above who contend that Paul created this tradition, Hans Lietzmann also sees this citation of its origin as evidence that Paul received this material in a vision.[29] Most interpreters, however, understand the expression in some way that allows that it belongs to a tradition that the church formulated before Paul received it. Joachim Jeremias and Gordon Fee assert that "from the Lord" indicates that the tradition goes back to the earthly Jesus.[30] In this study we have resisted making connections with the earthly Jesus since we know of him only through the interpretations in the

---

erste Brief an die Korinther, 4 vols., EKKNT 7.1-4 (Neukirchen-Vluyn: Neukirchener Verlag, 1991-2001), 3:29; Raymond F. Collins, *First Corinthians*, SP (Collegeville, MN: Liturgical Press, 1999), 425-26.

23. Schrage, *Erste Brief an die Korinther*, 3:29.

24. Even those who say that Paul created this material agree that it is being presented as tradition.

25. Hans-Josef Klauck cites Wis 14:15; Plato, *Theaet.* 198B; and Theon of Smyrna, *Exp. rer. math.* 1, where *paradidōmi* is used of passing on secrets in the mystery cults ("Presence in the Lord's Supper: 1 Corinthians 11:23-26 in the Context of Hellenistic Religious History," in *One Loaf, One Cup*, ed. Meyer, 61-62).

26. See the discussion above in ch. 2. So also William R. Farmer, "Peter and Paul, and the Tradition concerning 'The Lord's Supper' in 1 Corinthians 11:23-26," in *One Loaf, One Cup*, ed. Meyer, 36.

27. R. Collins comments that the recitative *hoti* suggests that the tradition had a life of its own (*First Corinthians*, 426).

28. Anders Eriksson, *Traditions as Rhetorical Proof: Pauline Argumentation in 1 Corinthians*, ConBNT 29 (Stockholm: Almqvist & Wiksell, 1998), 100.

29. Hans Lietzmann, *Mass and Lord's Supper: A Study in the History of the Liturgy*, trans. Dorothea H. G. Reeve (Leiden: Brill, 1979), 208 (original German published in 1926).

30. Jeremias, *Eucharistic Words of Jesus*, 101; Fee, *First Epistle to the Corinthians*, 548.

"In Remembrance of Me"

Gospels.³¹ But seeing this telling of the Last Supper as tradition does not require us to make any claim about the historical Jesus. A number of interpreters contend that saying it is "from the Lord" means only that it is a tradition whose ultimate source is "the Lord,"³² perhaps referring to the risen Christ as he was known in the community.³³ Schrage suggests that Paul says it is from the Lord to set it apart from "human traditions."³⁴ Peter Tomson makes the important observation that Paul refers to commands of Jesus four times in 1 Corinthians; the Gospels confirm that three of the four references are from Jesus. This suggests that Paul thinks this is (or at least he presents it as) a tradition that goes back to the earthly Jesus, not to a visionary experience.³⁵ Before we reach our final conclusion about this, it is important to consider whether there is good evidence for identifying the content of verses 23b-25 as non-Pauline.

A number of elements in these verses either do not appear elsewhere in Paul or are used differently than he uses them elsewhere. The term *anamnēsis* ("remembrance," "memory") is uncommon in the New Testament, where it appears only four times. Two of those instances are in verses 24b-25.³⁶ One of the other two uses of the term occurs in Luke's account of the words of institution at the Last Supper (22:19). Similarly, the verb *deipneō* ("to eat dinner") appears only four times in the New Testament. The only occurrence in Paul is in the phrase "after supper" (*meta to deipnēsai*) in 1 Cor 11:25. This is also the only place that Paul uses an infinitive as the object of the preposition *meta* ("after").³⁷ One of the other New Testament uses of this verb is found in Luke's narrative of the Last Supper, where he has the same prepositional phrase preceding Jesus's

---

31. Klauck comments that there is no historical certainty about there being a Last Supper or that it influenced the Lord's Supper ("Presence in the Lord's Supper," 57-58).

32. Robert H. Mounce, "Continuity of the Primitive Tradition: Some Pre-Pauline Elements in 1 Corinthians," *Int* 13 (1959): 421; Eriksson, *Traditions as Rhetorical Proof*, 102. Conzelmann says that Paul makes himself a link in a chain by citing tradition, but then asserts his independence with "from the Lord" (*1 Corinthians*, 196).

33. Jerome Kodell, *The Eucharist in the New Testament* (Collegeville, MN: Liturgical Press, 1988), 71, 76.

34. Schrage, *Erste Brief an die Korinther*, 3:30.

35. Peter J. Tomson, "La première épître aux Corinthiens comme document de la tradition apostolique de halakha," in *The Corinthian Correspondence*, ed. R. Bieringer, BETL 125 (Leuven: Leuven University Press, 1996), 466.

36. Jeremias lists this term as one of the elements that shows this material is a non-Pauline tradition (*Eucharistic Words of Jesus*, 104). Most of the vocabulary peculiarities highlighted in the next few paragraphs were listed by Jeremias. Subsequent commentators often cite his work on the terminology of this passage as determinative for seeing it as non-Pauline.

37. Jeremias, *Eucharistic Words of Jesus*, 104.

raising of the cup (22:20). These two commonalities may suggest that Paul and Luke draw on the same tradition in their recounting of this narrative. Tabor and Maccoby see this, instead, as evidence that Luke draws his account from Paul's composition. Again, determination of which seems more probable will have to await determination of whether this tradition is a Pauline composition.

The term *hosakis* ("as often as") appears only twice in Paul and one other time in the New Testament. In Paul it appears only in 1 Cor 11:25 and 26. It seems likely that the use of the term in verse 26 was prompted by its use in the tradition cited in verse 25.[38] Paul uses the verb *klaō* ("to break") only twice, both in 1 Corinthians and both in references to the Lord's Supper.[39] Besides appearing in Jesus's interpretation of the bread in 11:24, he uses it earlier in 10:16 in his argument against the Corinthians' participation in meals that included food sacrificed to other gods. The phrase "the bread we break," understood as the body of Christ, is a familiar enough traditional formulation that he can use it in an argument about another point. Thus Paul associates use of this verb with the Lord's Supper and uses it in no other connection. Beyond his scarce use of it, in 11:24 he uses it without an object; there is no grammatical designation of what is broken. This seems to assume that the audience is engaged in an act that is so familiar that there is no need to designate what is broken. Thus it points to a preformed text that is used often.

In addition to including rare terms, this passage has a number of other elements that are uncommon or unique in Pauline usage. One such non-Pauline element is the expression *kai eipen* ("and he said"). This combination of those terms appears only here in Paul.[40] Another is the way Paul uses the verb *paradidōmi* (whose most general meaning is "to give over"). At times he uses it to speak of God giving Christ or for Christ giving himself (e.g., Rom 4:25; 8:32; Gal 2:20). It is the verb he uses to tell the Corinthians to turn over to Satan the man who is sleeping with his father's wife (1 Cor 5:5). We have already seen

---

38. Richard Horsley comments that Paul's use of the term in v. 26 is "[p]icking up on" its use in the tradition in v. 25 (*1 Corinthians*, ANTC [Nashville: Abingdon, 1998], 161).

39. Andrew McGowan has argued powerfully that the designation "Lord's Supper" is a name Paul gave the banquet to address the Corinthian situation and does not represent a name the meal had prior to 1 Corinthians and that it does not become a common term for the meal until long after the first century ("The Myth of the 'Lord's Supper': Paul's Eucharistic Meal Terminology and Its Ancient Reception," *CBQ* 77 [2015]: 503–21). Since we are discussing the place where Paul does use that language, we will continue to employ that term here.

40. Jeremias, *Eucharistic Words of Jesus*, 104. Jeremias cites Heinz Schürmann, *Der Einsetzungsbericht Luke 22, 19–20* (Münster: Aschendorff, 1955), 10, 59–60, as his source for this observation.

that it is also used to describe the passing on of tradition (1 Cor 15:3; 11:23). But its appearance in 1 Cor 11:23b is the only time Paul uses it absolutely (without specifying who did the act) when it has the meaning of "betray." Verse 24 is also the only place Paul uses *eucharisteō* ("give thanks") to speak of a prayer over a meal. According to Heinz Schürmann, the phrases "this is my body" (v. 24) and "this is the cup" (v. 25) are also the only places in Paul where we find *touto* ("this") placed before the noun to which it relates.[41]

Jeremias asserts that the meaning of *sōma* ("body") in 11:24 is also clearly a non-Pauline use. He notes that this is the only time that Paul uses it to refer to the physical body of the earthly Jesus. Elsewhere, he argues, "body" of Christ always refers to the community; Paul even connects it to the community when recalling the eucharistic words in 10:16.[42] While body is a community metaphor in 10:17, "body of Christ" in 10:16 points to the elements of the Eucharist. It is set in opposition to eating what is on the table at a meal where there is food that has been sacrificed to another god. This use is obviously not a reference to the body of the earthly Jesus, but neither does it clearly point to the body as a community.[43] Still, this means that the expression "my body" is well known in Corinth as language associated with the Lord's Supper and that it is connected with the passion and death of Jesus. It also remains another example of an unusual Pauline usage in verses 23b–25.

The mention of the betrayal of Jesus may represent another non-Pauline feature of this liturgical tradition. Other than the crucifixion, Paul's letters seldom refer to events in the life of the earthly Jesus. In light of this tendency, Jerome Kodell argues that the mention of Jesus's betrayal here indicates that it was probably part of the tradition rather than coming from Paul.[44]

The many non-Pauline elements in 1 Cor 11:23b–25 demonstrate that Paul was not the author of this tradition. This makes it less likely that it is based on a visionary experience that Paul had. Jeremias notes that the presence of the article "the" before the reference to "cup" in verse 25 points to a preexistent tradition because it assumes that those present know its identity. He also thinks that "after the supper" sounds like instruction to the person presiding at the Eucharist.[45] This may help confirm that this is a well-known tradition in

---

41. Schürmann, *Einsetzungsbericht Luke 22, 19–20*, 12; cited in Jeremias, *Eucharistic Words of Jesus*, 104.

42. Jeremias, *Eucharistic Words of Jesus*, 104.

43. Thiselton asserts that the fellowship with the body of Christ here points to participation in the death of Jesus (*First Epistle to the Corinthians*, 762).

44. Kodell, *Eucharist in the New Testament*, 76.

45. Jeremias, *Eucharistic Words of Jesus*, 113.

Corinth, as do the references to the "cup of blessing," which is associated with the blood of Christ, and the "bread that we break," which is associated with Christ's body in 10:16–17.[46] Further, citing this understanding as part of his argument on another topic demonstrates that this interpretation is accepted by the Corinthians.[47] This tradition seems to serve as a cultic etiology.[48] It differs from other such originating explanations in the cultural context by taking place in real time rather than in mythic time. As an etiology, it both reflects and reinforces the practice of the supper.

While Paul did not compose the formulated liturgy in 11:23b–25, it remains possible that he was the person who initiated the ritual and gave its elements the meanings they have there. One must, then, compare the accounts of the Last Supper found in the Gospels with that in 1 Corinthians. Many commentators note that the account in Luke more closely matches Paul's than those in Mark and Matthew. Since Matthew's account is probably dependent on Mark, most of our comparisons will be between Luke and Mark.

Most interpreters contend that the account in Mark is based on a tradition that is older than the account in 1 Corinthians. This is the case in no small part because of the non-Greek aspects of Mark's syntax, many of which are identified as Semitisms.[49] The presence of Semitisms is evidence that Mark's account goes back to an Aramaic account of the supper.[50] Prominent among these features that reflect an Aramaic origin and Jewish custom is the wording of Jesus's prayers over the bread. In Mark 14:22, Jesus blesses the bread; in 1 Cor 11:24, he gives thanks. It was the custom among Jews, at least at festive meals, to begin the meal with a blessing of the bread.[51] Further evidence that "blessed" comes into Mark from Aramaic is that it lacks an explicit object. The usual

---

46. Wolfgang Schrage, "Einige Hauptprobleme der Diskussion des Herrenmahls im 1. Korintherbrief," in *Corinthian Correspondence*, ed. Bieringer, 192.

47. So also Francis J. Moloney, *A Body Broken for a Broken People: Eucharist in the New Testament* (Peabody, MA: Hendrickson, 1997), 160–62. Some interpreters see the mention of the cup before the bread in 10:16 as evidence that this was the original order of the Lord's Supper (so Mazza, *Origins of the Eucharistic Prayer*, 33). But this passing mention is too little evidence to support that claim. Mazza also cites Luke's account as evidence that the cup originally came before the bread. See below the discussion of that placement in relation to Hellenistic meal practices.

48. So R. Collins, *First Corinthians*, 428; Hofius, "Lord's Supper," 75.

49. Schrage, *Erste Brief an die Korinther*, 3:10.

50. Jeremias, *Eucharistic Words of Jesus*, 187.

51. Jeremias, *Eucharistic Words of Jesus*, 113, 174, where he gives examples. So also, among others, Kodell, *Eucharist in the New Testament*, 61; and Jean-Marie van Cangh, "Peut-on reconstituer le texte primitif de la Cène?" in *Corinthian Correspondence*, ed. Bieringer, 629.

meaning of the Greek verb *eulogeō* ("bless") was to praise someone or something. Thus the object would be specified. But the Hebrew equivalent term (*bērak*) often simply meant "to say grace," and thus did not need an object.[52]

Among other Semitisms is the expression "break bread" (Mark 14:22; 1 Cor 11:24). While the verb *klaō* ("break") is very rarely used to speak of sharing or distributing food in Greek that does not come from a Hebrew or Aramaic usage, it is regularly used in translating the Hebrew or Aramaic expression.[53] One clear example is Jer 16:7 LXX, where it is used of eating a funerary meal. The expression "fruit of the vine," which appears in Mark 14:25 but not in 1 Corinthians, was also a set liturgical formula within Judaism. Thus it seems to go back to an Aramaic account of the supper.[54] In addition, Mark's eschatological notation, in which Jesus says he will not partake of this meal again until he eats it in the kingdom, is introduced with "truly," *amēn*. This term occurs regularly in sayings of Jesus that appear in the Gospels, and it has the sense of "truly" only when used by Jesus. *Amēn* ("amen" or "truly") is a transliteration of a Hebrew term. It does not appear in Paul's account of the supper. Indeed, Paul's account does not include any mention of Jesus not eating the meal again until he does so in the kingdom. The only explicitly eschatological statement in 1 Cor 11:23–26 is in verse 26, which is not part of the tradition but rather Paul's interpretive application of it.[55] Interpreters often see the eschatological interpretation of the supper as one of its earliest elements.[56] This again indicates that Mark's form of the narrative is earlier than Paul's.

In Mark's account, Jesus says that his blood is "poured out for many" (14:24). Paul does not mention the blood of Jesus being poured out, but Luke does. Given that we have seen Paul cite other traditions that mention the blood of Jesus, he would not necessarily omit it here—even though it plays no role in his theology outside traditional material.[57] Further, if Luke had possessed Paul's formulation, he would have left out the reference to the pouring out of Jesus's blood because he does not usually have an expiation theology.[58]

---

52. Jeremias, *Eucharistic Words of Jesus*, 175. He cites Luke 9:16, where an object is added, as a demonstration that Greek finds the usage without an object difficult.
53. Jeremias, *Eucharistic Words of Jesus*, 176. See him for other examples.
54. Jeremias, *Eucharistic Words of Jesus*, 183; van Cangh, "Peut-on reconstituer?" 625.
55. The mention of the "new covenant" in v. 25 is an eschatological assertion, but it does not speak explicitly about the end or the coming of the kingdom.
56. See van Cangh, "Peut-on reconstituer?" 628, who argues that the eschatological words after the cup are older than those that interpret the cup as blood.
57. So also Conzelmann, *1 Corinthians*, 199.
58. Kodell, *Eucharist in the New Testament*, 60.

Perhaps, then, because he found it in Mark's account, Luke felt compelled to include it. In any case, it may well come from a tradition other than the one he and Paul both drew on.

Paul's account of the words over the cup differs further from Mark's. Paul identifies the recipients of the blessing in connection with the bread rather than with the blood and says that it is "for you" rather than "for many" (11:24). Jeremias identifies the "for many" as a Semitism that means "all," noting that Hebrew does not have a word for "all" with the sense of "sum total." Thus in Hebrew and Aramaic "many" often has an inclusive meaning.[59] Biblical examples of this use for *rabbîm* ("many") include Ps 109:30 and Isa 52:14. The reference to the "many" in Isa 52:14 is rendered "all" in the allusion to it in 1 En. 62:3 and 5.[60] Beyond the probability that the change to "all" is made to clarify its meaning for those who do not speak Aramaic, this is also the kind of change one might expect in a liturgical text.[61] Rather than remaining a general statement about who benefits from Jesus's death, this text now identifies those who receive the blessings as the participants in the rite.

A number of other stylized features of Paul's narrative indicate that its form is later than that found in Mark. Paul's account has Jesus tell the disciples to remember him after both the bread and the cup, while Mark's version does not contain the command at all. Its inclusion probably comes from its liturgical use,[62] and it clearly indicates that the supper is viewed as a memorial meal.[63] Its presence, then, suggests that Mark's narrative reflects an account composed before these liturgical elements were added. Luke's account has Jesus tell the "apostles" (22:14) to remember him after distributing the bread, but not after the cup. While Luke's version of the supper is much closer to Paul's than Mark's

---

59. Jeremias, *Eucharistic Words of Jesus*, 179–82; Kodell, *Eucharist in the New Testament*, 61. Among the examples Jeremias cites are Pirqe Abot 5:18; t. Sanh. 13.5; Sipre Deut. 27 on 3:24.

60. For these and other examples see J. Jeremias, "*polloi*," *TDNT* 6:536–45. Jeremias also identifies as Semitisms a number of other features of Mark's account (23 in all) that we have not mentioned. While it seems likely that he is correct in nearly all of these, those we have not mentioned seem less certain. Still, they provide more support for an early date for the composition of the narrative Mark records.

61. Kodell, *Eucharist in the New Testament*, 64; Eriksson, *Traditions as Rhetorical Proof*, 102–3.

62. R. Collins, *First Corinthians*, 427; van Cangh, "Peut-on reconstituer?" 630. Klauck refers to the addition of this command as a "historicizing" of the church's practice ("Presence in the Lord's Supper," 67). Fee, however, thinks Paul alters the tradition to emphasize remembrance (*First Epistle to the Corinthians*, 547).

63. Schrage, *Erste Brief an die Korinther*, 3:11; Dennis E. Smith, *From Symposium to Eucharist: The Banquet in the Early Christian World* (Minneapolis: Fortress, 2003), 189.

is, the absence of the command to remember Jesus after the cup indicates that it is not directly dependent on Paul. It is more likely that Luke and Paul are both dependent on the same tradition or related traditions than that Luke leaves out one of the commands to remember Jesus.[64] Furthermore, the double command gives the rite a balance. It is more likely that regular use would move the rite toward symmetry rather than away from it.[65] If Schrage is correct in seeing the repetition of the command as a shaping of the tradition to address the Corinthian situation,[66] its absence from Luke is further evidence that both Paul and Luke depend on an earlier tradition.

Van Cangh also sees the appearances of *hosakis* ("as often as") as an addition to the narrative from liturgical use.[67] We noted above that it appears only twice in Paul, once in the citation of the tradition and once in the verse that immediately follows (v. 26). This term, like the command to remember, does not appear in Mark. Given these two factors, the term does seem to come from the tradition Paul is citing. Since it does not appear in Luke's account, this again makes it less likely that he knows Paul's account as we have it in 1 Corinthians but instead relies on an earlier tradition that is similar to the one Paul knows.

Schrage understands "after the supper" (11:25) as a reflection on the practice of having the Lord's Supper within the communal meal.[68] It appears in both Luke (22:20) and Paul, and both have the object of the preposition *meta* ("after") be an articular infinitive. So this element of the tradition that Luke and Paul know seems to be early but still not known in the tradition Mark follows.

Calling Jesus "the Lord Jesus" is also a liturgical element in the narrative that draws on one of the church's earliest confessional formulae.[69] R. Collins, however, thinks it may be Paul who adds "Lord" to the account here.[70] We may leave that open as a possibility while noting that it does not appear in the Gospel accounts.

Another liturgical shaping of the narrative appears in its deleting of some of the story's concrete actions. In Mark's version, the narrative has Jesus distribute both the bread and the cup. In Luke, Jesus distributes only the first cup

---

64. And it seems more probable that Paul or the tradition would add a second call to remember Jesus than that either would drop it.
65. Kodell, *Eucharist in the New Testament*, 57, 60; R. Collins, *First Corinthians*, 427.
66. Schrage, *Erste Brief an die Korinther*, 3:40–41.
67. Van Cangh, "Peut-on reconstituer?" 630.
68. Schrage, *Erste Brief an die Korinther*, 3:12; also Conzelmann, *1 Corinthians*, 199.
69. Jeremias, *Eucharistic Words of Jesus*, 112; Eriksson, *Traditions as Rhetorical Proof*, 100.
70. R. Collins, *First Corinthians*, 427.

and the bread. Paul's account, however, contains no mention of the distribution of either; it includes only the acts and words that contribute to understanding the rite. As van Cangh notes, this is a characteristic of a secondary liturgical tradition.[71] Somewhat similarly, Paul's account does not make the Last Supper a Passover meal.[72] That detail seems to be another element that has dropped out of the telling as it becomes a liturgy.

The tradition Paul cites introduces the supper as having occurred "on the night on which he was betrayed" (11:23b). Some argue that this associates the meaning of the supper with Isa 53.[73] While this is possible, we are on more certain footing noting that it ties the supper to the wider passion narrative. Since Paul seldom mentions deeds or times in the life of the earthly Jesus, it probably appears in the tradition he is citing rather than being a Pauline creation.[74] That Luke does not have it may again suggest that he did not rely on Paul's formulation for his account of the supper. Alternatively, he could have seen it as superfluous because the timing is obvious in the narrative flow of his Gospel.

A number of interpreters argue that the combination of body and blood in this text had to take place after the story was being told among gentiles because within the Jewish thought world the blood is part of the body. Thus the pairing makes cultural sense only outside Judaism.[75] While this observation about the relationship between body and blood seems correct, Conzelmann notes that the pairing is not body and blood in Paul's account, but rather body and covenant.[76] This perhaps lessens the tension. It also points us to another divergence in the tradition. In the Pauline and Lukan tellings, the cup is the new covenant that is established through the blood of Jesus, but in Mark it is "my blood." The identification of the cup with a celebration of a covenant makes good sense within Jewish tradition and seems likely to be the older tradition.[77] Here, then, the Pauline and Lukan source seems to have preserved the earlier tradition.

One of the reasons some argue that the Lord's Supper tradition could not

---

71. Van Cangh, "Peut-on reconstituer?" 630.

72. R. Collins observes this about Paul's account (*First Corinthians*, 430).

73. Jeremias, *Eucharistic Words of Jesus*, 112-13; Mounce, "Continuity of the Primitive Tradition," 422.

74. Conzelmann remarks that these words betray "an established motif of the Passion kerygma" (*1 Corinthians*, 197).

75. Schrage, *Erste Brief an die Korinther*, 3:11-12; van Cangh, "Peut-on reconstituer?" 631.

76. Conzelmann, *1 Corinthians*, 199-200.

77. Kodell, *Eucharist in the New Testament*, 65; Smith, *From Symposium to Eucharist*, 190.

"In Remembrance of Me"

take the form we see in Paul at an early time or among Jewish believers is that drinking blood was too repugnant to Jews. The command against it, some argue, made it impossible for Jews to envision that Jesus could have told his disciples to drink blood. The strict prohibition against drinking blood is clear, and the careful adherence to food laws in the first century makes it obvious that it was taken seriously. But it is hard to think that it was more repulsive than the command to take up cannibalism (to eat "my body") that precedes it! John's Gospel, written for a church composed mostly of Jews, confirms that both were abhorrent. In John 6, which alludes to the Lord's Supper, Jesus tells the crowd that they must eat his flesh and drink his blood (vv. 50–59). The crowd's initial reaction is to reject eating Jesus's flesh; mention of his blood comes only after that first response. John acknowledges that this is difficult to comprehend and that some stop following Jesus because of it (vv. 60–61, 66–69). But the demand remains and does not drive away John's primarily Jewish church.

Furthermore, a careful reading of the tradition in 1 Corinthians renders the concern about Jews drinking blood moot in relation to its interpretation of the cup. A number of more recent commentators emphasize that the tradition in 11:23–25 does not identify the contents of the cup as blood.[78] Instead, "the cup is the new covenant." The covenant is ratified with the blood of Jesus, but that blood is not what is in the cup. Morna Hooker notes further that Paul does not tell the Corinthians to drink from the cup.[79]

The shedding of blood was associated with covenant initiation in the Hebrew Bible. For example, Moses sprinkled the people with blood to ratify the covenant between them and God (Exod 24:5–8).[80] In the tradition Paul cites, the blood of Jesus is "a symbol and mediation" of the covenant.[81]

---

78. Simon J. Kistemaker, *Exposition of the First Epistle to the Corinthians*, New Testament Commentaries (Grand Rapids: Baker, 1993), 396; Thiselton, *First Epistle to the Corinthians*, 759; Ben Witherington III, *Conflict and Community in Corinth: A Socio-Rhetorical Commentary on 1 and 2 Corinthians* (Grand Rapids: Eerdmans, 1995), 251; R. Collins, *First Corinthians*, 433; Conzelmann, *1 Corinthians*, 199–200. Neither does 1 Cor 10:16 clearly identify the contents of the cup as blood. The cup stands for fellowship or association with Christ's blood, but that does not mean the content of the cup is blood.

79. Morna Hooker, *Not Ashamed of the Gospel: New Testament Interpretations of the Death of Christ* (Grand Rapids: Eerdmans, 1994), 22–23. She adds here that Paul, as a good Jew, would not have told them to drink blood.

80. Kistemaker (*First Corinthians*, 396) and R. Horsley (*1 Corinthians*, 161) mention this precedent. We may add that the covenant with Abraham was initiated with the killing and splitting in half of multiple animals and God moving between the pieces.

81. R. Collins, *First Corinthians*, 433.

STEWARD OF GOD'S MYSTERIES

Interpreting the death of Jesus through covenant imagery sets this tradition clearly within a Jewish environment.[82] Richard Horsley identifies the biblical tradition of memorial meals that reenact founding events as "the background from which the celebration of the Lord's Supper as a ritual enactment in remembrance of Jesus' action, in the meal and on the cross, must be understood."[83] Referring to the *new* covenant sets this celebration apart from other Jewish memorial meals by recognizing the eschatological nature of Christ's death.[84]

Covenant banquets are well known in the Bible and elsewhere in the ancient Near East.[85] A particularly clear biblical example is the meal Isaac has with Abimelech and his advisors. They come asking to make peace and to enter into a covenant with Isaac. The relationship is sealed with a meal (Gen 26:26–33). Drinking the cup in this context means that one is in the covenant and is committed to maintaining that relationship.[86] There is, then, clear Jewish precedent for covenant meals and associating blood with the initiation of a covenant. The tradition Paul cites seems to envision the Lord's Supper as a covenant meal.[87] In addition to recognizing that the cup does not contain the blood of Jesus, Ben Witherington III argues that this tradition does not associate the breaking of the bread with the breaking of Jesus's body. As we have seen, speaking of "breaking the bread" was a traditional Hebrew/Aramaic way to refer to a meal.[88] Hooker further suggests that the ambiguity of the text allows that the meaning of this breaking is that the bread is to be shared.[89] Witherington, then, concludes that the tradition that Paul cites does not make the supper an explicit reenactment of the passion.[90]

Additionally, as we have seen in chapter 2, interpretations of Jewish martyrs had already used the language of bodies being given for others and the

---

82. Smith asserts that the idea of covenant being associated with the church's early memorial meal comes from Judaism (*From Symposium to Banquet*, 190).

83. R. Horsley, *1 Corinthians*, 161.

84. R. Collins, *First Corinthians*, 433.

85. R. Collins, *First Corinthians*, 433. His examples include Gen 14:18; 26:26–33; 31:43–54; Exod 24:9–11.

86. Kistemaker, *1 Corinthians*, 396; Thiselton, *First Epistle to the Corinthians*, 759.

87. R. Collins, *First Corinthians*, 427. Similarly, Ralph Martin says Paul's understanding is like the Jewish understanding of the Passover (*Worship in the Early Church* [Grand Rapids: Eerdmans, 1964], 122–23).

88. Witherington, *Conflict and Community*, 251.

89. Hooker, *Not Ashamed of the Gospel*, 22.

90. Witherington, *Conflict and Community*, 251. See below the argument of Angela Standhartinger that associates the tradition with dramatic retellings of the passion.

shedding of blood for the benefit of others.[91] So these ideas are not foreign to first-century Jewish thought.

While the accounts of the supper in 1 Corinthians and in Luke do not identify the contents of the cup as the blood of Jesus, those in Mark and Matthew do. This suggests that the different interpretations of the cup derive from separate traditions. In this case, the tradition Paul and Luke rely on seems earlier. Van Cangh, however, argues that the Markan version is older because it fits well with covenant theology and does not assume that the death of Jesus is expiatory. Further, he asserts that it is earlier because it is the more difficult reading and later developments are more likely to smooth out difficulties than to create them. That is, the initial tradition would have identified the contents of the cup as blood because that is the more difficult understanding. Jeremias contends that the expression "my blood of the covenant" (Mark 14:24) is early because it can be translated into Aramaic.[92] Whichever is older, both seem to be early and to persist into the time when the Synoptics were written. The differences may indicate that they represent separate developments of traditions about the Last Supper and the institution of the Lord's Supper.

Hal Taussig identifies the earliest, broadest, and most persistent understanding of the cup after supper to be its association with Jesus's blood. He sees this as pre-Pauline and as earlier than the command to remember Jesus or Jesus's eschatological remarks. He argues that the cup comes at the time of the meal when it was usual for libations to be offered. Noting that Rome demanded that a libation be offered to "the genius of the emperor," he views the cup associated with Jesus's death and blood as a "libational challenge to Rome."[93] It is a challenge because it celebrates the victory of Christ over the power of Rome, as the hymns to Christ resisted Rome by proclaiming Christ's cosmic rule.[94] Even if this political reading is not fully convincing or was less prominent in the minds of the earliest participants, it provides us with one more angle on how some in the early church could have understood the association of the cup with Jesus's blood.[95]

---

91. See also Smith, *From Symposium to Eucharist*, 190.

92. Jeremias, *Eucharistic Words of Jesus*, 193–95.

93. Hal Taussig, *In the Beginning Was the Meal: Social Experimentation and Early Christian Identity* (Minneapolis: Fortress, 2009), 131–32, 75.

94. Taussig, *In the Beginning*, 110, 131.

95. Taussig also argues that the reference to the covenant fits this interpretation because it points the participants to Judaism and to Judea's troubled history with Rome (*In the Beginning*, 131). R. Alan Streett also identifies the supper as anti-imperial and ties it, through the presence of prophets in the Corinthian church, to the critique of rulers seen in the Hebrew

We have seen that 1 Cor 11:23b–25 is composed of traditional material. It uses a great deal of vocabulary that is unusual in Paul, and it uses other terms in ways that are unusual for Paul. In addition, Paul gives attention to the blood of Christ only when he is citing traditional material. Comparison of this tradition with that in Mark (and thus Matthew, who follows Mark's account) shows a number of important differences. Still, some argue that the similarities, at least in the words of Jesus, are so close that all variations must go back to a single original form or to a historical event.[96] But the differences in the narratives of the event and in the theological ideas expressed suggest that there are disparate traditions, even if they developed in the same area. Looking at the words that Jesus speaks, Conzelmann concludes that it is unlikely that there was ever uniform wording.[97] We have also seen that some elements of the Markan tradition seem older than those in Paul. These include the several phrases that are Semitisms and the presence of the narrative details of distributing the bread and the cup.[98] We have also noted above that a number of things in the Pauline account seem later than the version in Mark. In addition, one should remember that Paul's version does not associate the supper with the Passover. At the same time, there are elements in the tradition Paul cites that seem earlier. This is particularly the case with the identification of the cup with the new covenant rather than with the blood of Jesus. Still, on the whole, Mark's account draws on a tradition that retains more elements of an earlier tradition.[99] It seems best to recognize that there were multiple versions of the Last Supper and the Lord's Supper tradition in the early church.[100] We have seen no evidence, including in the Didache, that any of them existed apart from a connection to a remembrance of the death of Jesus.[101]

Finally, we need to give some attention to the origins and development of the meal. As noted above, Maccoby asserts that it began as an annual remembrance of

---

prophets (*Subversive Meals: An Analysis of the Lord's Supper under Roman Domination during the First Century* [Eugene, OR: Wipf & Stock, 2013], 245–63); for the fuller argument about the relationship between the supper and prophecy, see 236–85.

96. So, e.g., Jeremias, *Eucharistic Words of Jesus*, 193; R. Collins, *First Corinthians*, 430.

97. Conzelmann, *1 Corinthians*, 201.

98. Jeremias identifies Mark 14:22–24, which contains this material, as the earliest parts of the Last Supper accounts (*Eucharistic Words of Jesus*, 100).

99. Kodell comments that neither the Pauline nor the Markan form "can claim primitiveness completely" (*Eucharist in the New Testament*, 60).

100. Mark Seifrid asserts that Paul composed what appears in these verses but drew on earlier elements of tradition ("Gift of Remembrance: Paul and the Lord's Supper in Corinth," *Concordia Journal* 42 [2016]: 127n2).

101. R. Collins, *First Corinthians*, 430.

"In Remembrance of Me"

the Last Supper. Maccoby also contends that the "breaking of the bread" referred to in Acts is not related to eucharistic practice.[102] More careful reconstructions of the relationship between a communal meal and the Lord's Supper seem to demonstrate that such a simple denial of the connection has fatal flaws.

Perhaps the first thing to notice is that our earliest evidence indicates that the communal meal and the Lord's Supper are connected. That is certainly the case in 1 Cor 11 because the problem Paul addresses is that the communal meal is not being conducted as it should be. They also seem connected in Paul's description of the Antioch incident in Gal 2:11–14.[103] There the dispute arises because the church composed of Jews and gentiles is about to sit down to a communal meal that could involve contact with food that Jews are not allowed to eat. This at least shows that a communal meal was part of many gatherings of the church, as Acts suggests. Conzelmann argues that the order of blessing the bread first and blessing the cup "after dinner" shows that the liturgy assumes that the meal takes places between these acts.[104] When Mark says that Jesus institutes the rite "as they were eating," it suggests that the cup comes after the meal[105] or while it is in progress.

Further, Dennis Smith notes that 1 Cor 11:17–18 and 11:21–22 seem to make gathering as the church and eating together "relatively synonymous."[106] Thus it seems the meal and accompanying rite were usually related in the churches' gatherings for worship. Smith finds this probable because the church met in houses and thus around tables.[107] The assumption that the church nearly always met in houses has recently been challenged. It seems that while some churches met in houses, others met in different spaces (gardens, rented halls, residential areas connected to workshops, perhaps upstairs in bath complexes, etc.).[108] While this complicates the picture of early church meetings and practices, it does not necessarily indicate that meals were less a part of their meetings. Many of these spaces are suitable for and even intended for the conduct of communal meals or banquets. We should, then, assume that meetings of the church regularly included communal meals and that those meals (at least often) included some type of celebration of the Lord's Supper.

---

102. Maccoby, "Paul and Eucharist," 250.
103. So also Smith, *From Symposium to Eucharist*, 176.
104. Conzelmann, *1 Corinthians*, 199.
105. So Jeremias, *Eucharistic Words of Jesus*, 121–22.
106. Smith, *From Symposium to Eucharist*, 176.
107. Smith, *From Symposium to Eucharist*, 177.
108. Edward Adams, *The Earliest Christian Meeting Places: Almost Exclusively Houses?* LNTS 450 (New York: Bloomsbury T. & T. Clark, 2013).

Some interpreters envision the Lord's Supper as a meal that included only bread and water as a continuation of the meal with Jesus before his death or of his usual eating practices. According to Lietzmann, in this meal the diners sensed the presence of Jesus and called for his return in the clouds. Such interpreters see this as separate from the memorial meal that we find in 1 Corinthians.[109] As Conzelmann notes, however, there is no evidence for that kind of celebration in the earliest church.[110] Lietzmann and those who have followed him fill in data that are lacking in the text with their interpretive hypothesis. Thus, as Mazza comments, this idea of two types of Eucharists "is more of a theological perspective than a plain showing of textual data."[111]

Interpreters commonly find the origins of the Lord's Supper in Jewish festive meals. Given that the church began in a Jewish context in Palestine, this seems most probable. The Didache certainly shows how the church's communal meal mirrored them, but also how the church sought to distinguish its meals from those of nonchurch members. But the church and its meal soon moved into predominantly gentile areas. Even while the church remained completely or predominantly Jewish, this move outside Palestine probably meant that the form of its communal meal was shaped in part by the prevailing meal practices of the world more generally. Indeed, the form would have been shaped by Hellenistic cultural practices even while the church remained in Palestine. We have come to recognize that Palestinian Judaism was not immune to influences from the prevailing culture. So, just as other groups that met for festive meals had particular practices that set them apart from others, such was also the case with Jewish meals. Yet we should also expect many similarities.

The similarities between Jewish covenant meals and celebrations such as the Passover, on the one hand, and Hellenistic memorial meals, on the other, likely meant that many (at least outside Judaism) saw them as equivalent, or nearly so. We have seen that the evidence indicates that the church's meal was associated with Jesus's death from the earliest times. This suggests that the church saw their meal as a memorial meal. Of course, a covenant meal was a type of memorial meal. In the broader world, memorial meals included family funerary meals and meals of other groups and associations. Smith argues that the closest parallel to the Lord's Supper among other groups is the Epicurean memorial meal that was said to have been instituted by Epicurus himself.[112]

---

109. For example, Lietzmann, *Mass and Lord's Supper*, 204, 205.
110. Conzelmann, *1 Corinthians*, 195.
111. Mazza, *Origins of the Eucharistic Prayer*, 3.
112. Smith, *From Symposium to Eucharist*, 188–89.

"In Remembrance of Me"

Angela Standhartinger also identifies funerary meals as the precedent that the supper draws on. She contends that the tradition Paul cites developed through reenactments of the passion in the form of a performance by someone in the church when they gathered for meals. She argues that the telling and enacting of the passion night events follow the practices of funerary banquets.[113] Thus what Paul quotes is the climax of an important scene. She also sees these regular performances, most likely done by women, as the reason for the diverse forms of the tradition that we find in the New Testament.[114]

We have seen above how Paul seems to assume that the church's meeting for worship will include a meal. Smith contends that we should not see this as unusual; rather, gathering around a meal was simply following "a practice common to all religious people and sectarian groups in the ancient world."[115] Thus having a common meal was only following "prevailing custom."[116] Smith goes on to contend that this means that Paul did not draw on the Passover for his understanding of the pattern of the meal.[117] This seems to assume perhaps too much distance between common practice of memorial meals and that of Jewish memorial meals. Still, Smith sees the formative pattern for the Lord's Supper to be the much more common banquet or symposium.[118] Taussig adds that Hellenistic communal meals served as ways for groups to express their ideals.[119] This identifies an important parallel between the church's meal and that of other associations because Paul's discussion of the Lord's Supper in 1 Cor 11 certainly assumes that it is to reflect the ideals of the church.

The importance of this connection between Hellenistic banquet practice and the Lord's Supper appears in the ways such meals were conducted. Hellenistic banquets, including memorial meals and other association meals, began with a full meal. After the meal came at least one libation that set what followed—a time of discussion or of entertainment—apart from the meal. The libation usually included a hymn to a god and often a prayer. That initial libation could be followed by several others to various gods.[120]

---

113. Angela Standhartinger, "Words to Remember—Women and the Origin of the 'Words of Institution,' " *Lectio Difficilior* 1 (2015): 1–25.
114. Standhartinger, "Words to Remember," 12–13. The predominance of women in such settings is drawn from cross-cultural settings rather than evidence of the first century.
115. Smith, *From Symposium to Eucharist*, 174.
116. Smith, *From Symposium to Eucharist*, 174.
117. Smith, *From Symposium to Eucharist*, 175.
118. Smith, *From Symposium to Eucharist*, 175.
119. Taussig, *In the Beginning*, 21–24.
120. See Taussig, *In the Beginning*, 50, 74–78.

Schrage thinks that the church meal began with the breaking of the bread and was concluded with the sharing of the cup, as evidenced by the "after supper" phrase (1 Cor 11:25).[121] Smith argues that this pattern of blessing the bread, full meal, and final cup of wine follows the normal features of the Hellenistic banquet. Thus this was the earliest way that the supper was celebrated.[122] This makes the full meal and the Lord's Supper inseparable. This fits the pattern we saw about meals at Qumran. They envisioned their entire communal meal as a sacramental event. If this was the original pattern of the supper, it may have undergone some development even before the time of 1 Corinthians.

Schrage recognizes that this picture is complicated when we take account of the poor being excluded from part of the meal, as they seem to be in 1 Cor 11:20–21.[123] This suggests that the more sacramental part of the Lord's Supper had been moved to the end of the meal. John Kloppenborg, however, has argued that the problem is not the late arrival of the poor but an unequal distribution of the food. The problem then is that those with higher status were designated to receive more food, as was common in various association meetings.[124] While the later arrival of the poor does seem to be the problem Paul addresses, the direct mention of the death of Jesus may still come at the end of the meal. If it is correct that Did. 9–10 contains the prayers for the meal that precedes the Lord's Supper proper, then the more sacramental part has been moved to the moment after the community's satiating meal. The order of events at the Hellenistic banquet may help us understand how this construction of the church's meal makes sense, and help us make sense of Luke's initial cup at the Last Supper.

We noted that banquets usually marked the move from the group meal to the program of discussion or entertainment by means of a libation that often included hymns and prayers. Perhaps the church moved from its communal meal to the more focused actions of worship through such a libation. The recitation of hymns and prayers connected with the libations would include the memorial bread and wine or might immediately follow them. This would account for Luke's cup of wine that begins the Lord's Supper; it is the initial libation that concludes the satiating meal.[125] It also makes sense of what we

---

121. Schrage, *Erste Brief an die Korinther*, 3:12–15.
122. Smith, *From Symposium to Eucharist*, 188.
123. Schrage, *Erste Brief an die Korinther*, 3:14–15.
124. John S. Kloppenborg, "Precedence at the Communal Meal in Corinth," *NovT* 58 (2016): 167–203.
125. This same conclusion about the order of events at the supper has also been reached by Streett, *Subversive Meals*, 38–41.

"In Remembrance of Me"

see in 1 Corinthians and the Didache. The "after supper" phrases in Paul's and Luke's account would then be an element of the tradition that reflected earlier practice or was the way the community remembered the institution of it. Klauck raises a practical matter that would encourage the church to have the more sacramental elements at the end of the meal. He notes that if the bread comes at the beginning of the meal, those who arrived late would miss it. So while the practice had changed, perhaps in part so that all were present for the whole of it, the liturgy had not changed to match the new practice.[126]

Whether the remembrance of the death of Jesus occurred in the middle of the fuller meal or at its end, the movement of Hellenistic banquets shows that it would be a recognizable and customary part of a religious community's communal meal. Observing this congruence does not mean that the earliest church would have abandoned Jewish prayers for various parts of the meal. So long as we remember that first-century Jews lived within Hellenistic culture, we should expect that they know its social practices and that those practices have influenced their own memorial and cultic meals. Hofius cites numerous examples from rabbinic literature of meals beginning with the breaking of bread and ending with a blessing of a cup.[127] We may see some of this confluence in the way Mark ends the story of the Last Supper; he has the participants sing a hymn at the end (14:26), just as Hellenistic banquets might have singing at the conclusion of the dinner portion of the night. Even if this is not a sign of Hellenistic banquets influencing Jewish festive meals, it shows that Mark thinks this is an appropriate end for a meeting centered on a religious meal. So we do not need to choose between Hellenistic communal meals and Jewish communal meals when thinking about how the church celebrated the Lord's Supper.[128]

At the least, setting the Lord's Supper in the context of Hellenistic banquets demonstrates again (that is, in addition to Qumran meals) that the early

---

126. Klauck, "Presence in the Lord's Supper," 65.

127. Hofius, "Lord's Supper," 84-86.

128. Klauck also warns against seeing too much division between Hellenism and Judaism. He cites the confluence of the use of the language of passing on of tradition (*paradidōmi*) as an example of the commonalities between Jewish practice and Hellenism ("Presence in the Lord's Supper," 58-59). Elisabeth Schüssler Fiorenza also groups together the practices of Greco-Roman religious associations, professional collegia, and Jewish festive meals (*In Memory of Her: A Feminist Theological Reconstruction of Christian Origins* [New York: Crossroad, 1983], 198). Konrad Vössing argues that Paul's instructions and use of this tradition have the goal of bringing together the parts of their gathering that involved singing, prophecy, and teaching with the eating of the Lord's Supper ("Das 'Herrenmahl' und 1 Cor. 11 im Kontext antiker Gemeinschaftsmähler," *JAC* 54 [2011]: 64 [where he assumes this is a known tradition], 67-68).

church would have no trouble incorporating a cultic or sacramental activity into its communal meal. Further, even seeing such a meal as a memorial meal that recalls a death, even a martyr's death, is not new or non-Jewish (as those who argue that Paul invented it assert) in this environment.

Our final task in this chapter is to consider where the traditions about the Lord's Supper and the accounts of its institution in Paul and the Gospels may have originated. We have already seen that Mark's account shows no influence from Paul. Further, the tradition Paul cites contains many words and ideas that are uncommon for Paul or are absent from his writings except in other citations of traditional material. Thus he is not its author, nor does it seem to come from his churches. The number of Semitisms in Mark's account indicates that it is based on an Aramaic original. This places it in the sphere of the Jerusalem church.[129] This means that the Jerusalem church associated the meal with the death of Jesus. We have seen that phrases such as "for many" indicate that it represents a telling of the story that took its form before it was influenced by its liturgical use.

The tradition Paul cites has been shaped by liturgical use. It has also been made to conform more to usual Greek syntax so that it no longer contains the Semitisms found in Mark's account. Many interpreters point to Antioch as the most likely place for Paul to have first gotten this tradition.[130] After all, this is the church that supported Paul as a missionary early in his career. It is also a church that had both Jewish and gentile members. Thus it would need to translate Aramaic traditions into Greek, and those traditions would begin to reflect more normal Greek syntax as they were repeated, including in their liturgical use. A number of interpreters see the tradition used in Antioch as dependent on the Jerusalem church, and so again on the earliest possible sources.[131]

---

129. So also Jeremias, *Eucharistic Words of Jesus*, 187; Kodell, *Eucharist in the New Testament*, 60; van Cangh, "Peut-on reconstituer," 629.

130. For example, Kodell, *Eucharist in the New Testament*, 71; Smith, *From Symposium to Eucharist*, 177. Mounce asserts that Paul received the tradition while he was in Damascus but that it was formulated in Antioch ("Continuity of the Primitive Tradition," 421-22). Martin Hengel contends that it goes back at least to the time Paul was in Syria and Cilicia (*Studies in Early Christology* [Edinburgh: T. & T. Clark, 1995], 43).

131. So, e.g., R. Collins, *First Corinthians*, 426, 428. William Farmer asserts that Paul got his information about the supper (though he does not say the wording of the tradition) from Peter when he visited with him in Jerusalem as reported in Gal 2 ("Peter and Paul, and the Tradition concerning 'The Lord's Supper' in 1 Corinthians 11:23-26," in *One Loaf, One Cup*, ed. Meyer, 54).

Conclusion

Our examination of the tradition Paul cites in 1 Cor 11:23-26 shows that Paul is not its author and not the inventor of the cultic meal that memorializes the death of Jesus. Even if Did. 9-10 is an account of a Eucharist in the more liturgical sense, it does not demonstrate that Paul was the one to connect the meal and the death of Jesus. Although not explicit, the reference to the spiritual food and drink that comes through Christ may well allude to Jesus's death. Further, our examination of the Gospel accounts and 1 Cor 11 shows that Paul is drawing on non-Pauline and preformed tradition in his account of the institution of the supper. The vocabulary and style of 1 Cor 11:23-25 point to a well-used preformed piece. Our comparisons with the Gospel narratives of the Last Supper also show that they are not dependent on the account that appears in 1 Corinthians. Even Luke's account of the supper that is drawn from the same stream of tradition as Paul's is not dependent on the form of it that appears in 1 Cor 11. The Mark/Matthew version rests on a tradition not only older than Paul's letter, but older than the tradition that Paul cites.

Although we cannot reconstruct the exact form of the tradition (there was probably not just one version of it in circulation)[132] and cannot know whether or how much of it might go back to Jesus, we can be confident that its attachment to the death of Jesus predates Paul's entrance into the church.[133] If it is correct that this form of the tradition developed in Syria or Arabia, it shows that the church in that area understood Jesus's death as a covenant sacrifice and perhaps, in some sense, vicarious. Moreover, John Carroll and Joel Green seem correct when they assert that this tradition assumes a passion narrative.[134] This passage indicates that churches in regions outside Palestine understood Jesus's death as central to the faith and as vicarious (in some sense) in the years that immediately follow his death.[135]

---

132. So, e.g., R. Collins, *First Corinthians*, 430. Fee, for example, thinks Paul alters the tradition to emphasize remembrance (*First Epistle to the Corinthians*, 547).

133. This may well have been one of the things about the church's understanding of Jesus that led Paul to oppose it.

134. John Carroll and Joel Green, *The Death of Jesus in Early Christianity* (Peabody, MA: Hendrickson, 1995), 120. So also G. François Wessels, "The Historical Jesus and the Letters of Paul," in *The New Testament Interpreted: Essays in Honour of Bernard C. Lategan*, ed. Ciliers Breytenbach, Johan C. Thom, and Jeremy Punt, NovTSup 124 (Leiden: Brill, 2006), 33.

135. If the tradition goes back to the Jerusalem church, then it is further evidence of a sustained focus on Jesus's death in the earliest days of the church.

In 1 Cor 11, Paul is writing to correct what he sees as misconduct when the church gathers to worship and to celebrate the Lord's Supper. While he provides other reasons for them to change their practice, his use of this tradition is a significant part of his argument that supports his demands. His citation of it reminds them of the meal's purpose and suggests how it should be conducted. Once again, then, we see Paul relying on earlier church tradition as a basis for his instruction to his churches.

CHAPTER 7

"I Handed On to You . . . What I Received"

We have now explored how Paul draws on preformed tradition in a number of places in his letters, which give clear evidence that he regularly uses prior tradition when he makes theological assertions about a wide range of beliefs. We have seen that these traditions come from various branches of the church, including the church in Jerusalem. We will now pull together what we have found and consider what it says about Paul's place within and his relationship to the wider and earlier church.

Paul's Dependence on Earlier Tradition

Paul's beliefs about the centrality and meaning of the death of Jesus rely on and conform to the meanings it was given before he was in the church. The tradition he cites in 1 Cor 15:3b–5 demonstrates that the Jerusalem church understood the death of Jesus to be vicarious. It is important to recognize that this tradition has no comment about how the death of Jesus deals with sin. It asserts that it does so without setting out any atonement theory. Claiming that it deals with sin does not suggest a substitutionary theory, and it does not exclude it.[1] This brief tradition asserts only that his death

---

1. Cilliers Breytenbach eschews the term *substitutionary* and uses *interchange* to avoid the theological baggage of the former. Still he sees a number of places in Paul where Christ does take the place of sinners (*Grace, Reconciliation, Concord: The Death of Christ in Graeco-Roman Metaphors*, NovTSup 135 [Leiden: Brill, 2010], 75, 114).

was "for our sins." Other traditions and other comments use a wide variety of metaphors to envision how Jesus's death accomplishes this, but this early one does not. This tradition about the meaning of Jesus's death developed, it seems, before the church began admitting gentiles. It interprets that death with categories that are within the thought world of first-century Judaism and through its reading of Scripture. This confession further identifies Jesus as the Messiah.

The centrality of the Jewish thought world in interpretations of Jesus's death is confirmed by the tradition Paul cites in Rom 3:24–26. In this confession, the death of Jesus is given the function of a place of atonement, probably identified with the lid of the ark of the covenant. Even the idea that such a death might be vicarious is found in Jewish literature of the period when it is interpreting the deaths of martyrs (4 Maccabees). Further, the notion that Christ "became sin for us" is also at home in a Jewish context, as the allusion to Isa 53 in the tradition that appears in 2 Cor 5:21 shows.

Beyond explicitly mentioning Scripture, other indications that the earliest church placed importance on interpreting Jesus's death through Scripture appear in the allusions to the Hebrew Bible in traditions Paul cites. The tradition Paul mentions in Rom 4:25 ("handed over for our trespasses") is based on an interpretation of Isa 53:12. The confessions he cites in 2 Cor 5:21 and Gal 3:13 also seem to relate to this Isaiah text. Texts such as Pss 110:1 and 8:7 played a crucial role in the development of the church's understandings of Christ and his roles. Such contacts with the Hebrew Bible point us to a community concerned with maintaining continuity with God's previous acts in relation to Israel. Such a concern places us in a Jewish context.

Other traditions Paul cites point us to a time when the church had begun to admit gentiles. The tradition that says Jesus's death was "for us all" (Rom 8:32, 34) is an example. The already established understanding of Jesus's death as vicarious is expanded so that its effect covers gentiles as well as believing Jews. This explicit expansion of the efficacy of Jesus's death suggests that this kind of meaning was central to what it meant to be in the church.

The extent of Paul's reliance on traditions and beliefs that were in the church before him may be seen in Rom 4:25. The tradition he cites there may interpret the death and resurrection of Jesus as an event that gives believers justification. If that term is part of the tradition rather than a Pauline insertion, it suggests that a central way Paul speaks of the meaning of Jesus in Romans and Galatians, and what many have seen as his signature doctrine, is drawn from the tradition rather than being an idea that originates with or is first given prominence by Paul.

"I Handed On to You . . . What I Received"

These continuities do not indicate that there was a single way that the earliest churches interpreted Jesus's death. The varied imagery in these traditions indicates that they drew on many ideas and texts to interpret it. Still, all saw it as in some way vicarious. This does not suggest that they had a single or clear atonement theology. The early tradition recited in 1 Cor 15:3–5 leaves completely open how Jesus's death deals with sin; it simply asserts that it does. This central belief could then be explicated in multiple ways, not all of which would be coherent with one another.

We have seen in this study that Paul's understanding of the identity of Jesus is also dependent on the Christology of those in the church before him. The traditions he cites demonstrate that the church quickly developed a complex and exalted Christology. The Aramaic term *Maranatha* shows that the earliest believers proclaimed that Jesus was Lord and saw him as one who could be present with them and who would be God's eschatological agent. One of the earliest understandings of Jesus was that he was the one God raised from the dead. This death and resurrection quickly became so central that one of the church's primary ways of thinking of God was as the one who raised Jesus.

Some of the most exalted claims about Christ seem to develop in relation to Ps 110:1. In its earliest times, as evidenced by its use in so many different texts, the church interpreted the experienced resurrection but current absence of Jesus through this psalm. They came to speak of him as being exalted to the right hand of God, a claim that was unique within first-century Judaism. Paul inserts a tradition based on this psalm in Rom 8:34. This tradition of applying Ps 110:1 to Jesus assigns him a heavenly post and a place of power at God's throne. He is seen as the one in position to wield God's power. This understanding of Jesus was current and widespread in the church before Paul's influence. It also develops in a church that knows Scripture and uses it to interpret Jesus. Paul accepts this understanding of the position of Christ but is not its originator.

Jesus was also called the Son of God within the predominantly Jewish branch of the church, as the tradition in Rom 1:3–4 and appearance of that title in the Didache show. Jesus is also quickly and widely named as the one sent by God, as seen by this way of speaking of Jesus in Rom 8:3, Gal 4:4, and so much early church literature. While this does not necessarily mean they saw him as preexistent, it did come to mean this quite early for at least some (e.g., the Johannine church). The tradition Paul cites in 1 Cor 8:6 takes the step of identifying Jesus as preexistent and assigns him the role of God's agent in creation. It seems to come from a church in which the Shema is important. The Jewish theological background that makes this move feasible is the wisdom tradition. It had already made the hypostasis of God's wisdom the active agent in creation. The significant move that the church makes is to apply this understanding of how characteristics of God can be both distinct from God's being, in some way, and attributed to a human. This move was made by those who formulated the tradition Paul accepts and uses in his argument in 1 Corinthians.

Even if those who think Paul formulated 1 Cor 8:6 are correct, he does not think this assertion of Christ's preexistence needs any defense. Since he uses this statement to argue against participation in meals that involve other gods, he does not see it as a violation of the recognition and worship of the one God of Israel. Nor does he think that the Corinthians, among whom there are at least some Jewish members, will see it as a violation. It may be that Rom 9:5 is the earliest place where the noun *theos* ("god") is applied to Jesus. If the doxology at the end of this verse addresses Jesus rather than God, then Paul is the earliest extant author to use it of Jesus. Again, however, he does not seem to think his assertion is controversial. The doxology is not necessary to his argument and he gives it no defense. So he can write it to a church he did not found (even if it was founded under his auspices) and that he is asking to support his mission. He does not think this is new to the Roman church.

Even if Paul composed the formula in 1 Cor 8:6 and addresses the doxology of Rom 9:5 to Jesus, he has not pushed much beyond what was already in the tradition. Jesus had already been seen as the one who wields God's power and sovereignty. The tradition had also already identified Jesus as the coming eschatological judge. If the liturgy of Phil 2:6–11 is non-Pauline, it had already claimed that Jesus possesses the "name above all names," which is "Lord." That exaltation brings him near to being identified with God. The tradition does this with language drawn from the Hebrew Bible and so points us again to a church that hears those resonances. So this claim about Jesus probably comes from the predominantly Jewish church.

Paul, then, is not the one creating christological doctrines in the early church. The acclamations of Jesus as Son of God and as Lord come from the Aramaic-speaking church and the exaltation of him to the right hand of God comes from the predominantly Jewish segment of the church that interprets Jesus through Scripture. It is also likely that the segment of the church that recites the Shema proclaims Christ as the preexistent agent of creation. Paul accepts what the earlier church and those outside his sphere confess about who Jesus is. He then uses those understandings of Jesus to offer advice and instruction on other matters to his churches.

"I Handed On to You... What I Received"

Our study has shown that many elements of Paul's understandings of salvation are drawn from earlier church traditions. Before Paul, the church confessed that forgiveness of sins comes through Christ, as the traditions in Gal 2:20 and Rom 3:24–26 make evident. Paul asserts in Gal 2:16 that all Jewish church members recognize that justification comes through Christ. While they do not draw the same implications about gentile Torah observance that he does, his argument assumes that they agree about the premise. Neither is Paul the first to assert that baptism identifies one with Christ in a way that brings salvation. The liturgies that he cites in Gal 3:27–28 and Rom 6:3 show this clearly, while 1 Cor 6:11 shows that the tradition sees baptism as the place at which one's sins are forgiven. The Didache's structure, baptismal formula, and recognition of the transition that occurs at baptism show that its church also practices a baptism in the name of the Father, Son, and Holy Spirit that cleanses the baptizands and makes them fit for full interaction with the community.

This salvation involves more than membership in an earthly kingdom. The tradition in 1 Thess 1:9–10 includes avoiding eschatological wrath as part of salvation. The identification with Christ that occurs at baptism was understood to include the believer in Christ's resurrection and to have eschatological consequences in the present. The overcoming of gender, social class, and ethnic distinctions is part of the salvation that the tradition in Gal 3:27–28 professes. The tradition Paul cites in 2 Cor 4:14 asserts that believers will be raised with Christ at the eschaton.

Paul was not the first to assert that the salvation the church offers includes a transearthly eschatological aspect. Long before he became a member, the Aramaic church proclaimed Jesus as the Lord whom they called upon to return with the well-known *Maranatha* (1 Cor 16:22; Did 10.6). The belief in his exaltation to the position of power in heaven was accomplished through the use of Pss 110:1 and 8:7. This acclamation of Jesus's position places him over all other cosmic powers. The tradition incorporated in 1 Cor 15:24–28 goes so far as to make Christ himself the one who subdues those powers. These understandings of the work of Christ emerged in churches that used Scripture to interpret what he had accomplished. These predominantly Jewish churches already envisioned a transearthly kingdom as a goal of what God was accomplishing in Christ. At the same time, the traditions in Rom 14:9; 1 Thess 1:9–10; and 4:14–17 show that Christ was seen as both eschatological judge and as the one who saves believers in that judgment. The evidence of the Didache also shows that believers outside Paul's influence looked to a transearthly life that was a gift received through Christ (4.8; 9.4; 10.2).

In a different way, the preformed material in 1 Thess 4:14–17 (and 1 Cor 15:50–52, if it does quote a tradition) also shows that the church before Paul looked for a transearthly salvation. These traditions speak of being bodily transformed so that believers are suited to life in a different realm. Some elements suggest that this tradition goes back to the Palestinian church, while others point to the Hellenistic Jewish church. Either way, it develops before and outside Paul's influence. The discussion of the parousia in 1 Thess 4:14–17 may be a place where Paul contributes to the growing tradition. He may be the one who adds that those who die before the end will not be disadvantaged. If that is the case, he adopts the established tradition and makes a new point using it. While Paul draws out new implications and develops ambiguous assertions, those in the church before him have cosmic eschatological expectations and see Christ bringing a transearthly existence for believers. These beliefs grew among the Aramaic-speaking church members and did not need ideas that were not already in Judaism to develop in the ways we have seen.

However much Paul contributed to the shaping of church worship through his mission work and his letters, he was not the first person to identify the church's communal meal as a memorial of the death of Jesus. Our study of 1 Cor 11:23–26 indicates that he was not the author of that narrative of the Last Supper. If one compares the 1 Corinthians account with those in the Gospels, it is evident that elements of the Markan account are more ancient than the version Paul cites. The differences in Luke's account also suggest that Luke did not have the version found in 1 Corinthians. The Semitisms in Mark show that his version is dependent on an account of the supper that came from the Aramaic-speaking church. The differences suggest that there was no single account of the Last Supper from which the various versions developed. Still, all who celebrated it saw it as a memorial meal that was related to the death of Jesus. Even if the consensus of Didache scholars is wrong and the meal in chapters 9–10 does include the Lord's Supper, it has allusions to Jesus's death and the salvation it brings. Finally, while Paul is often accused of asking believers to drink blood, a careful reading of 1 Cor 11 shows that he does not identify the contents of the cup as blood.

In all of these central doctrines of the church, Paul is often directly dependent on the church before him or outside his influence for the beliefs he espouses. We have seen that the tradition contains a diversity of expressions of most of these teachings, but that they also have some commonalities. Some of these commonalities were the product of the church's initial existence within Torah-observant Judaism. Others were pressed upon them by the originating events that brought the church into existence. Central among these was the execution of Jesus and believers' experience of his resurrected presence in their midst. No one who wanted to continue to honor the person or teachings of Jesus could do so without giving significant attention to interpreting his death.

The Early Church and the Death of Jesus

When present-day scholars envision communities that form their identity in relation to Jesus but do not give extended attention to the meaning of his death by crucifixion, they fail to grasp the effects such a death has on a community. Alan Kirk argues from social memory studies that violence brings such social disruption that communities must institute commemorative activities to retain social identity.[2] Furthermore, he argues, violence "poses a particularly difficult challenge to the hermeneutical impulse" because it "generates a sense of fragmentation, of the disintegration of a moral and social order previously experienced as stable and routine."[3] This would particularly be the case if the acknowledged leaders of one's own religion initiated the violence that was carried out by the overlord who claimed to sustain peace and order. As Kirk says,

> The death of Jesus, through political violence, would bring about the sort of radically altered situation, dissolution of previous group frameworks, and discontinuity from all that had gone before such that if the community were to survive it would need to reconstitute its memory, and with the same stroke the coherence of its own social and moral identity, in the context of intense commemorative activities.[4]

All who remained favorably disposed toward Jesus to such an extent that they preserved his teaching or viewed him as a messenger from God would have had to give this kind of attention to the dramatic form of his death.[5]

Beyond the internal necessity of interpreting Jesus's death, anyone who would continue to value his life and/or teaching to such an extent that they

---

2. Alan Kirk, "The Memory of Violence and the Death of Jesus in Q," in *Memory, Tradition, and Text: Uses of the Past in Early Christianity*, ed. Alan Kirk and Tom Thatcher, SemeiaSt 52 (Atlanta: SBL Press, 2005), 191.

3. Kirk, "Memory of Violence," 193.

4. Kirk, "Memory of Violence," 206. Notably, Kirk argues that the Q community gave extensive attention to interpreting and commemorating Jesus's death.

5. On the difficulty of interpreting the crucifixion, see also Breytenbach, *Grace, Reconciliation, Concord*, 61–62.

formed their group identity around them had to develop responses to outsiders who interpreted the death of Jesus by giving crucifixion one of its usual meanings. We noted above that the Jerusalem church would have had to reject explicitly those meanings (e.g., that Jesus was a criminal or a false messiah) and provide alternative meanings. Any kind of adherence to Jesus after his crucifixion would have entailed the same demand. Such a death demands an apology to outsiders. The books in the Nag Hammadi library demonstrate that even docetic gnostics had to give Jesus's death a meaning and assign it a significance—even if that was radically different from what we have seen in the evidence of Paul's letters.[6]

Our survey of those Paul opposes and our exploration of the traditions he cites give no indications that any wing of the church that Paul interacts with or knows questioned the importance of Jesus's death in the formulation of their identity. Neither do we see evidence that he knows of people who try to follow Jesus's teachings or are favorably disposed toward any aspect of his life or ministry that do not give prominence to Jesus's death as a salvific event.

François Wessels reports that in a 2002 presentation at the University of Stellenbosch, John Dominic Crossan asserted that there were four types of early Christianity: Thomas Christianity, which cared only for the teaching of Jesus and opposed apocalyptic views; Pauline Christianity, which made the death and resurrection of Jesus central; Q Christianity, which cared only about Jesus's sayings and emphasized the wisdom aspect of his teaching; and Exegetical Christianity, which manipulated Scripture for apologetic purposes. Crossan added that these groups were so different from one another they would not recognize that they belonged to the same religious group.[7] (If this is truly the case, it seems inappropriate for us to force them into a single group or identify them all as [legitimate?] ancestors of the developing church.[8]) Our

---

6. It seems more likely that the earliest interpretations gave it the meanings we have seen evidence for in the earlier time than that the gnostic meaning developed immediately following Jesus's death. This is particularly the case since Gnosticism was probably not a developed system in the first century.

7. These statements are reported by Wessels in "The Historical Jesus and the Letters of Paul," in *New Testament Interpreted*, ed. Cilliers Breytenbach, Johan C. Thom, and Jeremy Punt (Leiden: Brill, 2006), 29n1. Crossan mentions three of these kinds of "Christianity" together in *The Birth of Christianity* (San Francisco: HarperSanFrancisco, 1998), 409-11. He does not mention "Exegetical Christianity" in this earlier work.

8. Crossan's decision to call all four "church" seems to be an attempt to legitimate their interpretation of Jesus.

"I Handed On to You . . . What I Received"

examination of what Paul knows about other adherents to Jesus, however, suggests that Crossan arrives at an unlikely reconstruction.⁹

As we have seen, any group that would carry forward the teaching of Jesus would be required to give significant attention to the form of his death simply to justify their continuing attachment to the teaching of an executed criminal. If we give full weight to the devastation brought on Jesus's followers by his death, we must acknowledge that any group that remained positively disposed toward Jesus, and certainly any group that would form its identity around remembrance of him or his teachings, had to give that event a meaning that allowed the community to interpret Jesus in ways contrary to what his death apparently indicated. Such adherents might use Jesus's death to accuse others of sin or ignorance, but they could not ignore it. That a single document (e.g., the Gospel of Thomas) does not give attention to interpreting Jesus's death is not sufficient evidence to claim that his death had no place in the theology of the community it served or represented. The same is true for the community that produced Q. Not only do we not know how much material beyond what Matthew and Luke copy might have been in such a document, we also have no reason to think that all of the community's important beliefs would appear in this one document. After all, if we only had 1 Thessalonians or 2 Corinthians (or both) from Paul, we would never know that justification by faith had a substantive place in his theology.

A hundred years or perhaps even a few decades after the event, some kinds of adherence to the teaching of Jesus that gave little attention to his death could emerge. By then the shocking nature of his death had been muted by both the passage of time and prior interpretation. But in the wake of the actual events, no such distance was possible because the experience was still fresh in the minds of both believers and nonbelievers. Jesus's death demanded

---

9. If Crossan's point is that different people interpreted the words and deeds of Jesus differently, we should grant this point immediately. After all, that is why some urged that he should be crucified and others claimed that he was bringing the kingdom of God. But Crossan seems here to work with the primitivist notion that implicitly assumes that if an idea was early, it has validity as an interpretation of Jesus. (Of course, this creates the problem that many understood him to be a false messiah. Is that an equally valid interpretation because it is early?) However, at an earlier time, Crossan veered away from that primitivist inclination, claiming that narrative accounts of Jesus give a fuller picture than a discourse gospel (*Four Other Gospels: Shadows on the Contours of Canon* [Chicago: Winston, 1985], 186). Crossan does draw on a wider range of materials than we have in this study, but most are significantly later than the letters of Paul. The exception to this is Q, but the work of Kirk ("Memory of Violence," esp. 195-206) gives sound reasons for thinking that the "Q community" gave attention to Jesus's death.

sustained attention from all who wanted to maintain some attachment to him or his teaching.

Even Crossan's separation of "Exegetical Christianity" from "Pauline Christianity" seems to miss the essential links Paul makes with reading Scripture and the claim of the earliest confession of any length we have, that of 1 Cor 15. There we see the pre-Pauline church, the church of the 30s and 40s, using Scripture to interpret the event that is most difficult to explain, Jesus's violent death as a political criminal. The group that uses Scripture to defend its adherence to Jesus is not separate from the group that emphasizes the death and resurrection of Jesus or the group that values his wisdom teaching. Forming one's identity around Jesus demanded an interpretation of his death that allowed adherents to continue to identify him as the kind of person whose teachings have value. Furthermore, our study suggests that the view we find in Paul is not "Paul's" in the sense that he originated it. Rather, he constantly draws on earlier traditions, including some that reach back into the Jerusalem church of the first few years of the church's existence.

Perhaps some reticence to acknowledge how important discussion and explanation of Jesus's death was in forming the identity of anyone who held a favorable view of Jesus stems from our culture's limitations on the meaning of dying for others. Outside biblical materials, a significant body of material demonstrates that the Greco-Roman world possessed various ways to interpret a person's death so that the person became a martyr for some cause or institution (one's city, a philosophy, etc.).[10] For example, adherents to Socrates's teaching had to interpret his death in a way that allowed them to continue following his philosophy after his death as a criminal. Such a death could not simply be ignored. Some (e.g., Epictetus, *Disc.* 4.1.168-69) who interpreted Socrates's death (and the deaths of other philosophers, warriors, and others) saw it as vicarious, though not expiatory. The point here is simply that such deaths could not be ignored and were often seen as vicarious without any implication that they were expiatory. There was so much attention to such deaths that Seneca can say they are "droned to death in all the schools" (*Ep.* 24.6).[11] If we recognize that the ancient definition of "vicarious" was broader than

---

10. See Jeffrey B. Gibson, "Paul's 'Dying Formula': Prolegomena to an Understanding of Its Import and Significance," in *Celebrating Romans: Template for Pauline Theology: Essays in Honor of Robert Jewett*, ed. Sheila E. McGinn (Grand Rapids: Eerdmans, 2004), 20-41; David Seeley, *The Noble Death: Graeco-Roman Martyrology and Paul's Concept of Salvation*, JSNTSup 28 (Sheffield: Sheffield Academic Press, 1990).

11. See Seeley, *Noble Death*, 124-29. He cites this Epictetus passage and other writers who speak of vicarious deaths.

expiation, we open ourselves to more historically credible reconstructions of what sense various kinds of communities who formed their identity in relation to Jesus made of his violent death as a political criminal. We can be certain, however, that no Jesus-affirming community could ignore it.

We have given extensive attention to the impact of the death of Jesus because so many of the other beliefs about Jesus grew out of the interpretations given to his death and resurrection.[12] Belief in his exaltation to a position of power is dependent on belief in his resurrection and what that signifies about the meaning of his death. The Christology that developed is then rooted both in interpretations of Jesus's death and resurrection and in belief in his exaltation. His death and resurrection also ground the beliefs in the eschatological character of his ministry. His resurrection to a different kind of life is seen as a sign that he has in some way participated in the transformation of the end time. Without interpretations that contend that his death validates his ministry, even Jesus's own claims to be an eschatological figure prove impossible to continue to hold. Finally, the church's understandings of salvation are based on its understandings of Jesus's death and the nature of his resurrection.

Putting Paul in His Place[13]

We have not discussed all of Paul's uses of preexisting formulations of the faith. His surprisingly numerous citations of earlier tradition indicate that he expects his churches to recognize these statements as allusions to the tradition that defines the identity of the church. Moreover, these citations suggest that he belongs within the mainstream of the first-century church in much that he teaches. Such extensive dependence discredits any claim that Paul was the founder of Christianity or the one who invented the Christ-cult idea or the idea that Jesus's death was vicarious. The various reasons we have seen for tracing some of the traditions to the Palestinian church and the predominantly Jewish Hellenistic church show that there were substantive continuities, even as there were significant differences in claims about Jesus and in understandings of what his ministry, death, and resurrection accomplished.

The theological debates in Paul's letters and the variety of traditions he

---

12. Similarly, Breytenbach asserts that the phrase "Christ died for us" is more foundational to Paul's theology than images of reconciliation or justification (*Grace, Reconciliation, Concord*, 126).

13. For this phrase I am indebted to Victor P. Furnish's 1993 SBL Presidential Address, "On Putting Paul in His Place," *JBL* 113 (1994): 3–17.

cites indicate that many within the early church were engaged in the theological enterprise. The teachings that take hold are not simply handed down from apostles or recognized leaders. Rather, those who experienced the presence of God through Christ in their churches worked to give expression to the meaning of that experience. They spontaneously exclaimed something about Jesus or wrote liturgies and hymns. Some developed confessions for baptism, others for their communal meals. As these were formulated, they were no doubt topics of debate, as even the stories of different views in the book of Acts reveal. The forms they finally take are honed into shape by debate, by trading materials between churches, and by compromise. A significant range of differences in beliefs and practices remained and were acceptable to many, including Paul. Of course, those differences led to tensions and arguments, and sometimes were seen to be too great to be admissible. But even the decisions that some beliefs or practices put a person out of the community had to be argued for and accepted by individual local churches.

The diversity of the language and imagery we have seen in the traditions Paul cites points to this kind of theologizing activity in the early church. It validates the approach to understanding the history of the church that rejects the great man or hero model. The names and identities of those who led in the composition of these traditions are lost to us. But their work captured the experience of their fellow believers so accurately and powerfully that it shaped how communities beyond their own would recognize the experience and so claim that interpretation of it. Their work as theologians comes to us through the letters of Paul. His citations of their work show us not only some of the variety of expressions of the faith that existed, but also that the church's beliefs were not the products of a few domineering leaders. Those who were recognizable leaders seem to have been listening to and adopting the expressions of the faith that other members were formulating. They saw these confessions and liturgies as authentic expressions of what God was doing in their midst.

Paul accepts both the theology that these traditions embody and the very form they take. We have seen Paul use these traditions in multiple ways. His citations of these formulations often provide support for a belief he wants his church to adopt. When he cites the tradition about Jesus's death and resurrection in 1 Cor 15:3–5, it is not to argue that Jesus has been raised but to argue that believers will have a resurrection like Christ's. Similarly, his citation of the preformed description of the parousia in 1 Thess 4:16–17 is not an argument for the reality of it but rather the basis for his assurance about believers who had died. On other occasions Paul uses traditions to argue for a certain kind

"I Handed On to You ... What I Received"

of behavior within a church. When he cites the liturgy of Christ's incarnation and exaltation in Phil 2:6–11, it is not to argue that Jesus has been exalted but rather to present Jesus's willingness to put the good of others before his own as a model for how to live within the church. Again, Paul does not argue for the belief that the tradition asserts in such places. He expects his churches to recognize these preformed traditions and to grant them some sort of authority. Only if the readers know them and have some attachment to them will they serve to strengthen Paul's arguments.

We have also seen, however, that Paul is willing to reinterpret the traditions he received. He engaged in that interpretation and modification in 1 Cor 15:24–28. There he inserts qualifications and interpretations to make the message more coherent with his theology and not just the use he puts it to. Breytenbach sees another example of Paul taking a tradition and giving it new meaning in his use of the confession that Christ died "for us." He asserts that Paul broadens it to mean that Christ died for all.[14] The assertion that the dead rise "first" in the parousia may be another kind of modification. He is drawing implications from the tradition that others had not seen—and that may not have been there until he added or changed a word. So we see the dialogue continuing even as he and his churches cede some recognizable authority to the traditions.

His use of preformed traditional material indicates that, as Paul founds his churches, he provides them with these formulations of the wider church's beliefs. Their appearances in his letters are not his readers' first acquaintance with them. This use of traditional material suggests that he sees himself and his work in continuity with the earlier and wider church. As we noted, his passing on of formulae such as *Maranatha* indicates that he consciously and intentionally conforms the beliefs, practices, and worship of his churches to those in Jerusalem. Even as he argues that some practices of gentile believers must be different from those of Jewish believers, he does so on the basis of shared beliefs that were already encapsulated in set formulae (e.g., Gal 3:27–28).

Paul's contributions to the church's theological tradition are, then, interpretations of what was believed in the church before he joined or was influential. This does not mean those contributions were insignificant. From as early as Acts and Ephesians his contributions were seen as vital to the expansion of the church. Acts presents him as one of the two most important apostles. Paul was clearly the most successful missionary to gentiles of the first generation of the church. That by itself makes him an important figure who shaped

14. Breytenbach, *Grace, Reconciliation, Concord*, 122–26.

the church as he sided with those who insisted that gentile members were full members *as gentiles*. Within Pauline circles of the second generation, he was also seen as central to the church's life. The author of Ephesians (perhaps following Paul's own statement in Gal 1:11–12) speaks of the revelation given to Paul (Eph 3:3–4). But this clearly does not mean that the revelation was to Paul alone or that his revelation was different from the rest of the church, as is evident in the passage that immediately precedes this reference to the revelation given Paul. In 2:20 the same author says that the church that includes the gentiles is built on the "apostle*s* and prophets." The context for the revelation to Paul, then, is the teaching of the other apostles and other church members who are recipients of revelations; the most foundational of those revelations came to them before Paul was in the church.

The combination of Paul's reliance on prior tradition and his interpretation of it has long been recognized by New Testament interpreters. We have just highlighted some examples. Over fifty years ago Bultmann gave regular attention to identifying traditions Paul cites and looking for ways Paul adds layers of meaning to them. For example, he identified Rom 6:2–8 as a citation of an early baptismal formula that the Hellenistic church had expanded to interpret baptism as a rite that gave victory over death. He then saw Paul add the idea of incorporation into Christ to that Hellenistic formulation.[15] Bultmann, then, sees what appears in Rom 6 as the third iteration of that tradition. Bultmann was among those who see even Paul's distinctive view of faith to rest on prior tradition.[16] While Bultmann's criteria for identifying traditional material were not as stringent as those we have used, his careful attention to what preceded Paul and how Paul used that material demonstrates Paul's dependence on tradition and his application of it in new settings.

We should also acknowledge that much of later Christian theology has been a series of responses to what we read in Paul's letters. His letters have clearly been extremely influential in the history of the church and Christian theology.[17] After all, those letters are our earliest account of what the earliest believers in Christ thought and did. Echoing Harnack, Wayne Meeks speaks of

---

15. Rudolf Bultmann, *Theology of the New Testament*, trans. Kendrick Grobel, 2 vols. (New York: Scribner's Sons, 1951, 1955), 1:140–41. See also his discussion of Paul's interpretation of baptism at 1:298. For Bultmann's views of Pauline additions to the interpretation of the death of Jesus, see 1:45.

16. Bultmann, *Theology*, 1:90.

17. For an account of Paul's importance for the church in the centuries that follow him, see Furnish, "On Putting Paul in His Place," 3–17.

Paul's thought as the "ferment" of Christian thought.[18] But this later and continuous use of his letters and thought does not mean that Paul was the originator of the central and foundational doctrines of the church. Meeks goes on to say,

> Perhaps the most significant discovery about Paul in this [twentieth] century's scholarship has been the recognition of his Christian precedents. Paul cannot be called the "second founder of Christianity." ... Christianity in the "Pauline" form—with sacraments, cultic worship of Jesus as Lord, Gentile members, and the doctrines of pre-existence and atoning death of Christ—had already been "founded" before Paul became first its persecutor and then its missionary.[19]

We have seen many of these predecessors of Paul in this study. It is Paul's presentation and use of these beliefs that have helped make him so important in later developments.

Paul is not, then, the author or originator of the early church's theology. He seldom develops new assertions about Christ's nature or work or other theological doctrines beyond what is found in the traditions he cites. He seems to have contributed little to the development of those kinds of doctrines. His influence and his genius are seen in the ways he is able to bring those beliefs into new environments. He is able to draw implications from those beliefs that further explicate a belief or show its relevance to an ethical issue. He is the person we see responding to new questions and problems that predominantly gentile churches raise. He takes what the church confesses about God, Christ, salvation, or some other topic and uses it to argue for how believers in his churches should relate to the world around them, conduct their own assemblies, and understand their own identity and fate.[20] He is not the first to bring gentiles into the church without requiring the same kind of Torah observance that Jews keep, but he provides that act a theological foundation from the church's already believed confessions and liturgies. He is not the first to assert that God had raised Jesus from the dead, but he draws out the implications of that belief for the eschatological hope of believers. Neither

---

18. Meeks, "The Christian Proteus," in *The Writings of St. Paul*, Norton Critical Edition (New York: Norton, 1972), 435.

19. Meeks, *Writings of St. Paul*, 440.

20. The study of Paul's use of quotations of Scripture by Katja Kujanpää ("From Eloquence to Evading Responsibility: The Rhetorical Functions of Quotations in Paul's Argumentation," *JBL* 123 [2017]: 185–202) arrived too late for me to use its insights to talk about Paul's use of traditional materials.

is he the first to claim that Christ had ascended to God's right hand, but he does draw implications for how to live as the church from that response of God to Christ's self-giving death. And while he is not the one who authored the liturgy for the Lord's Supper, he uses it to correct unacceptable behavior at the communal meal.

Paul is his churches' leading *interpreter* of the beliefs expressed in the church's earlier traditions. He is performing the pastoral task of helping his churches understand how to embody their faith. As the most successful missionary we know of in the first generation of the church, he became the person who interpreted the beliefs of the church for a new ethnocultural setting. He took up the mission to gentiles and the task of helping them embody the church's faith. His great accomplishment was to be able to lead others to adopt that faith and to show those predominantly gentile churches how to conduct their lives in ways that honored and reflected the character of the "God who raised Jesus from the dead."

Bibliography

Adams, Edward. *The Earliest Christian Meeting Places: Almost Exclusively Houses?* LNTS 450. New York: Bloomsbury T. & T. Clark, 2013.
Ascough, Richard S. "A Question of Death: Paul's Community-Building Language in 1 Thessalonians 4:13–18." *JBL* 123 (2004): 509–30.
Bachmann, Michael. "Zwei Ebenen oder eher ein Niveau? Zur Entgegensetzung innerhalb von Gal 2, 16a." *BZ* 59 (2015): 112–16.
Barclay, John M. G. *Obeying the Truth: A Study of Paul's Ethics in Galatians.* SNTW. Edinburgh: T. & T. Clark, 1988.
———. " 'That You May Not Grieve, Like the Rest Who Have No Hope' [1 Thess 4:13]: Death and Early Christian Identity." In *Not in the Word Alone: The First Epistle to the Thessalonians.* Edited by Morna D. Hooker, 131–53. Monograph Series of Benedictina. Rome: St. Paul's Abbey, 2003.
Barnett, Paul. *The Second Epistle to the Corinthians.* NICNT. Grand Rapids: Eerdmans, 1997.
Barrett, C. K. "Deuteropauline Ethics: Some Observations." In *Theology and Ethics in Paul and His Interpreters: Essays in Honor of Victor Paul Furnish,* edited by Eugene Lovering and J. L. Sumney, 161–72. Nashville: Abingdon, 1996.
———. "Paul's Opponents in 2 Corinthians." *NTS* 17 (1971): 233–54.
———. *The Second Epistle to the Corinthians.* HNTC. New York: Harper & Row, 1973.
Barth, Markus. "Traditions in Ephesians." *NTS* 30 (1984): 3–25.
Barton, Stephen C. "Eschatology and the Emotions in Early Christianity." *JBL* 130 (2011): 571–91.
Bates, Matthew W. "A Christology of Incarnation and Enthronement: Romans

1:3–4 as Unified, Nonadoptionist, and Nonconciliatory." *CBQ* 77 (2015): 107–27.
Bauckham, Richard. *God Crucified: Monotheism and Christology in the New Testament*. Grand Rapids: Eerdmans, 1998.
———. *Jesus and the God of Israel*. Grand Rapids: Eerdmans, 2008.
Baur, F. C. *Paul the Apostle of Jesus Christ: His Life and Works, His Epistles and Teachings*. 2 vols. London: Williams & Norgate, 1873–75. Repr., 2 vols. in 1, Peabody, MA: Hendrickson, 2003.
Best, Ernest. *A Commentary on the First and Second Epistles to the Thessalonians*. BNTC. London: Black, 1972.
Betz, Hans Dieter. *Galatians: A Commentary on Paul's Letter to the Churches in Galatia*. Hermeneia. Philadelphia: Fortress, 1979.
Betz, Johannes. "The Eucharist in the *Didache*." In *The Didache in Modern Research*, edited by Jonathan A. Draper, 244–75. AGJU 37. Leiden: Brill, 1996.
Betz, Otto. "Adam." In *Theologische Realenzyklopädie*, edited by G. Krause and G. Müller, 1:414–24. Berlin: de Gruyter, 1977.
Bird, Michael F. "The Incident at Antioch (Gal. 2.11–14)." In *Earliest Christian History: History, Literature, and Theology: Essays from the Tyndale Fellowship in Honor of Martin Hengel*, edited by Michael F. Bird and Jason Maston, 329–61. WUNT 2/320. Tübingen: Mohr Siebeck, 2012.
Bobertz, Charles A. "Ritual Eucharist within Narrative: A Comparison of Didache 9–10 with Mark 6:31–44; 8:1–9." In *Ascetica, Liturgica, Orientalia, Critica et Philologica, First Two Centuries*, edited by J. Baun, A. Cameron, M. Edwards, and M. Vinzent, 93–99, StPatr 45. Leuven: Peeters, 2010.
Boer, Martinus C. de. *The Defeat of Death: Apocalyptic Eschatology in 1 Corinthians 15 and Romans 5*. JSNTSup 22. Sheffield: JSOT Press, 1988.
———. *Galatians: A Commentary*. NTL. Louisville: Westminster John Knox, 2011.
———. "Paul's Use of a Resurrection Tradition in 1 Cor 15,20–28." In *The Corinthian Correspondence*, edited by R. Bieringer, 639–51. BETL 125. Leuven: Leuven University Press, 1996.
Boers, Hendrikus. "2 Corinthians 5:14–6:2: A Fragment of Pauline Christology." *CBQ* 64 (2002): 527–47.
Bonnard, Pierre. *L'épitre de Saint Paul aux Philippiens*. CNT 10. Neuchâtel: Delachaux & Niestlé, 1950.
Borgen, Peder. "Crucified for His Own Sins—Crucified for Our Sins: Observations on a Pauline Perspective." In *The New Testament and Early Christian Literature in Greco-Roman Context: Studies in Honor of David E. Aune*, edited by John Fotopoulos, 17–35. NovTSup 122. Leiden: Brill, 2006.
———. "Openly Portrayed as Crucified: Some Observations on Gal 3:1–14." In *Christology, Controversy and Community: New Testament Essays in Hon-*

our of David R. Catchpole, edited by David G. Horrell and Christopher M. Tuckett, 345–53. NovTSup 99. Leiden: Brill, 2000.

Boring, M. Eugene. *1 & 2 Thessalonians: A Commentary*. NTL. Louisville: Westminster John Knox, 2015.

———. *Sayings of the Risen Jesus: Christian Prophecy in the Synoptic Tradition*. SNTSMS 46. Cambridge: Cambridge University Press, 1982.

Bornkamm, Günther. "The Revelation of Christ to Paul on the Damascus Road and Paul's Doctrine of Justification and Reconciliation: A Study in Galatians 1." Translated by J. M. Owen. In *Reconciliation and Hope: New Testament Essays on Atonement and Eschatology Presented to L. L. Morris on His 60th Birthday*, edited by Robert Banks, 90–103. Grand Rapids: Eerdmans, 1974.

Bradshaw, Paul F. "The Status of Jesus in Early Christian Prayer Texts." In *Portraits of Jesus: Studies in Christology*, edited by Susan E. Myers, 249–60. WUNT 321. Tübingen: Mohr Siebeck, 2012.

Bradshaw, Paul F., and Maxwell Johnson. *The Eucharistic Liturgies: Their Evolution and Interpretation*. Collegeville, MN: Liturgical Press, 2012.

Branick, Vincent P. "Source and Redaction Analysis of 1 Corinthians 1–3." *JBL* 101 (1982): 251–69.

Breytenbach, Cilliers. *Grace, Reconciliation, Concord: The Death of Christ in Graeco-Roman Metaphors*. NovTSup 135. Leiden: Brill, 2010.

Bruce, F. F. *1 & 2 Thessalonians*. WBC 45. Waco: Word, 1982.

———. *The Epistle to the Galatians: A Commentary on the Greek Text*. NIGTC. Grand Rapids: Eerdmans, 1982.

Bultmann, Rudolf. *The Second Letter to the Corinthians*. Edited by Erich Dinkler. Translated by Roy A. Harrisville. Minneapolis: Augsburg, 1985.

———. *Theology of the New Testament*. Translated by Kendrick Grobel. 2 vols. New York: Scribner's Sons, 1951, 1955.

Burchard, Christoph. "Nicht aus Werken des Gesetzes gerecht, sondern Glauben an Jesus Christus—seit wann?" in *Frühes Christentum*, ed. Hermann Lichtenberger, 405–15. Vol. 3 of *Geschichte—Tradition—Reflexion: Festschrift für Martin Hengel zum 70. Geburtstag*, edited by Hubert Cancik, Hermann Lichtenberger, and Peter Schäfer. Tübingen: Mohr, 1996.

———. "Satzbau und Übersetzung von 1 Thess 1,10." *ZNW* 96 (2005): 272–73.

Burton, Ernest deWitt. *A Critical and Exegetical Commentary on the Epistle to the Galatians*. ICC. Edinburgh: T. & T. Clark, 1921.

Bussmann, Claus. *Themen der paulinischen Missionspredigt auf dem Hintergrund der spätjüdisch-hellenistischen Missionsliteratur*. EHS series 23, Theologie 3. Bern: Lang, 1971.

Byrne, Brendan. *Romans*. SP. Collegeville, MN: Liturgical Press, 1996.

Campbell, Alastair. "Dying with Christ: The Origin of a Metaphor." In *Baptism, the New Testament and the Church: Historical and Contemporary Studies in*

Honour of R. E. O. White, edited by Stanley E. Porter and Anthony R. Cross, 273–93. JSNTSup 171. Sheffield: Sheffield Academic Press, 1999.

Campbell, Douglas A. *The Rhetoric of Righteousness in Romans 3:21–26*. JSNTSup 65. Sheffield: JSOT Press, 1992.

Cangh, Jean-Marie van. "Peut-on reconstituer le texte primitif de la Cène? (1 Co 11,23–26 par. Mc 14,22–26)." In *The Corinthian Correspondence*, edited by R. Bieringer, 623–37. BETL 125. Leuven: Leuven University Press, 1996.

Carey, Greg. "Apocalyptic Discourse as Constructive Theology." *PRSt* 40 (2013): 19–34.

Carroll, John, and Joel Green. *The Death of Jesus in Early Christianity*. Peabody, MA: Hendrickson, 1995.

Chester, Andrew. "Resurrection and Transformation." In *Auferstehung—Resurrection*, edited by Friedrich Avemarie and Hermann Lichtenberger, 47–77. WUNT 135. Tübingen: Mohr Siebeck, 2001.

Collange, Jean-François. *The Epistle of Saint Paul to the Philippians*. Translated by A. W. Heathcote. London: Epworth, 1979.

Collins, Adela Yarbro. "Psalms, Philippians 2:6–11, and the Origins of Christology." *BibInt* 11 (2003): 361–72.

Collins, Raymond F. *First Corinthians*. SP. Collegeville, MN: Liturgical Press, 1999.

———. "Paul as Seen through His Own Eyes." In *Studies on the First Epistle to the Thessalonians*, 175–208. BETL 66. Leuven: Leuven University Press, 1984.

———. "Paul's Early Christology." In *Studies on the First Letter to the Thessalonians*, 253–84. BETL 66. Leuven: Leuven University Press, 1984.

———. "Tradition, Redaction and Exhortation in 1 Thess 4, 13–5, 11." In *Studies on the First Letter to the Thessalonians*, 154–72. BETL 66. Leuven: Leuven University Press, 1984.

———, ed. *The Thessalonian Correspondence*. BETL 87. Leuven: Leuven University Press, 1990.

Conzelmann, Hans. *1 Corinthians: A Commentary on the First Epistle to the Corinthians*. Translated by James W. Leitch. Hermeneia. Philadelphia: Fortress, 1975.

———. "On the Analysis of the Confessional Formula in 1 Corinthians 15:3–5." *Int* 20 (1965): 15–25.

Cosby, Michael R. "Hellenistic Formal Receptions and Paul's Use of *apantēsis* in 1 Thessalonians 4:17." *BBR* 4 (1994): 15–33.

Cosgrove, Charles H. *The Cross and the Spirit: A Study in the Argument and Theology of Galatians*. Leuven: Peeters, 1988.

———. "Justification in Paul: A Linguistic and Theological Reflection." *JBL* 106 (1987): 653–70.

Cousar, Charles B. *Philippians and Philemon: A Commentary*. NTL. Louisville: Westminster John Knox, 2009.

Cranfield, C. E. B. *A Critical and Exegetical Commentary on the Epistle to the Romans*. 2 vols. ICC. Edinburgh: T. & T. Clark, 1975-1979.
Crossan, John Dominic. *The Birth of Christianity*. San Francisco: HarperSan Francisco, 1998.
———. *Four Other Gospels: Shadows on the Contours of Canon*. Chicago: Winston, 1985.
Cullmann, Oscar. *The Christology of the New Testament*. Translated by Shirley C. Guthrie and Charles A. M. Hall. Philadelphia: Westminster, 1959.
———. *The Earliest Christian Confessions*. Translated by J. K. S. Reid. London: Lutterworth, 1949.
Dahl, Nils. *The Crucified Messiah and Other Essays*. Minneapolis: Augsburg, 1974.
———. "Paul and the Church at Corinth according to 1 Corinthians 1:10–4:21." In *Christian History and Interpretation: Studies Presented to John Knox*, edited by W. R. Farmer, C. F. D. Moule, and R. R. Niebuhr, 313–35. Cambridge: Cambridge University Press, 1967.
Das, A. Andrew. "Another Look at *ean mē* in Galatians 2:16." *JBL* 119 (2000): 529–39.
Deichgräber, Reinhard. *Gotteshymnus und Christushymnus in der frühen Christenheit: Untersuchungen zur Form, Sprache und Stil der frühchristlichen Hymnen*. SUNT. Göttingen: Vandenhoeck & Ruprecht, 1967.
Denies, Roland. "Christology between Pre-Existence, Incarnation and Messianic Self-Understanding." In *Earliest Christian History: History, Literature, and Theology: Essays from the Tyndale Fellowship in Honor of Martin Hengel*, edited by Michael F. Bird and Jason Maston, 75–116. WUNT 2/320. Tübingen: Mohr Siebeck, 2012.
Do, Toan J. "The LXX Background of *hilastērion* in Rom 3,25." In *The Letter to the Romans*, edited by Udo Schnelle, 641–57. BETL 226. Leuven: Peeters, 2009.
Donfried, Karl P. "The Cults of Thessalonica and the Thessalonian Correspondence." *NTS* 31 (1985): 350–51.
Draper, Jonathan A. "Eschatology in the Didache." In *Eschatology of the New Testament and Some Related Documents*, edited by Jan G. van der Watt, 567–82. WUNT 2/315. Tübingen: Mohr Siebeck, 2011.
Dunn, James D. G. "1 Corinthians 15:45—Last Adam, Life-Giving Spirit." In *Christ and Spirit in the New Testament: Studies in Honour of Charles Francis Digby Moule*, edited by Barnabas Lindars and Stephen S. Smalley, 127–41. Cambridge: Cambridge University Press, 1973.
———. *Baptism in the Holy Spirit: A Re-examination of the New Testament Teaching on the Gift of the Spirit in Relation to Pentecostalism Today*. SBT 2/15. Naperville, IL: Allenson, 1970.
———. " 'Baptized' as Metaphor." In *Baptism, the New Testament and the Church: Historical and Contemporary Studies in Honour of R. E. O. White*,

edited by Stanley E. Porter and Anthony R. Cross, 294-310. JSNTSup 171. Sheffield: Sheffield Academic Press, 1999.
———. *Christology in the Making; A New Testament Inquiry into the Origins of the Doctrine of the Incarnation.* 2nd ed. Grand Rapids: Eerdmans, 1989.
———. *The Epistle to the Galatians.* BNTC. Peabody, MA: Hendrickson, 1993.
———. "How Controversial Was Paul's Christology?" In *From Jesus to John: Essays on Jesus and New Testament Christology in Honour of Marinus de Jonge*, edited by Martinus C. de Boer, 148-67. JSNTSup 84. Sheffield: JSOT Press, 1993.
———. "Jesus—Flesh and Spirit: An Exposition of Romans 1:3-4." *JTS* 24 (1973): 40-68.
———. "The New Perspective on Paul." *BJRL* 65 (1983): 95-122.
———. "Paul's Understanding of the Death of Jesus as a Sacrifice." In *Sacrifice and Redemption: Durham Essays in Theology*, edited by S. W. Sykes, 35-56. Cambridge: Cambridge University Press, 1991.
———. *Romans 1-8.* WBC 38A. Waco: Word, 1988.
———. *Romans 9-16.* WBC 38B. Waco: Word, 1988.
———. "The Theology of Galatians: The Issue of Covenantal Nomism." In *Thessalonians, Philippians, Galatians, Philemon.* Vol. 1 of *Pauline Theology*, edited by Jouette M. Bassler, 125-46. Minneapolis: Fortress, 1991.
———. *The Theology of Paul the Apostle.* Grand Rapids: Eerdmans, 1998.
du Toit, David. "Theologische Themen: Christologische Hoheitstitel." In *Paulus Handbuch*, edited by Friedrich W. Horn, 294-99. Tübingen: Mohr Siebeck, 2013.
Eastman, Susan Grove. "Philippians 2:6-11: Incarnation as Mimetic Participation." *JSPHL* 1 (2011): 1-22.
Ehrman, Bart D., ed. and trans. *Apostolic Fathers.* 2 vols. LCL. Cambridge: Harvard University Press, 2003.
Elias, Jacob W. " 'Jesus Who Delivers Us from the Wrath to Come' (1 Thess 1:10): Apocalyptic and Peace in the Thessalonian Correspondence." In *Society of Biblical Literature 1992 Seminar Papers*, 121-32. SBLSP 31. Atlanta: Scholars Press, 1992.
Ellis, E. Earle. "Preformed Traditions and Their Implications for Pauline Christology." In *Christology, Controversy and Community: New Testament Essays in Honour of David R. Catchpole*, edited by David G. Horrell and Christopher M. Tuckett, 303-20. NovTSup 99. Leiden: Brill, 2000.
———. "Traditions in 1 Corinthians." *NTS* 32 (1986): 481-502.
Eriksson, Anders. *Traditions as Rhetorical Proof: Pauline Argumentation in 1 Corinthians.* ConBNT 29. Stockholm: Almqvist & Wiksell, 1998.
Ernst, Josef. *Die Briefe an die Philipper, an Philemon, an die Kolosser, an die Epheser.* RNT. Regensburg: Pustet, 1974.
Farmer, William R. "Peter and Paul, and the Tradition concerning 'The Lord's

Supper' in 1 Corinthians 11:23-26." In *One Loaf, One Cup: Ecumenical Studies of 1 Cor. 11 and Other Eucharistic Texts*, edited by Ben F. Meyer, 35-55. NGS 6. Macon, GA: Mercer University Press, 1993.

Fee, Gordon D. *The First Epistle to the Corinthians*. NICNT. Grand Rapids: Eerdmans, 1987.

———. "Philippians 2:5-11: Hymn or Exalted Prose?" *BBR* 2 (1992): 29-46.

Feldman, Louis H. *Studies in Hellenistic Judaism*. AGJU 30. Leiden: Brill, 1996.

Fitzmyer, Joseph A. "The Aramaic Background of Philippians 2:6-11." *CBQ* 50 (1988): 470-83.

———. "The Christology of the Epistle to the Romans." In *The Future of Christology: Essays in Honor of Leander E. Keck*, edited by Abraham J. Malherbe and Wayne A. Meeks, 81-90. Minneapolis: Fortress, 1993.

———. *Romans: A New Translation with Introduction and Commentary*. AB 33. New York: Doubleday, 1993.

———. "The Semitic Background of the New Testament *Kyrios*-Title." In *A Wandering Aramean: Collected Aramaic Essays*, 115-43. SBLMS 25. Missoula, MT: Scholars Press, 1979.

Fotopoulos, John. "Arguments concerning Food Offered to Idols: Corinthian Quotations and Pauline Refutations in a Rhetorical *Partitio* (1 Corinthians 8:1-9)." *CBQ* 67 (2005): 611-31.

———. "Paul's Curse of Corinthians: Restraining Rivals with Fear and *Voces Mysticae* (1 Cor 16:22)." *NovT* 56 (2014): 275-309.

Fredriksen, Paula. *From Jesus to Christ: The Origins of the New Testament Images of Jesus*. 2nd ed. New Haven: Yale University Press, 2000.

Friedrich, Gerhard. "Ein Tauflied hellenistischer Judenchristen: 1. Thess. 1,9f." *TZ* 21 (1965): 502-16.

Fuller, Reginald H. "First Corinthians 6:1-11: An Exegetical Paper." *ExAud* 2 (1986): 96-104.

———. *The Foundations of New Testament Christology*. New York: Scribner's Sons, 1965.

———. *The Mission and Achievement of Jesus*. SBT 1/12. London: SCM, 1954.

Furnish, Victor P. *II Corinthians: A New Translation with Introduction and Commentary*. AB 32A. Garden City, NY: Doubleday, 1984.

———. " 'He Gave Himself [Was Given] . . .': Paul's Use of a Christological Assertion." In *The Future of Christology: Essays in Honor of Leander E. Keck*, edited by Abraham J. Malherbe and Wayne A. Meeks, 109-21. Minneapolis: Fortress, 1993.

———. *Jesus according to Paul*. Understanding Jesus Today. Cambridge: Cambridge University Press, 1993.

———. "The Jesus-Paul Debate: From Baur to Bultmann." In *Paul and Jesus: Collected Essays*, edited by A. J. M. Wedderburn, 17-50. New York: T. & T. Clark, 2004.

———. "On Putting Paul in His Place." *JBL* 113 (1994): 3–17.
———. *The Theology of the First Letter to the Corinthians.* New Testament Theology. Cambridge: Cambridge University Press, 1999.
Georgi, Dieter. *The Opponents of Paul in Second Corinthians.* Philadelphia: Fortress, 1986.
Gerhardsson, Birger. "Evidence for Christ's Resurrection according to Paul: 1 Cor 15:1–11." In *Neotestamentica et Philonica: Studies in Honor of Peder Borgen*, edited by David E. Aune, Torrey Seland, and Jarl H. Ulrichsen, 73–91. NovTSup 106. Leiden: Brill, 2003.
Gibson, Jeffrey B. "Paul's 'Dying Formula': Prolegomena to an Understanding of Its Import and Significance." In *Celebrating Romans: Template for Pauline Theology: Essays in Honor of Robert Jewett*, edited by Sheila E. McGinn, 20–41. Grand Rapids: Eerdmans, 2004.
Gnilka, Joachim. *Der Philipperbrief.* HTKNT. Freiburg: Herder, 1968.
Goodwin, D. R. "Ean mē in Gal ii. 16." *JBL* (1886): 122–27.
Gray, Patrick. *Paul as a Problem in History and Culture: The Apostle and His Critics through the Centuries.* Grand Rapids: Baker Academic, 2016.
Green, Joel B. "From 'John's Baptism' to 'Baptism in the Name of the Lord Jesus': The Significance of Baptism in Luke-Acts." In *Baptism, the New Testament and the Church: Historical and Contemporary Studies in Honour of R. E. O. White*, edited by Stanley E. Porter and Anthony R. Cross, 157–72. JSNTSup 171. Sheffield: Sheffield Academic Press, 1999.
Gundry, Judith M. "Jesus-Tradition and Paul's Opinion about the Widow Remaining as a Widow (1 Cor 7:40)." In *Portraits of Jesus: Studies in Christology*, edited by Susan E. Myers, 175–200. WUNT 321. Tübingen: Mohr Siebeck, 2012.
Gundry, Robert H. "A Brief Note on 'Hellenistic Formal Receptions and Paul's Use of *apantēsis* in 1 Thessalonians 4:17.'" *BBR* 6 (1996): 39–41.
———. "The Hellenization of Dominical Tradition and Christianization of Jewish Tradition in the Eschatology of 1–2 Thessalonians." *NTS* 33 (1987): 161–78.
Hafemann, Scott. *Suffering and the Spirit: An Exegetical Study of II Cor. 2:14–3:3 within the Context of the Corinthian Correspondence.* WUNT 2/19. Tübingen: Mohr Siebeck, 1986.
Hahn, Ferdinand. *The Titles of Jesus in Christology: Their History in Early Christianity.* Translated by Harold Knight and George Ogg. New York: World, 1969.
Harnack, Adolf. *Mission and Expansion of Christianity.* Translated and edited by James Moffatt. 2 vols. New York: Putnam's Sons, 1908.
Harnisch, Wolfgang. *Eschatologische Existenz: Ein exegetischer Beitrag zum Sachanliegen von 1 Thessalonicher 4:13–5:11.* FRLANT 110. Göttingen: Vandenhoeck & Ruprecht, 1973.

Hartman, Lars. *"Into the Name of the Lord Jesus": Baptism in the Early Church.*
SNTW. Edinburgh: T. & T. Clark, 1997.
Hay, David. *Glory at the Right Hand: Psalm 110 in Early Christianity.* SBLMS 18.
Nashville: Abingdon, 1973.
Hellerman, Joseph H. "Vindicating God's Servants in Philippi and in Philippians:
The Influence of Paul's Ministry in Philippi and upon the Composition of
Philippians 2:6-11." *BBR* 20 (2010): 85-102.
Hellholm, David. "The Impact of the Situational Contexts for Paul's Use of Baptismal Traditions in His Letters." In *Neotestamentica et Philonica: Studies in Honor of Peder Borgen*, edited by David E. Aune, Torrey Seland, and Jarl H. Ulrichsen, 147-75. NovTSup 106. Leiden: Brill, 2003.
Hengel, Martin. *Between Jesus and Paul: Studies in the Earliest History of Christianity.* Translated by John Bowden. Philadelphia: Fortress, 1983.
―――. "Confessing and Confession." In *Earliest Christian History: History, Literature, and Theology: Essays from the Tyndale Fellowship in Honor of Martin Hengel*, edited by Michael F. Bird and Jason Maston, 589-623. WUNT 2/320. Tübingen: Mohr Siebeck, 2012.
―――. *Studies in Early Christology.* Edinburgh: T. & T. Clark, 1995.
Hengel, Martin, and Anna Maria Schwemer. *Paul between Damascus and Antioch: The Unknown Years.* Translated by John Bowden. Louisville: Westminster John Knox, 1997.
Herzer, Jens. "Theologische Themen: Passion und Auferstehung Jesu Christi: Paulus und die urchristliche Tradition." In *Paulus Handbuch*, edited by Friedrich W. Horn, 285-94. Tübingen: Mohr Siebeck, 2013.
Hill, Charles E. "Paul's Understanding of Christ's Kingdom in I Corinthians 15:20-28." *NovT* 30 (1988): 297-320.
Hill, Wesley. *Paul and the Trinity: Persons, Relations, and the Pauline Letters.* Grand Rapids: Eerdmans, 2015.
Hofius, Otfried. " 'Einer ist Gott—Einer ist Herr': Erwägungen zu Struktur und Aussage des Bekenntnisses 1. Kor 8,6." In *Eschatologie und Schöpfung: Festschrift für Erich Grässer zum siebzigsten Geburtstag*, edited by Martin Evang, Helmut Merklein, and Michael Wolter, 95-108. BZNW 89. Berlin: de Gruyter, 1997.
―――. "The Lord's Supper and the Lord's Supper Tradition: Reflections on 1 Corinthians 11:23b-25." In *One Loaf, One Cup: Ecumenical Studies of 1 Cor. 11 and Other Eucharistic Texts*, edited by Ben F. Meyer, 75-115. NGS 6. Macon, GA: Mercer University Press, 1993.
Hogeterp, Albert L. A. *Expectations of the End: A Comparative Traditio-Historical Study of Eschatological, Apocalyptic and Messianic Ideas in the Dead Sea Scrolls and the New Testament.* STDJ 83. Leiden: Brill, 2009.
Holladay, Carl. *Theios anēr in Hellenistic Judaism: A Critique of the Use of This*

Category in New Testament Christology. SBLDS 40. Missoula, MT: Scholars Press, 1977.

Holleman, Joost. *Resurrection and Parousia: A Traditio-Historical Study of Paul's Eschatology in 1 Corinthians 15*. NovTSup 84. Leiden: Brill, 1996.

Holtz, Traugott. "Das Alte Testament und das Bekenntnis der frühen Gemeinde zu Jesus Christus." In *Christus Bezeugen: Festschrift für Wolfgang Trilling zum 65. Geburtstag*, edited by Karl Kertelge, Traugott Holtz, and Claus-Peter März, 55–66. ETS 59. Leipzig: St. Benno, 1988.

Hooker, Morna. "1 Thessalonians 1.9–10: A Nutshell—But What Kind of a Nut?" In *Frühes Christentum*, edited by Hermann Lichtenberger, 435–48. Vol. 3 of *Geschichte—Tradition—Reflexion: Festschrift für Martin Hengel zum 70. Geburtstag*, edited by Hubert Cancik, Hermann Lichtenberger, and Peter Schäfer. 3 vols. Tübingen: Mohr Siebeck, 1996.

———. "The Letter to the Philippians: Introduction, Commentary, and Reflections." *NIB* 11:467–549.

———. *Not Ashamed of the Gospel: New Testament Interpretations of the Death of Christ*. Grand Rapids: Eerdmans, 1994.

Horrell, David G. *The Social Ethos of the Corinthian Correspondence: Interests and Ideology from 1 Corinthians to 1 Clement*. SNTW. Edinburgh: T. & T. Clark, 1996.

Horsley, G. H. R., and Stephen Llewelyn, eds. *New Documents Illustrating Early Christianity*. Vols. 2 and 3. North Ryde, NSW: Ancient History Documentary Research Centre, Macquarie University, 1982–1983.

Horsley, Richard A. *1 Corinthians*. ANTC. Nashville: Abingdon, 1998.

———. "Gnosis in Corinth: 1 Cor. 8.1–6." *NTS* 27 (1979): 32–51.

Horst, Pieter van der. "The Egyptian Beginning of Anti-Semitism's Long History." Jerusalem Center for Public Affairs website. http://jcpa.org/article/the-egyptian-beginning-of-anti-semitism's-long-history. Accessed 4/11/2016.

Howard, Tracy L. "The Literary Unity of 1 Thessalonians 4:13–5:11." *GTJ* 9 (1988): 163–90.

Hunn, Debbie. "*Ean mē* in Galatians 2:16: A Look at Greek Literature." *NovT* 49 (2007): 281–90.

Hunter, A. M. *Paul and His Predecessors*. Rev. ed. London: SCM, 1961.

Hurtado, Larry W. *How on Earth Did Jesus Become God? Historical Questions about Earliest Devotion to Jesus*. Grand Rapids: Eerdmans, 2005.

———. "Jesus' Divine Sonship in Paul's Epistle to the Romans." In *Romans and the People of God: Essays in Honor of Gordon D. Fee on the Occasion of His 65th Birthday*, edited by Sven K. Soderlund and N. T. Wright, 217–33. Grand Rapids: Eerdmans, 1999.

———. *Lord Jesus Christ: Devotion to Jesus in Earliest Christianity*. Grand Rapids: Eerdmans, 2003.

———. "Pre-70 CE Jewish Opposition to Christ-Devotion." *JTS* 50 (1999): 35–58.

Jeremias, Joachim. *The Eucharistic Words of Jesus*. Translated by Norman Perrin. 1966. Repr. Philadelphia: Fortress, 1977.

———. *New Testament Theology*. New York: Scribner, 1971.

Jervell, Jacob. *Imago Dei: Gen 1,26f. im Spätjudentum, in der Gnosis und in den paulinischen Briefen*. FRLANT 58. Göttingen: Vandenhoeck & Ruprecht, 1960.

Jewett, Robert. *Romans: A Commentary*. Hermeneia. Minneapolis: Fortress, 2007.

———. *The Thessalonian Correspondence: Pauline Rhetoric and Millenarian Piety*. Philadelphia: Fortress, 1986.

Jipp, Joshua W. "Ancient, Modern, and Future Interpretations of Romans 1:3–4: Reception History and Biblical Interpretation." *JTI* 3 (2009): 241–59.

Johnston, J. William. "Which 'All' Sinned? Rom 3:23–24 Reconsidered." *NovT* 53 (2011): 153–64.

Jonge, Henk J. de. "The Historical Jesus' View of Himself and His Mission." In *From Jesus to John: Essays on Jesus and New Testament Christology in Honour of Marinus de Jonge*, edited by Martinus C. de Boer, 21–37. JSNTSup 84. Sheffield: Sheffield Academic Press, 1993.

———. "The Original Setting of the *Christos apethanen hyper* Formula." In *The Thessalonian Correspondence*, edited by Raymond F. Collins, 229–35. BETL 87. Leuven: Leuven University Press, 1990.

Käsemann, Ernst. *Commentary on Romans*. Translated by Geoffrey W. Bromiley. Grand Rapids: Eerdmans, 1980.

———. *New Testament Questions of Today*. Translated by W. J. Montague. Philadelphia: Fortress, 1969.

———. *Perspectives on Paul*. Translated by Margaret Kohl. Philadelphia: Fortress, 1969.

———. "Zur Verständnis von Römer 3.24–26." *ZNW* 43 (1950/1951): 150–54.

Keck, Leander E. *Romans*. ANTC. Nashville: Abingdon, 2005.

———. "The Law and 'The Law of Sin and Death' (Rom 8:1–4): Reflections on the Spirit and Ethics in Paul." In *The Divine Helmsman: Studies on God's Control of Human Events, Presented to Lou H. Silberman*, edited by J. L. Crenshaw and S. Sandmel, 41–58. New York: Ktav, 1980.

Kertelge, Karl. "Das Verständnis des Todes Jesu bei Paulus." In *Der Tod Jesu: Deutungen im Neuen Testament*, edited by Karl Kertelge, 114–36. QD 74. Freiburg: Herder, 1976.

———. "Jesus Christus verkündigen als den Herren (2 Kor 4,5)." In *Christus Bezeugen: Festschrift für Wolfgang Trilling zum 65. Geburtstag*, edited by Karl Kertelge, Traugott Holtz, and Claus-Peter März, 227–36. ETS 59. Leipzig: St. Benno, 1988.

Kieffer, René. "L'Eschatologie en 1 Thessaloniciens dans une perspective rhétorique." In *The Thessalonian Correspondence*, edited by Raymond F. Collins, 206-19. BETL 125. Leuven: Leuven University Press, 1990.

Kim, Seyoon. "Jesus the Son of God as the Gospel [1 Thess 1:9-10 and Rom 1:3-4]." In *Earliest Christian History: History, Literature, and Theology: Essays from the Tyndale Fellowship in Honor of Martin Hengel*, edited by Michael F. Bird and Jason Maston, 117-41. WUNT 2/320. Tübingen: Mohr Siebeck, 2012.

Kirk, Alan. "The Memory of Violence and the Death of Jesus in Q." In *Memory, Tradition, and Text: Uses of the Past in Early Christianity*, edited by Alan Kirk and Tom Thatcher, 191-206. SemeiaSt 52. Atlanta: SBL Press, 2005.

Kistemaker, Simon J. *Exposition of the First Epistle to the Corinthians*. New Testament Commentaries. Grand Rapids: Baker, 1993.

Kittel, Gerhard, and Gerhard Friedrich, eds. *Theological Dictionary of the New Testament*. Translated by Geoffrey W. Bromiley. 10 vols. Grand Rapids: Eerdmans, 1964-1976.

Kittredge, Cynthia Briggs. *Community and Authority: The Rhetoric of Obedience in the Pauline Tradition*. HTS 45. Harrisburg, PA: Trinity Press International, 1998.

———. "Rethinking Authorship in the Letters of Paul: Elisabeth Schüssler Fiorenza's Model of Pauline Theology." In *Walk in the Ways of Wisdom: Essays in Honor of Elisabeth Schüssler Fiorenza*, edited by Shelly Matthews, Cynthia Briggs Kittredge, and Melanie Johnson-Debaufre, 318-33. Harrisburg, PA: Trinity Press International, 2003.

Klauck, Hans-Josef. "Presence in the Lord's Supper: 1 Corinthians 11:23-26 in the Context of Hellenistic Religious History." In *One Loaf, One Cup: Ecumenical Studies of 1 Cor. 11 and Other Eucharistic Texts*, edited by Ben F. Meyer, 57-74. NGS 6. Macon, GA: Mercer University Press, 1993.

Klausner, Joseph. *From Jesus to Paul*. Translated by William F. Stinespring. New York: Macmillan, 1943.

Kloppenborg, John. "An Analysis of the Pre-Pauline Formula 1 Cor 15:3b-5 in Light of Some Recent Literature." *CBQ* 40 (1978): 351-67.

———. "Precedence at the Communal Meal in Corinth." *NovT* 58 (2016): 167-203.

Knoch, Otto. " 'Do This in Memory of Me!' (Luke 22:20; 1 Corinthians 11:24ff.): The Celebration of the Eucharist in the Primitive Christian Communities." In *One Loaf, One Cup: Ecumenical Studies of 1 Cor. 11 and Other Eucharistic Texts*, edited by Ben F. Meyer, 1-10. NGS 6. Macon, GA: Mercer University Press, 1993.

Kodell, Jerome. *The Eucharist in the New Testament*. Collegeville, MN: Liturgical Press, 1988.

Koester, Helmut. "The Purpose of the Polemic of a Pauline Fragment (Philippians III)." *NTS* 8 (1961/1962): 317-32.

Kramer, Werner. *Christ, Lord, Son of God*. Translated by Brian Hardy. SBT 1/50. London: SCM, 1966.
Kraus, Wolfgang. *Der Tod Jesu als Heiligtumsweihe. Eine Untersuchung zum Umfeld der Sühnevorstellung in Römer 3,25–26a*. WMANT 66. Neukirchen-Vluyn: Neukirchener Verlag, 1991.
———. "Paulus als Heidenmissionar: Zwischen Damaskus und Antiochien." In *Paulus Handbuch*, edited by Friedrich W. Horn, 91–98. Tübingen: Mohr Siebeck, 2013.
Kreitzer, L. Joseph. *Jesus and God in Paul's Eschatology*. JSNTSup 19. Sheffield: JSOT Press, 1987.
Kujanpää, Katja. "From Eloquence to Evading Responsibility: The Rhetorical Functions of Quotations in Paul's Argumentations." *JBL* 136 (2017): 185–202.
Lake, Kirsopp, trans. *Apostolic Fathers*. 2 vols. LCL. Cambridge: Harvard University Press, 1912.
Lambrecht, Jan. "Paul's Christological Use of Scripture in 1 Cor. 15.20–28." In *Pauline Studies: Collected Essays*, 134–40. BETL 115. Leuven: Leuven University Press, 1994.
———. *Second Corinthians*. SP. Collegeville, MN: Liturgical Press, 1999.
———. "Thanksgivings in 1 Thessalonians 1–3." In *The Thessalonian Correspondence*, edited by Raymond F. Collins, 183–205. BETL 87. Leuven: Leuven University Press, 1990.
Lategan, Bernard C. "Reconsidering the Origin and Function of Galatians 3:28." *Neot* 46 (2012): 274–86.
LaVerdiere, Eugene. *The Eucharist in the New Testament and the Early Church*. Collegeville, MN: Liturgical Press, 1996.
Legarreta-Castillo, Felipe de Jesús. *The Figure of Adam in Romans 5 and 1 Corinthians 15: The New Creation and Its Ethical and Social Reconfiguration*. Minneapolis: Fortress, 2014.
Lichtenberger, Hermann. "Auferstehung in den Qumranfunden." In *Auferstehung—Resurrection*, edited by Friedrich Avemarie and Hermann Lichtenberger, 79–91. WUNT 135. Tübingen: Mohr Siebeck, 2001.
Lietzmann, Hans. *Mass and Lord's Supper: A Study in the History of the Liturgy*. Translated by Dorothea H. G. Reeve. Leiden: Brill, 1979. Originally published as *Messe und Herrenmahl: Eine Studie zur Geschichte der Liturgie*. Berlin: de Gruyter, 1926.
Lindemann, Andreas. "Die Auferstehung der Toten: Adam und Christus nach 1.Kor 15." In *Eschatologie und Schöpfung: Festschrift für Erich Grässer zum siebzigsten Geburtstag*, edited by Martin Evang, Helmut Merklein, and Michael Wolter, 155–67. BZNW 89. Berlin: deGruyter, 1997.
———. "Paulus und die korinthische Eschatologie: Zur These von einer 'Entwicklung' im paulinischen Denken." *NTS* 37 (1991): 373–99.

Lohmeyer, Ernst. *Kyrios Jesus: Eine Untersuchung zu Phil. 2,5–11.* SHAW. Heidelberg: Winter, 1928.

Longenecker, Richard N. *The Christology of Early Jewish Christianity.* SBT 2/17. Naperville, IL: Allenson, 1970.

———. *Galatians.* WBC 41. Dallas: Word, 1990.

———. "The Nature of Paul's Early Eschatology." *NTS* 31 (1985): 85–95.

———. *New Wine into Fresh Wineskins: Contextualizing the Early Christian Confessions.* Peabody, MA: Hendrickson, 1999.

Lüdemann, Gerd. *Opposition to Paul in Jewish Christianity.* Translated by M. Eugene Boring. Minneapolis: Fortress, 1989.

———. *Paul, Apostle to the Gentiles: Studies in Chronology.* Translated by F. Stanley Jones. Philadelphia: Fortress, 1984.

Lyons, George. *Pauline Autobiography: Toward a New Understanding.* SBLDS 73. Atlanta: Scholars Press, 1985.

Macaskill, Grant. "The Atonement and Concepts of Participation." In *Earliest Christian History: History, Literature, and Theology: Essays from the Tyndale Fellowship in Honor of Martin Hengel,* edited by Michael F. Bird and Jason Maston, 363–80. WUNT 2/320. Tübingen: Mohr Siebeck, 2012.

Maccoby, Hyam. *The Mythmaker: Paul and the Invention of Christianity.* New York: Harper & Row, 1987.

———. "Paul and the Eucharist." *NTS* 37 (1991): 247–67.

Mack, Burton. *A Myth of Innocence: Mark and Christian Origins.* Philadelphia: Fortress, 1988.

Malherbe, Abraham. " 'Gentle as a Nurse': The Cynic Background to 1 Thessalonians 2." *NovT* 12 (1970): 203–17.

———. *The Letters to the Thessalonians: A New Translation with Introduction and Commentary.* AB 32B. New York: Doubleday, 2000.

Marshall, I. Howard. "The Development of the Concept of Redemption in the New Testament." In *Reconciliation and Hope: New Testament Essays on Atonement and Eschatology Presented to L. L. Morris on His 60th Birthday,* edited by Robert Banks, 153–69. Grand Rapids: Eerdmans, 1974.

Martin, Ralph P. *2 Corinthians.* WBC 40. Waco: Word, 1986.

———. *Carmen Christi: Philippians ii. 5–11 in Recent Interpretation and in the Setting of Early Christianity.* Rev. ed. Grand Rapids: Eerdmans, 1983.

———. *Worship in the Early Church.* Grand Rapids: Eerdmans, 1964.

Martin, Troy. "The Covenant of Circumcision (Gen 17:9–14) and the Situational Antithesis of Gal 3:28." *JBL* 122 (2003): 111–25.

Martyn, J. Louis. *Galatians: A New Translation with Introduction and Commentary.* AB 33A. New York: Doubleday, 1997.

———. *Theological Issues in the Letters of Paul.* Nashville: Abingdon, 1997.

Masson, Charles. *Les deux épitres de Saint Paul aux Thessaloniciens.* CNT 11a. Neuchâtel: Delachaux & Niestlé, 1957.

Matera, Frank J. *II Corinthians: A Commentary.* NTL. Louisville: Westminster John Knox, 2003.
———. *Galatians.* SP. Collegeville, MN: Liturgical Press, 1992.
Mazza, Enrico. "Didache 9–10: Elements of a Eucharistic Interpretation." In *The Didache in Modern Research*, edited by Jonathan A. Draper, 276–99. AGJU 37. Leiden: Brill, 1996.
———. *The Origins of the Eucharistic Prayer.* Collegeville, MN: Liturgical Press, 1995.
McGowan, Andrew Brian. "The Myth of the 'Lord's Supper': Paul's Eucharistic Meal Terminology and Its Ancient Reception." *CBQ* 77 (2015): 503–21.
Mearns, Christopher L. "Early Eschatological Development in Paul: The Evidence of 1 Corinthians." *JSNT* 22 (1984): 19–35.
Meeks, Wayne A. "The Christian Proteus." In *The Writings of St. Paul*, edited by Wayne A. Meeks, 435–44. Norton Critical Edition. New York: Norton, 1972.
———. "Image of the Androgyne: Some Uses of a Symbol in Earliest Christianity." *HR* 13 (1974): 165–208.
Merklein, Helmut. "Der Theologe als Prophet: Zur Function prophetischen Redens im theologischen Diskurs des Paulus." *NTS* 38 (1992): 402–29.
Meyer, Ben F. "The Pre-Pauline Formula in Rom. 3.25–26a." *NTS* 29 (1983): 198–208.
Michaels, J. Ramsey. "Everything That Rises Must Converge: Paul's Word from the Lord." In *To Tell the Mystery: Essays on New Testament Eschatology in Honor of Robert H. Gundry*, edited by Thomas E. Schmidt and Moisés Silva, 182–95. JSNTSup 100. Sheffield: JSOT Press, 1994.
Minns, Denis, and Paul Parvis, eds. *Justin, Philosopher and Martyr: Apologies.* Oxford Early Christian Texts. Oxford: Oxford University Press, 2009.
Mitchell, Margaret M. *Paul and the Rhetoric of Reconciliation: An Exegetical Investigation of the Language and Composition of 1 Corinthians.* Louisville: Westminster John Knox, 1991.
Moloney, Francis J. *A Body Broken for a Broken People: Eucharist in the New Testament.* Peabody, MA: Hendrickson, 1997.
Moo, Douglas. *The Epistle to the Romans.* NICNT. Grand Rapids: Eerdmans, 1996.
Morris, Leon. *The Epistle to the Romans.* Pillar. Grand Rapids: Eerdmans, 1988.
Moss, Candida R., and Joel S. Baden. "1 Thessalonians 4.13–18 in Rabbinic Perspective." *NTS* 58 (2012): 199–212.
Mounce, Robert H. "Continuity of the Primitive Tradition: Some Pre-Pauline Elements in 1 Corinthians." *Int* 13 (1959): 417–24.
Müller, Ulrich B. *Der Brief des Paulus an die Philipper.* THKNT 11.1. Leipzig: Evangelische Verlagsanstalt, 1993.
———. *Prophetie und Predigt im Neuen Testament: Formgeschichtliche Unter-*

suchungen zur urchristlichen Prophetie. SNT 10. Gütersloh: Gütersloher Verlagshaus, 1975.

Mussner, Franz. *Der Galaterbrief.* HTKNT 9. Freiburg: Herder, 1974.

Nanos, Mark. "Intruding 'Spies' and 'Pseudo-Brethren': The Jewish Intra-Group Politics of Paul's Jerusalem Meeting (Gal 2:1–10)." In *Paul and His Opponents*, edited by Stanley E. Porter, 59–97. PS 2. Leiden: Brill, 2005.

———. *The Irony of Galatians.* Minneapolis: Fortress, 2002.

Neufeld, Vernon H. *The Earliest Christian Confessions.* NTTS 5. Leiden: Brill, 1963.

Niederwimmer, Kurt. *The Didache: A Commmentary.* Translated by Linda M. Maloney. Hermeneia. Minneapolis: Fortress, 1998.

Öhler, Markus. "Bausteine aus frühchristlicher Theologie." In *Paulus Handbuch*, edited by Friedrich W. Horn, 497–504. Tübingen: Mohr Siebeck, 2013.

Orr, William F., and James A. Walther. *1 Corinthians: A New Translation with Introduction and Commentary.* AB 32. Garden City, NY: Doubleday, 1976.

Osiek, Carolyn. *Philippians, Philemon.* ANTC. Nashville: Abingdon, 2000.

Pahl, Michael. *Discerning the "Word of the Lord": The "Word of the Lord" in 1 Thessalonians 4:15.* LNTS 389. London: T. & T. Clark, 2009.

Pearson, Birger A. "Hellenistic-Jewish Wisdom Speculation and Paul." In *Aspects of Wisdom in Judaism and Early Christianity*, edited by Robert L. Wilken, 43–66. Notre Dame: University of Notre Dame Press, 1975.

———. *The Pneumatikos-Psychikos Terminology in 1 Corinthians.* SBLDS 12. Missoula, MT: Scholars Press, 1973.

Pearson, Brook W. R. "Baptism and Initiation in the Cult of Isis and Serapis." In *Baptism, the New Testament and the Church: Historical and Contemporary Studies in Honour of R. E. O. White*, edited by Stanley E. Porter and Anthony R. Cross, 42–62. JSNTSup 171. Sheffield: Sheffield Academic Press, 1999.

Pede, E. Di, and A. Wénin. "Le Christ Jésus et l'humain de l'Eden: L'hymne aux Philippiens (2,6–11) et le début de la Genèse." *RTL* 43 (2012): 225–41.

Peterson, Erik. "Die Einholung des Kyrios." *ZST* 1 (1930): 682–702.

Porter, Stanley E. "Did Paul Have Opponents in Rome and What Were They Opposing?" In *Paul and His Opponents*, edited by Stanley E. Porter, 149–68. PS 2. Leiden: Brill, 2005.

Reinach, Théodore. *Textes d'auteurs grecs et romains relatifs au Judaïsme.* Hildesheim: Olms, 1963.

Reumann, John. "The Gospel of the Righteousness of God: Pauline Reinterpretation in Romans 3:21–31." *Int* 20 (1966): 432–52.

———. "Philippians 3:20–21—A Hymnic Fragment?" *NTS* 30 (1984): 593–609.

———. *Philippians: A New Translation with Introduction and Commentary.* AB 33B. New Haven: Yale University Press, 2008.

Richard, Earl. *First and Second Thessalonians*. SP. Collegeville, MN: Liturgical Press, 1995.

Ridderbos, Herman. "The Earliest Confession of the Atonement in Paul." In *Reconciliation and Hope. New Testament Essays on Atonement and Eschatology Presented to L. L. Morris on His 60th Birthday*, edited by Robert Banks, 76–89. Grand Rapids: Eerdmans, 1974.

Rigaux, Béda. *Les épîtres aux Thessaloniciens*. EB. Paris: Gabalda, 1956.

———. "Tradition et rédaction dans 1 Th. V.1–10." *NTS* 21 (1975): 318–34.

Roetzel, Calvin. *The Letters of Paul: Conversations in Context*. Atlanta: John Knox, 1975.

Romanov, Andrey. "*Heis kyrios* and *hēmeis* in 1 Corinthians 8:6: An Investigation of the First Person Plural in Light of the Lordship of Jesus Christ." *Neot* 49 (2015): 47–74.

———. "Through One Lord Only: Theological Interpretation of the Meaning of *dia* in 1 Cor 8,6." *Bib* 96 (2015): 391–415.

Rordorf, Willy. "The Didache." In *The Eucharist of the Early Christians*, by Rordorf et al., 1–23. Translated by Matthew J. O'Connell. New York: Pueblo, 1978. Originally published as *L'Eucharistie des premiers chrétiens*. Paris: Beauchesne, 1976.

Sandt, Hubertus Waltherus Maria van de. "Why Does the Didache Conceive of the Eucharist as a Holy Meal?" *VC* 65 (2011): 1–20.

Schippers, R. "The Pre-Synoptic Tradition in I Thessalonians ii 13–16." *NovT* 8 (1966): 223–34.

Schlier, Heinrich. *Der Brief an die Galater*. 11th ed. KEK 7. Göttingen: Vandenhoeck & Ruprecht, 1951.

Schmithals, Walter. *Gnosticism in Corinth: An Investigation of the Letters to the Corinthians*. Translated by John E. Steely. Nashville: Abingdon, 1971.

———. *Paul and the Gnostics*. Translated by John E. Steely. Nashville: Abingdon, 1972.

———. "The Pre-Pauline Tradition in 1 Corinthians 15:20–28." *PRSt* 20 (1993): 357–80.

———. *The Theology of the First Christians*. Translated by O. C. Dean Jr. Louisville: Westminster John Knox, 1997.

Schneider, Sebastian. "1 Kor 15,51–52: Ein neuer Lösungsvorschlag zu einer alten Schwierigkeit." In *The Corinthian Correspondence*, edited by R. Bieringer, 661–69. BETL 125. Leuven: Leuven University Press, 1996.

Schoedel, William R. *Ignatius of Antioch: A Commentary on the Letters of Ignatius of Antioch*. Hermeneia. Philadelphia: Fortress, 1985.

Schrage, Wolfgang. "Einige Hauptprobleme der Diskussion des Herrenmahls im 1. Korintherbrief." In *The Corinthian Correspondence*, edited by R. Bieringer, 191–98. BETL 125. Leuven: Leuven University Press, 1996.

———. *Der erste Brief an die Korinther*. 4 vols. EKKNT 7.1–4. Neukirchen-Vluyn: Neukirchener Verlag, 1991–2001.

———. *The Ethics of the New Testament*. Translated by David E. Green. Philadelphia: Fortress, 1988.

Schürmann, Heinz. *Der Einsetzungsbericht Luke 22, 19–20*. Münster: Aschendorff, 1955.

Schüssler Fiorenza, Elisabeth. *In Memory of Her: A Feminist Theological Reconstruction of Christian Origins*. New York: Crossroad, 1983.

———. *Rhetoric and Ethic: The Politics of Biblical Studies*. Minneapolis: Fortress, 1999.

Schweizer, Eduard. "What Do We Really Mean When We Say, 'God Sent His Son...'?" In *Faith and History: Essays in Honor of Paul W. Meyer*, edited by John T. Carroll, Charles H. Cosgrove, and E. Elizabeth Johnson, 298–312. Atlanta: Scholars Press, 1990.

Scroggs, Robin. *The Last Adam: A Study in Pauline Anthropology*. Philadelphia: Fortress, 1966.

———. "Paul and the Eschatological Woman." *JAAR* 40 (1972): 283–303.

———. "Paul: Myth Remaker. The Refashioning of Early Ecclesial Traditions." In *Pauline Conversations in Context: Essays in Honor of Calvin J. Roetzel*, edited by Janice Capel Anderson, Philip Sellew, and Claudia Setzer, 87–101. JSNTSup 221. Sheffield: Sheffield Academic Press, 2002.

———. *The People's Jesus: Trajectories in Early Christianity*. Minneapolis: Fortress, 2001.

Seeley, David. *The Noble Death: Graeco-Roman Martyrology and Paul's Concept of Salvation*. JSNTSup 28. Sheffield: Sheffield Academic Press, 1990.

Seifrid, Mark A. "Gift of Remembrance: Paul and the Lord's Supper in Corinth." *Concordia Journal* 42 (2016): 119–29.

———. *The Second Letter to the Corinthians*. Pillar. Grand Rapids: Eerdmans, 2014.

Sellin, Gerhard. "Das 'Geheimnis' der Weisheit und das Rätsel der 'Christuspartei' (zu 1 Kor 1–4)." *ZNW* 73 (1982): 69–96.

Shillington, V. George. *Jesus and Paul before Christianity: Their World and Work in Retrospect*. Eugene, OR: Cascade, 2011.

Slee, Michelle. *The Church in Antioch in the First Century CE: Communion and Conflict*. JSNTSup 244. Sheffield: Sheffield Academic Press, 2003.

Smith, Dennis E. *From Symposium to Eucharist: The Banquet in the Early Christian World*. Minneapolis: Fortress, 2003.

Standhartinger, Angela. "Words to Remember—Women and the Origin of the 'Words of Institution.'" *Lectio Difficilior* 1 (2015): 1–25.

Sterling, Greg E. "'The Image of God': Becoming like God in Philo, Paul, and Early Christianity." In *Portraits of Jesus: Studies in Christology*, edited by Susan E. Myers, 157–73. WUNT 2/321. Tübingen: Mohr Siebeck, 2012.

Stettler, Hanna. "Did Paul Invent Justification by Faith?" *TynBul* 66 (2015): 161–96.
Streett, R. Alan. *Subversive Meals: An Analysis of the Lord's Supper under Roman Domination during the First Century*. Eugene, OR: Wipf & Stock, 2013.
Stuhlmacher, Peter. *Reconciliation, Law, and Righteousness: Essays in Biblical Theology*. Translated by Everett R. Kalin. Philadelphia: Fortress, 1997.
Sumney, Jerry L. "The Resurrection of the Body in Paul." *HBT* 31 (2009): 12–26.
―――. "The Search for the Opponents of Paul." In *Paul Unbound: New Approaches to the Study of the Apostle*, edited by Mark Given, 55–70. Peabody, MA: Hendrickson, 2009.
―――. *Servants of Satan, False Brothers, and Other Opponents of Paul*. JSNTSup 188. Sheffield: Sheffield Academic Press, 1999.
―――. "Studying Paul's Opponents: Advances and Challenges." In *Paul and His Opponents*, edited by Stanley E. Porter, 7–58. PS 2. Leiden: Brill, 2005.
Tabor, James D. *Paul and Jesus: How the Apostle Transformed Christianity*. New York: Simon & Schuster, 2012.
Talbert, Charles H. "The Problem of Pre-existence in Philippians 2:6–11." *JBL* 86 (1967): 141–53.
Tannehill, Robert C. *Dying and Rising with Christ: A Study in Pauline Theology*. BZNW 32. Berlin: Töpelmann, 1967.
Taussig, Hal. *In the Beginning Was the Meal: Social Experimentation and Early Christian Identity*. Minneapolis: Fortress, 2009.
Theobald, Michael. "Die Briefe des Paulus: Römerbrief: Literarische Kennzeichen des Schreibens." In *Paulus Handbuch*, ed. Friedrich W. Horn, 220–27. Tübingen: Mohr Siebeck, 2013.
―――. "Strukturen: Kontingenz und Kohärenz." In *Paulus Handbuch*, edited by Friedrich W. Horn, 512–17. Tübingen: Mohr Siebeck, 2013.
―――. "Theologische Grundoptionen als Garanten theologischer 'Kohärenz.'" In *Paulus Handbuch*, edited by Friedrich W. Horn, 515–17. Tübingen: Mohr Siebeck, 2013.
Thiselton, Anthony C. *The First Epistle to the Corinthians: A Commentary on the Greek Text*. NIGTC. Grand Rapids: Eerdmans, 2000.
Thompson, Marianne Meye. *The God of the Gospel of John*. Grand Rapids: Eerdmans, 2001.
Thrall, Margaret E. *A Critical and Exegetical Commentary on the Second Epistle to the Corinthians*. 2 vols. ICC. Edinburgh: T. & T. Clark, 1994–2000.
Thurston, Bonnie, and Judith Ryan. *Philippians and Philemon*. SP. Collegeville, MN: Liturgical Press, 2005.
Tilling, Chris. *Paul's Divine Christology*. 2012. Repr. Grand Rapids: Eerdmans, 2015.
Tobin, Thomas H. "The Use of Christological Traditions in Paul: The Case of

Rom 3:21–26." In *Portraits of Jesus: Studies in Christology*, edited by Susan E. Myers, 229–45. WUNT 2/321. Tübingen: Mohr Siebeck, 2012.

Tomson, Peter J. "La Première Épître aux Corinthiens comme document de la tradition apostolique de halakha." In *The Corinthian Correspondence*, edited by R. Bieringer, 459–70. BETL 125. Leuven: Leuven University Press, 1996.

Tuckett, Christopher M. "Synoptic Tradition in 1 Thessalonians?" In *The Thessalonian Correspondence*, edited by Raymond F. Collins, 160–82. BETL 87. Leuven: Leuven University Press, 1990.

Villiers, Pieter G. R. de. "In the Presence of God: The Eschatology of 1 Thessalonians." In *Eschatology of the New Testament and Some Related Documents*, edited by Jan G. van der Watt, 302–32. WUNT 2/315. Tübingen: Mohr Siebeck, 2011.

Vollenweider, Samuel. "Der 'Raub' der Gottgleichheit: Ein religionsgeschichtlicher Vorschlag zu Phil 2.6(–11)." *NTS* 45 (1999): 413–33.

Vossing, Konrad. "Das 'Herrenmahl' und 1 Cor. 11 im Kontext antiker Gemeinschaftsmähler." *JAC* 54 (2011): 40–72.

Waaler, Erik. *The Shema and the First Commandment in First Corinthians: An Intertextual Approach to Paul's Re-reading of Deuteronomy*. WUNT 2/253. Tübingen: Mohr Siebeck, 2008.

Walton, Steven. "How Mighty a Minority Were the Hellenists?" In *Earliest Christian History: History, Literature, and Theology: Essays from the Tyndale Fellowship in Honor of Martin Hengel*, edited by Michael F. Bird and Jason Maston, 303–27. WUNT 2/320. Tübingen: Mohr Siebeck, 2012.

Wanamaker, Charles A. *The Epistles to the Thessalonians: A Commentary on the Greek Text*. NIGTC. Grand Rapids: Eerdmans, 1990.

Ware, James. "The Resurrection of Jesus in the Pre-Pauline Formula of 1 Cor 15.3–5." *NTS* 60 (2014): 475–98.

Watson, Francis. *Paul, Judaism, and the Gentiles: Beyond the New Perspective*. Rev. ed. Grand Rapids: Eerdmans, 2007.

Wedderburn, A. J. M. *Baptism and Resurrection: Studies in Pauline Theology against Its Graeco-Roman Background*. WUNT 44. Tübingen: Mohr Siebeck, 1987.

Weiss, Alexander. "Christus Jesus als Weihegeschenk oder Sühnemal?" *ZNW* 105 (2014): 294–302.

———. "Hellenistic Christian Traditions in Romans 6." *NTS* 29 (1983): 337–55.

Wengst, Klaus. "Der Apostel und die Tradition: Zur theologischen Bedeutung urchristlicher Formeln bei Paulus." *ZTK* 69 (1972): 145–62.

———. *Christologische Formeln und Lieder des Urchristentums*. SNT 7. Gütersloh: Gütersloher Verlagshaus, 1972.

Wenham, David. *Paul and Jesus: The True Story*. Grand Rapids: Eerdmans, 2002.

———. *Paul: Follower of Jesus or Founder of Christianity?* Grand Rapids: Eerdmans, 1995.

Wessels, G. François. "The Historical Jesus and the Letters of Paul." In *The New Testament Interpreted: Essays in Honour of Bernard C. Lategan*, edited by Cilliers Breytenbach, Johan C. Thom, and Jeremy Punt, 27–51. NovTSup 124. Leiden: Brill, 2006.
White, Joel R. " 'Peace and Security' (1 Thessalonians 5.3): Is It Really a Roman Slogan?" *NTS* 59 (2013): 382–96.
———. " 'Peace' and 'Security' (1 Thess 5.3): Roman Ideology and Greek Aspiration." *NTS* 60 (2014): 499–510.
Williams, Sam K. *Galatians*. ANTC. Nashville: Abingdon, 1997.
———. *Jesus' Death as Saving Event: The Background and Origin of the Concept*. HDR 2. Missoula, MT: Scholars Press, 1975.
Wilson, Barrie. *How Jesus Became Christian*. New York: St. Martin's, 2008.
Windisch, Hans. "Der erste Petrusbrief." In *Die katholischen Briefe*. HNT 4.2. Tübingen: Mohr Siebeck, 1911.
Witherington, Ben, III. *Conflict and Community in Corinth: A Socio-Rhetorical Commentary on 1 and 2 Corinthians*. Grand Rapids: Eerdmans, 1995.
———. *Grace in Galatia: A Commentary on Paul's Letter to the Galatians*. Grand Rapids: Eerdmans, 1998.
———. *Jesus, Paul, and the End of the World: A Comparative Study in New Testament Eschatology*. Downers Grove, IL: InterVarsity Press, 1992.
———. *Paul's Letter to the Philippians: A Socio-Rhetorical Commentary*. Grand Rapids: Eerdmans, 2011.
Wolter, Michael. "The Distinctiveness of Paul's Eschatology." In *Eschatology in the New Testament and Some Related Documents*, edited by Jan G. van der Watt, 416–26. WUNT 2/315. Tübingen: Mohr Siebeck, 2011.
Wrede, William. *Paul*. Translated by Edward Lummis. London: Green, 1907.
Wright, N. T. "The Letter to the Romans: Introduction, Commentary, and Reflections." *NIB* 10:393–770.
———. *Paul and the Faithfulness of God: Parts III and IV*. Christian Origins and the Question of God 4. Minneapolis: Fortress, 2013.
Yeo, Khiok-khng. *Rhetorical Interaction in 1 Corinthians 8 and 10: A Formal Analysis with Preliminary Suggestions for a Chinese, Cross-Cultural Hermeneutic*. BibInt 9. Leiden: Brill, 1995.
Young, Francis M. *The Use of Sacrificial Ideas in Greek Christian Writers from the New Testament to John Chrysostom*. Patristic Monograph Series 5. Cambridge, MA: Philadelphia Patristic Foundation, 1979.
Ysebaert, Joseph. *Greek Baptismal Terminology*. Nijmegen: Dekker & Van de Vegt, 1962.
Ziesler, John A. *Paul's Letter to the Romans*. TPINTC. Philadelphia: Trinity Press International, 1989.

Index of Authors

Ascough, Richard S., 109

Bachmann, Michael, 79
Baden, Joel S., 111
Barclay, John M. G., 12, 104
Barrett, C. K., 11, 65
Barth, Markus, 16
Bates, Matthew W., 54–55
Bauckham, Richard, 41, 43, 47–48, 58–60, 62–63, 66, 100
Baur, F. C., 11
Best, Ernest, 36, 89, 104–5, 107, 122
Betz, Hans Dieter, 33–34, 37, 50–51, 64, 73, 75, 78, 81
Betz, Johannes, 130, 135
Betz, Otto, 113
Bird, Michael F., 42, 53, 55
Bobertz, Charles A., 136
Boer, Martinus C. de, 14, 43, 50, 52, 115–17, 119–20
Bonnard, Pierre, 12
Borgen, Peder, 21, 35, 75
Boring, M. Eugene, 11, 72, 89, 107
Bornkamm, Günther, 90
Bradshaw, Paul, 134
Breytenbach, Cilliers, 21–22, 25, 27, 38, 40, 157, 159, 165–66, 169, 171
Bruce, F. F., 72–73, 89, 105, 107

Bultmann, Rudolf, 22, 24, 27, 42, 44, 58, 64, 72, 82–84, 102, 105, 172
Burchard, Christoph, 78, 89
Burton, Ernest deWitt, 12
Bussmann, Claus, 16–17, 90, 101–2
Byrne, Brendan, 43–44, 50, 53–54, 64, 71, 93

Campbell, Alastair, 23
Campbell, Douglas A., 23, 84
Cangh, Jean-Marie van, 142–46, 149, 156
Carey, Greg, 23
Carroll, John, 52, 157
Chester, Andrew, 115
Collange, Jean-François, 31
Collins, Adela Yarbro, 28
Collins, Raymond, 10, 35–36, 49, 56, 60–61, 63, 74, 82–83, 98, 108–9, 112, 115, 117, 119–23, 125–26, 138, 142, 144–48, 150, 156–57
Conzelmann, Hans, 21–22, 35, 49, 60–61, 82, 92, 116–17, 120, 125, 137, 139, 143, 145–47, 150–52
Cosby, Michael R., 110
Cosgrove, Charles H., 52, 73, 80–81
Cousar, Charles B., 29, 57
Cranfield, C. E. B., 23, 26, 35, 43–44, 54, 68, 71, 77, 83–84
Crossan, John Dominic, 166–68

Index of Authors

Cullmann, Oscar, 22, 44-45, 47, 62

Dahl, Nils, 11, 22, 24-25, 27, 81
Das, Andrew, 78, 80
Davies, W. D., 113
Deichgräber, Reinhard, 28, 30-31, 45, 60, 73
Denies, Roland, 21, 55, 57
Do, Tan J., 24
Donfried, Karl J., 10
Draper, Jonathan A., 130, 135-36
Dunn, James D. G., 12, 24, 26, 32-33, 35, 42-44, 48-49, 51-54, 57, 60, 62-64, 66-68, 71-74, 77, 80, 85-86, 114, 120, 124
Du Toit, David, 45

Eastman, Susan Grove, 28, 58
Ehrman, Bart D., 48, 56, 130
Elias, Jacob W., 101
Ellis, E. Earle, 16, 36
Eriksson, Anders, 36, 60-61, 74, 138-39, 144-45
Ernst, Josef, 13

Farmer, William R., 11, 156
Fee, Gordon, 28, 56, 60, 137-38, 144, 157
Feldman, Louis H., 6
Fitzmyer, Joseph A., 24, 26-27, 30, 32, 43, 46, 48-49, 68, 71, 78, 85-86, 91, 123
Fotopoulos, John, 22, 61, 97-98
Fredriksen, Paula, 22, 25
Friedrich, Gerhard, 88, 101-2
Fuller, Reginald H., 33, 45, 50, 54, 81
Furnish, Victor P., 26-27, 32-33, 36-37, 42, 49, 65, 103, 169, 172

Georgi, Dieter, 11
Gerhardsson, Birger, 21-23
Gibson, Jeffrey B., 168
Gnilka, Joachim, 13
Goodwin, D. R., 80
Gray, Patrick, 2
Green, Joel, 157
Gundry, Robert H., 105, 110

Hafemann, Scott, 11
Hahn, Ferdinand, 45-46, 48-49, 54
Harnack, Adolf von, 1, 88, 172
Harnisch, Wolfgang, 9-10, 127
Hartman, Lars, 35, 76-77, 82
Hay, David, 30, 32, 46-48
Hellerman, Joseph H., 28
Hellholm, David, 35, 75-76
Hengel, Martin, 21, 25, 31, 42, 45-47, 50, 58-59, 61, 156
Hill, Charles E., 115
Hill, Wesley, 42, 58-59, 63, 119-20
Hofius, Otfried, 136, 142, 155
Hogeterp, Albert L., 110
Holladay, Carl, 11
Holleman, Joost, 109, 129, 131
Holtz, Traugott, 43-44
Hooker, Morna, 30-31, 57, 88-90, 104, 147-48
Horrell, David G., 16, 22, 36
Horsley, G. H. R., 85
Horsley, Richard A., 10, 73, 113, 140, 147-48
Horst, Pieter van der, 6
Howard, Tracy L., 111
Hunn, Debbie, 80
Hunter, A. M., 21, 26, 51, 71, 84, 114, 124
Hurtado, Larry W., 21-22, 26, 31, 45-46, 49, 51, 57, 59, 61-63

Jeremias, Joachim, 21, 26-27, 92, 137-46, 149-51, 156
Jervell, Jacob, 65
Jewett, Robert, 9-10, 24, 26, 32, 35-37, 41-42, 50, 53-55, 64, 68, 71, 77-78, 83-84, 86-88, 93, 95, 124, 168
Jipp, Joshua W., 55
Johnson, Maxwell, 134
Johnstone, J. William, 84
Jonge, Henk J. de, 14, 36, 38

Käsemann, Ernst, 24, 26, 32, 36, 38, 54, 82, 84, 87
Keck, Leander E., 26-27, 35, 43, 50, 54, 64, 78, 83, 93
Kertelge, Karl, 37, 43-44

INDEX OF AUTHORS

Kieffer, René, 122
Kim, Seyoon, 53–55
Kirk, Alan, 165, 167
Kistemaker, Simon J., 147–48
Kittredge, Cynthia Briggs, 8–9, 29–30
Klauck, Hans-Josef, 138–39, 144, 155
Klausner, Joseph, 1
Kloppenborg, John, 64, 91, 154
Kodell, Jerome, 139, 141–44, 146, 150, 156
Koester, Helmut, 13
Kramer, Werner, 42–43, 49–50, 64, 71–72, 84, 89–90, 102, 124
Kraus, Wolfgang, 86
Kreitzer, L. Joseph, 115
Kujanpää, Katja, 173

Lake, Kirsopp, 130
Lambrecht, Jan, 10, 65, 117–18
Lategan, Bernard C., 74
Legarreta-Castillo, Felipe de Jesús, 117
Lichtenberger, Hermann, 79, 88, 110, 115
Lietzmann, Hans, 138, 152
Lindemann, Andreas, 111, 113, 115, 125
Lohmeyer, Ernst, 29–30
Longenecker, Richard N., 16, 49, 78, 81, 84, 122
Lovering, Eugene, 11
Lüdemann, Gerd, 11, 89–91, 107–9
Lyons, George, 12

Maccoby, Hyam, 1, 4–7, 14, 20, 70, 96, 133–35, 140, 150–51
Mack, Burton, 2
Malherbe, Abraham, 10, 26, 36, 43, 72, 90, 102, 105, 110, 122, 127
Marshall, I. Howard, 83–84
Martin, Ralph P., 29–30, 33, 36, 42, 57, 65, 102, 148
Martin, Troy, 74
Martyn, J. Louis, 25–27, 35, 50, 73, 75, 77, 79, 81, 84
Masson, Charles, 10
Matera, Frank J., 33, 52, 65–66
Mazza, Enrico, 130, 136, 142, 152
McGowan, Andrew Brian, 140
Meeks, Wayne A., 26, 43, 75, 99, 172–73

Merklein, Helmut, 113, 125
Meyer, Ben F., 25, 29, 136, 138, 156
Michaels, J. Ramsey, 105, 125
Minns, Denis, 134
Mitchell, Margaret M., 11
Moloney, Francis J., 142
Moo, Douglas, 23, 26, 32, 35, 50, 53–54, 64, 71, 78, 84, 93, 124, 147
Morris, Leon, 53
Moss, Candida R., 111
Mounce, Robert H., 139, 146, 156
Müller, Ulrich B., 30, 56, 105–7, 123
Mussner, Franz, 12
Myers, Susan E., 84n56

Nanos, Mark, 12
Neufeld, Vernon H., 15–16, 26, 32, 41, 43–46, 53, 55, 71–72
Niederwimmer, Kurt, 56, 129–30, 135–37

Öhler, Markus, 29, 43–44
Orr, William F., 60
Osiek, Carolyn, 56

Pahl, Michael, 106
Parvis, Paul, 134
Pearson, Birger, 10
Pede, E. Di, 57
Peterson, Erik, 110
Porter, Stanley E., 9, 12–13

Reinach, Théodore, 6
Reumann, John, 13, 28–29, 57–59, 81–83, 87
Richard, Earl, 89, 105, 107, 112, 122
Ridderbos, Herman, 83
Rigaux, Béda, 10, 121, 127
Roetzel, Calvin, 55
Romanov, Andrey, 60, 62
Rordorf, Willy, 135–37

Sandt, Hubertus Waltherus Maria van de, 135
Schlier, Heinrich, 52
Schmithals, Walter, 10–11, 116–17, 119
Schneider, Sebastian, 126

Index of Authors

Schoedel, William R., 103
Schrage, Wolfgang, 60, 63, 74, 82, 92, 113, 115, 120, 137–39, 142, 144–46, 154
Schürmann, Heinz, 140–41
Schüssler Fiorenza, Elisabeth, 4, 8, 15, 155
Schweizer, Eduard, 52
Schwemer, Anna Maria, 46n26
Scroggs, Robin, 44, 54–55, 59, 75, 114
Seeley, David, 168
Seifrid, Mark A., 65–66, 150
Sellin, Gerhard, 10, 113
Shillington, V. George, 14
Slee, Michelle, 135
Smith, Dennis, 144, 146, 148–49, 151–54, 156
Standhartinger, Angela, 148, 163
Stettler, Hanna, 79
Streett, R. Alan, 149, 154
Stuhlmacher, Peter, 21–22, 25–27
Sumney, Jerry L., 9–11, 132

Tabor, James D., 1, 3, 5, 7, 14, 20, 48, 56, 70, 75–76, 96, 133–35, 140
Talbert, Charles H., 57
Tannehill, Robert C., 77
Taussig, Hal, 149, 153
Theobald, Michael, 44
Thiselton, Anthony C., 61, 74, 113–15, 137, 141, 147–48
Thompson, Marianne Meye, 69
Thrall, Margaret E., 42, 66, 102
Thurston, Bonnie, 28, 30
Tilling, Chris, 46, 60–61, 98
Tobin, Thomas H., 84
Tomson, Peter J., 139

Tuckett, Christopher, M., 16, 22, 36, 109

Villiers, Pieter G. R. de, 102, 110, 112
Vollenweider, Samuel, 57
Vossing, Konrad, 155

Waaler, Erik, 60
Walther, James A., 60
Wanamaker, Charles A., 90, 104–5, 121–22
Ware, James, 23
Watson, Francis, 12, 37, 40
Wedderburn, A. J. M., 95
Weiss, Alexander, 25
Wengst, Klaus, 42–44, 46, 60, 62, 71, 73, 102–3, 109, 124
Wénin, A., 57
Wessels, G. François, 157, 166
White, Joel R., 121
Williams, Sam K., 21, 24–25, 52, 65, 78–79
Wilson, Barrie, 1–4, 7, 20, 48, 56, 67, 76, 96, 108, 131, 133–35
Windisch, Hans, 124
Witherington, Ben, III, 28–29, 52, 57, 123, 147–48
Wolter, Michael, 113
Wrede, William, 1, 2
Wright, N. T., 23, 26, 32, 51, 60, 121

Yeo, Khiok-khng, 61
Ysebaert, Joseph, 35

Ziesler, John A., 35, 44, 53–54, 68, 78, 83

Index of Subjects

Abba, 49, 98
Adam, 113–14, 120
Adoption, 52
Antioch, 19, 25, 44, 151, 156
Anti-Semitism, 6–7
Apostleship, 11, 12, 13, 55, 102–3, 171–72
Aramaic expression/style, 18, 21, 30, 45–46, 49, 66–67, 76–77, 89–90, 97–98, 128, 130, 132, 142–44, 148–49, 156, 161–64
Aramaic-speaking church, 18, 21, 30, 45–46, 49, 54, 66–67, 76–77, 90, 97–98, 128, 130, 132, 142–44, 148–49, 156, 161–64
Ark of the covenant, 24–25, 39, 86, 160
Ascension, 48, 49, 174. *See also* Exaltation
Atonement, 23–25, 32, 39–40, 80, 86, 92, 95, 159–61, 173

Baptism, 3, 9, 30, 35–36, 48, 51, 56, 74–78, 81–82, 95, 99, 101, 103–4, 123, 136, 163, 170, 172

Christ: blood of, 23–24, 83, 86–87, 142–44, 146–50, 164; and creation, 61–63, 67, 161–62; descent of, 20, 41, 70; image of God, 65–66; preexistence of, 51–52, 55–58, 61, 67, 161–62, 169; sending of, 50–52, 57–58, 67, 73, 161; Son of God, 3, 31, 41, 50–56, 64–65, 67, 72–73, 76, 78, 90, 116, 118, 161–63; Son of Man, 85, 108, 128; Word, 63. *See also* Earthly (human) Jesus; Identification with Christ—"with Jesus"
Christology: Adamic, 29, 51–52, 57, 66, 113–14, 120, 129; adoptionist, 6, 20, 54; bipartite, 55, 62
Circumcision, 7, 11–12, 99
Communal and cultic meals, 46, 48, 56, 97, 134–37, 140, 142–46, 148–49, 151, 152–57. *See also* Meal/banquet/symposium
Covenant, 25, 39, 73, 79, 87, 94–95, 98, 143, 146–50, 152, 157
Creation, mediated by Christ, 61–63, 67, 161–62
Crucifixion, 3, 21, 23, 33, 37–38, 87, 141, 165–67

Damascus, 25, 90, 156
Davidic descent, 53–56, 66, 137
Day of Atonement, 80, 86, 92
Death, vicarious. *See* Vicarious death
Descent of Christ, 20, 41, 70

Earthly (human) Jesus, 1–7, 13–15, 40–41,

Index of Subjects

43, 47, 50–51, 53–54, 76, 79, 96, 105–6, 122, 131–32, 138–39, 141, 146, 152
Earthly kingdom, 5, 47, 70, 96, 109, 119–20, 128–31, 163
Ebionites, 5–6, 96
Enthronement. *See* Exaltation
Eschatological interpretation or agent/figure, 13, 22, 31–32, 34, 45–46, 48, 54–55, 67, 77, 87, 90–91, 95, 96–100, 102–4, 108, 111, 114, 120, 125, 128–32, 148, 161–64, 169, 173
Eschatology, 1, 9–10, 12–13, 22, 24, 34, 45–48, 54–55, 62, 72, 77, 79, 81, 87, 89–92, 94–95, 96–132, 143, 148–49, 161–64, 169, 173; overrealized, 9–10, 13
Exaltation, 29–30, 32, 39, 41, 46–49, 51, 54–60, 66–67, 72, 96–100, 102–5, 111, 119–20, 128, 161–63, 169, 171, 174
Expiation, 21, 24, 27, 38, 86, 143, 149, 168–69

Forgiveness, 23, 25, 40, 73, 79–80, 82, 86, 92, 94–95, 159, 163

Glory/glorification, 90, 91
Glory of God, 59
Gnosticism/Gnostics, 6, 10–11, 13, 20, 31, 65, 75, 166
Greek (language), 28, 45, 65, 76–77, 97, 102, 142–43, 156

Hellenism/Hellenistic: church, 21, 24, 27, 29–31, 39, 46, 49, 62–63, 87, 91, 100, 102, 106, 120, 164, 169, 172; communal meals, 142, 152–56; Hellenistic thought, 6, 22, 27–29, 39–40, 45, 72, 85, 105, 138, 152, 155, 168
Historical Jesus, 14, 105–6, 111, 139, 143, 150, 166
Historical method, 2, 4–19, 133–35, 150, 166–70
Holy/holiness, 35, 54, 56, 81–82, 92, 134–35
Holy Spirit, 9–11, 13, 46, 53–56, 71, 76, 78, 82, 112, 163

Identification with Christ—"with Jesus," 35–36, 73–77, 81, 91, 95, 99, 103–4, 109, 111, 114, 128–29, 163
Image of God, Christ as, 65–66
Incarnation, 31, 39, 41, 55, 58, 171

Jerusalem church, 5–6, 9, 11–12, 21–23, 27, 29–30, 38, 45, 54–55, 67, 72, 98, 105, 134, 156–57, 159, 166, 168, 171. *See also* Palestinian church
Jesus. *See* Earthly (human) Jesus; Historical Jesus; Teaching of Jesus
Jesus movement, 2, 5, 20, 67, 96
John the Baptist, 75–76, 101
Judaism, 3, 5–6, 12–13, 15, 20, 22, 25, 27, 33–34, 41, 46–48, 59, 62, 81, 103, 110, 113, 134–35, 143, 146, 148–49, 152, 155, 160–61, 164; apocalyptic, 63, 75, 77, 90, 99, 113, 115, 121–22, 128, 132; Hellenistic, 10–11, 18, 22, 24, 34, 40, 62, 65–66, 86, 102, 119; Palestinian, 23, 25, 34, 39, 45–46, 81, 134–35, 152, 161, 164; Second Temple, 47–48, 59, 62, 79, 90
Justification, 26–28, 35, 73, 78–81, 87, 94–95, 160, 163–64, 167, 169

Kingdom, 47, 81, 96, 115–16, 118–19, 123, 125, 143, 167; earthly, 5, 47, 70, 96, 109, 115, 120, 128–31, 163; transearthly, 47, 109–12, 119–20, 126, 128–32, 163

Lamb, 58, 92; Passover, 91–93
Libertine, 13

Maranatha, 45–46, 48–49, 66–67, 97–98, 132, 134, 136, 161, 163, 171
Martyrs/martyrdom, 22, 34, 38–39, 86–87, 94, 132, 148, 156, 160, 168
Meal/banquet/symposium, 134–40, 142–43, 148, 151–56, 170; memorial meals, 137, 144, 148, 152–57, 164; ritual meals in Judaism, 134–36, 142–43, 146, 148, 152–56. *See also* Communal and cultic meals
Messiah (Christ as), 3, 21–22, 37–39, 43, 47, 66, 99, 160, 166–67

201

INDEX OF SUBJECTS

Overrealized eschatology, 9–10, 13

Palestinian church, 4–5, 21–25, 27, 38–40, 43–46, 63, 103–4, 152, 157, 164, 169
Parousia, 10, 34, 66, 89–90, 104, 107–8, 111–12, 115, 120–22, 126–27, 131, 164, 170–71
Passover, 92, 134, 146, 148, 150, 152–53; Passover lamb, 91–93
Persecution, 104
Preexistence of Christ. *See* Christ: preexistence of
Purification, 86

Q, 1–2, 51, 89–90, 101, 121–22, 130–33, 165–67
Qumran, 46, 50, 79–81, 110, 135, 154–56

Reconciliation, 33, 169
Redemption (*lytron*), 52, 83, 85, 87, 94–95
Rescue, 89–91, 101
Resurrection: of the dead, 34, 42, 49, 53–54, 64, 72, 75, 102–5, 107–13, 115–16, 126, 128–29, 131, 170; of Jesus, 3, 13, 20, 22–23, 26, 29, 34, 38–39, 43, 45–47, 49, 54–55, 66–67, 71–73, 87–88, 96, 100, 102–4, 106, 111–13, 115–17, 124, 128–29, 132–33, 160–61, 163, 165–66, 168–70

Sacrifice, 6, 25, 33–34, 85, 140–41; of atonement, 83, 86, 92; of covenant initiation, 87, 157; for sin, 25, 34, 39, 92
Second coming, 96–32

Semiticism/Semitic character of language, 16, 18, 27, 29–30, 54, 142–44, 150, 156, 164
Sending (of Christ), 50–52, 57–58, 67, 73, 161
Septuagint, 18, 24, 27, 39, 46–47, 49, 85–87, 102, 127, 143
Shema, 41, 61–62, 161–62
Sins, 20, 22–24, 33, 70, 82–83, 86–88, 94–95, 160, 163
Socrates, 168
Spirit. *See* Holy Spirit
Stephen circle, 25
Suffering: of believers, 28, 36, 91; of Christ, 36, 91
Suffering servant, 22, 33
Symposium. *See* Meal/banquet/symposium
Syria, 25, 39, 156–57

Teaching of Jesus, 1–4, 14–15, 40, 122, 164–68
Temple worship, 6, 25, 39, 86–87, 134–35
Torah observance by Gentiles, 11–13, 52, 69, 73, 78–81, 163, 173

Vicarious death, 21, 33, 38, 40, 74, 157, 159–61, 168–69

Wisdom, 10, 166, 168; as an hypostasis, 52, 62–63, 162; wisdom tradition, 18, 29, 52, 62–63, 66, 162
Wrath, 89–91, 94, 101, 127, 163

Index of Scripture and Other Ancient Texts

HEBREW BIBLE

Genesis
1:26	65
1:27	75, 99, 129
14:18	148
15:8–11	87
17:9–14	74
26:26–33	148
31:43–54	148
31:50–54	87

Exodus
6:6	85
13:13	85
13:15	85
19:6	127
21:8	85
23:33	93
24:4–8	87
24:5–8	147
24:9–11	148
25:17–22	5
29:23	24
34:34	89
40:23	24

Leviticus
24:8	24

Deuteronomy
3:24	144
7:8	85
8:10	136
9:26	85
13:5	85
28:25	93

2 Samuel
7:14	51

Psalms
2:7	51
8	114, 116–19, 120, 128, 163
8:4–6	114
8:6–7	59, 66
8:7	116, 119, 160
24:22 (LXX)	85
25:11 (LXX)	85
32:1	40
53:5	24
91:12	93
109:30	144
110	30, 32, 46–48, 49, 98, 116–19, 120, 128
110:1	46, 47, 58, 59, 66, 100, 116, 119, 160, 161, 163
110:4	47

Proverbs
8:27–30	62

Isaiah
8:14	93
28:16	93
29:21	93
41:14	85
43:1	85
43:14	85
43:20–21	127
45:23	59
52:14	144
53	22, 26, 27, 39, 92, 146, 160
53:7	92
53:11	26
53:12	26, 160
59:11	102
59:20	89, 101

Jeremiah
7:25	52
13:16	102
16:7 (LXX)	143

INDEX OF SCRIPTURE AND OTHER ANCIENT TEXTS

Ezekiel
2:3 — 52

Daniel
4:32 — 85
7:13–14 — 128
12:1–3 — 111
12:3 — 131

Haggai
1:12 — 52

Zechariah
3:1 — 85

NEW TESTAMENT

Matthew — 54, 66–67, 96, 108, 129, 130–31, 142, 149, 150, 157, 167
3:7 — 89, 101
7:6 — 76
10:32 — 132
11:21–23 — 131
11:25 — 51
11:27 — 58, 100
12:38–42 — 131
12:46–50 — 6
13:24–30 — 131
13:36–43 — 131
13:41 — 131
13:43 — 131
17:9 — 107
19:28 — 132
20:28 — 85
22:44 — 46
23:39 — 132
24 — 132
24:3 — 108, 131
24:8 — 121
24:19 — 121
24:27 — 108, 131
24:29–31 — 105
24:31 — 106
24:37 — 108, 131
24:37–39 — 121
24:39 — 108, 131
24:42 — 123
24:43 — 122, 123
25 — 131
25:13 — 123
25:30 — 131
26:64 — 46
28:17 — 66
28:19 — 78

Mark — 142–45, 146, 149, 150, 156, 157, 164
10:45 — 85
12:25 — 107
12:35–37 — 47
12:36 — 46
13:8 — 121
13:17 — 121
13:34 — 123
13:35 — 123
13:37 — 123
14:22 — 142, 143, 151
14:22–24 — 150
14:24 — 143, 149
14:25 — 143
14:26 — 155
14:62 — 46
16:19 — 47

Luke — 54, 85, 121, 139–40, 142, 143–46, 149, 154–55, 157, 164, 167
1:4 — 121
1:68 — 85
2:38 — 85
3:7 — 89, 101
9:16 — 143
10:13–15 — 131
10:21–22 — 51
10:22 — 58, 100
11:29–32 — 131
12:8 — 132
12:37 — 123
12:39 — 122, 123
12:45 — 123
13:35 — 132
16:31 — 107
17:26 — 121
20:42–43 — 47
21:23 — 121
21:34 — 121
21:34–36 — 122
22:14 — 144
22:19 — 139
22:20 — 140, 143, 145
22:29–30 — 132
22:69 — 47
24:21 — 85
24:46 — 107

John — 89, 92, 93, 107–8, 133, 147
1 — 52
1:1 — 65
1:29 — 92
1:36 — 92
3:35 — 58, 100
3:36 — 101
6:50–59 — 147
6:60–61 — 147
6:66–69 — 147
11:23 — 107
11:24 — 107
11:25–26 — 105
13:3 — 58, 100
16:15 — 58, 100

Acts — 3, 9, 44, 47, 75, 92, 95, 121, 151, 170, 171
2:24 — 121
2:33 — 47
2:34–35 — 47
2:38 — 78
3:15 — 42
4:10 — 42
5:14 — 44
5:23 — 121
5:31 — 47
7:55–56 — 47

Index of Scripture and Other Ancient Texts

8:16	78	7:4	42, 70–71	1:30	83
8:32	92	7:24	89, 101	2:2	37
10:36	58, 100	8	52	2:7	61
10:42	124	8:3	50–53, 61, 161	2:8	37
10:48	78	8:3–4	50	3:12	93
11:26	44	8:11	42–43, 70–71, 72, 103	4:20	116
13:30	42			5:5	140
13:33	51	8:15	49, 98	5:7	91, 92, 93
16	28	8:17	91	6:9	116
17:3	107	8:23	83	6:10	81, 116
19:5	78	8:27	32	6:11	35–36, 81–82, 95, 163
22:16	35	8:32	26, 64–65, 73, 112, 140, 160, 161		
23:6–8	111			6:14	42, 49, 103
		8:32–34	31–32	6:18	83
Romans	13, 37, 40, 51, 55, 67, 86, 87, 88, 89, 95, 112, 160, 164	8:34	32, 47, 160	7:10	4
		9:5	53, 68, 162	7:14	35
		9:32–33	93–94	8	61
1–5	90, 101	9:33	107	8:1–4	61
1:3–4	53–56, 67, 160	10:8	124	8:4	41
1:13	23, 83	10:9	42, 44, 45–49, 124	8:6	52, 60–64, 67, 161, 162
1:16–17	88	11:2	32		
1:23	126	11:16	112	8:9	93
2:4	82	11:26	89, 101	8:11	36
2:7	126	11:36	41, 62	9:25	126
3	83	13:12–14	123	10:7	72, 107
3:10–18	88	14:9	34, 64, 124, 128, 163	10:16	83, 147
3:24–26	23–25, 82–83, 88, 94, 95, 160, 163			10:16–17	142
		14:13	93	10:17	141
3:25	86	14:15	36	11	87, 151, 153, 157, 158, 164
3:25–26	39	14:17	116		
3:26	72, 83	14:20	93	11:17–18	151
3:30	41	14:21	93	11:20–21	154
4:7	40	15:3	64	11:21	123
4:24	42, 44–45	15:12	72, 107	11:21–22	151
4:24–25	42, 73	15:31	89, 101	11:23	133, 141
4:25	26–28, 39, 42, 140, 160	16:5	112	11:23–25	137–50, 157
				11:23–26	134, 157, 164
5:8	36	**1 Corinthians**	10, 62, 63, 98, 113, 126, 138, 139, 140, 142–47, 152, 154–55, 162	11:24	141, 142, 143
5:9	83			11:25	83, 139, 140, 154
5:14	113			11:26	140, 143
5:18	26			11:27	83
6:1–2	13	1:13	37	12:3	44, 72
6:2–8	172	1:13–15	78	12:13	74, 99–100, 129
6:3	35, 77–78, 95, 163	1:17	37	12:26	91
6:3–5	78	1:18	37	14:8	106, 125
6:4	42	1:23	37	15–16	112

205

15	21, 39, 128, 168	5:14	36	5:24	37
15:1–11	112	5:15	43, 72	6:12	37
15:3	138, 141	5:18–21	33	6:14	37
15:3–5	15, 20–23, 27, 37, 38–39, 159, 161, 170	5:21	33–34, 160	6:17	37
		8–9	19		
15:4	42	8:9	58	**Ephesians**	47, 171, 172
15:12	42	8:24	83	1:9	83
15:20	42, 112, 113	11:4	72	1:14	127
15:20–28	112–20, 128	11:21–29	3	1:20	42
15:21–22	113	11:31	68	1:20–22	47, 59
15:22	113	12:2	106	1:20–23	117, 118
15:23	107, 115	12:4	106	1:22	58, 100
15:24–28	68, 112, 117–20, 163, 171	13:4	37	2:6	47
				3:3–4	172
15:25	47	**Galatians**	12, 27, 33, 50–51, 65, 75, 95, 160	4:6	41
15:27–28	58, 100			5:2	26
15:28	117			5:5	116
15:42–54	126	1:1	42	5:6	101
15:45	113	1:4	26, 73	5:18	123
15:50	116	1:11–12	133, 172	5:25	26
15:50–52	125, 128, 164	1:16	65	5:26	81
15:51–52	110, 126	2	9, 156		
15:52	106, 126	2:1–5	19	**Philippians**	13
15:53	130	2:10	19	1:28	83
15:58	42	2:11–14	151	2	39, 128
16:1–4	19	2:15	78	2:3–5	31
16:13	123	2:16	27, 42, 78–81, 94, 163	2:6–8	52
16:15	112			2:6–11	28–31, 56–60, 61, 65, 66, 100, 128, 162, 171
16:22	45, 97–98, 128, 163	2:20	26, 64–65, 72–74, 94, 140, 163		
				2:8	37
2 Corinthians	11, 12, 103, 167	3	74	2:9	58
		3:1	37	2:9–11	58, 59, 66, 117
1:7	42	3:10	34	2:10	68, 72
1:10	89, 101	3:13	33–34, 160	2:11	44, 58
2:9	29	3:20	41	3:18	37
3:7	93	3:26–28	95, 100	3:21	58, 100
3:16	89	3:27–28	74–77, 81, 99, 103, 114, 129, 163, 171		
4:4	65			**Colossians**	47
4:4–5	65			1:15	65
4:4–6	65	4:4	50–53, 61, 161	2:12	42
4:10	72	4:4–5	50, 51	3:1	47
4:11	72	4:6	49, 98	3:6	101
4:14	42–43, 72, 102–4, 105, 109, 128, 163	4:9	89	3:11	74
		4:20	126		
5	33	5:11	37	**1 Thessalonians**	9–10,
5:6	42	5:21	116		

Index of Scripture and Other Ancient Texts

	101, 105, 126, 129, 131, 167
1–5	101
1:9–10	88–91, 94, 100–102, 128, 163
1:10	42, 101
2–5	107, 108
2:1	101
2:16	101
4	128
4:13–18	104–12
4:14	34, 71–72, 104, 107, 117, 164
4:14–17	72, 128
4:15	105, 106, 117, 125
4:15–17	105, 126
4:16	72, 106, 107, 125
4:16–17	108, 109–11, 170
4:17	106
5	123
5:1–3	120
5:1–11	122
5:2	122
5:2–3	120, 122, 127, 129
5:6	123
5:6–8	120, 123, 127, 132
5:7	123
5:8	123
5:9–10	36, 127
5:10	36, 123
5:20	106

2 Thessalonians
2:14	127

1 Timothy
1:17	126
2:6	26

2 Timothy
2:8	54
4:1	124

Titus
2:14	26, 85
3:5	81

Hebrews
1:2	58, 100
1:3	47, 65, 117
1:5	51
1:13	117
2:5–9	114
2:8	58, 100, 117
2:10	61
5:5	51
5:6	47
5:10	47
6:20	47
7:3	47
7:8	47
7:15–17	47
7:21	47
7:24–25	47
7:28	47
8:1	47
9:12	85
10:12–13	47
10:22	81
10:39	127
12:2	47
12:19	106

James
	96, 108, 133
2:7	76
3:1	42
5:7	108, 131
5:8	108

1 Peter
	59, 93
1:4	126
1:18	42, 85
1:19	92
1:21	42
1:23	126
2:6	93
2:9	127
3:18–22	47, 59
3:21–22	117, 118
3:22	47
4:5	124

2 Peter
1:16	108
3:4	108
3:10	122
3:12	108

Jude
9	106

Revelation
	47, 59, 89, 92, 105
1:10	106–7
3:2	123
3:3	122, 123
3:21	47
4:1	106–7
5	58
5:6	92
5:9	92
5:9–10	66
5:12	92
6:9–11	132
6:16	101
6:17	101
8:2	106–7
8:6	106–7
8:13	106–7
9:14	106–7
11:18	101
14:10	101
16:15	122, 123
16:19	101
19:15	101
22:20	98

DEUTERO-CANONICAL WORKS

Wisdom of Solomon
8:4–6	62
9:9	62
14:15	138
16:6–7	101
18:20–21	101

INDEX OF SCRIPTURE AND OTHER ANCIENT TEXTS

Sirach
2:6–8 — 102

1 Maccabees
1:11–15 — 7

2 Maccabees
1:8 — 24
1:15 — 24

2 Esdras
16:37–39 — 121

4 Maccabees — 2, 24, 39, 86–87, 94, 160
8:12 — 24
17:21–22 — 86
17:22 — 86

OLD TESTAMENT PSEUDEPIGRAPHA

2 Baruch — 115
29–31 — 115

1 Enoch — 115
48:1–4 — 63
62:3 — 144
62:5 — 144
70–71 — 111
91:9–14 — 115
104:2 — 111
104:4 — 111
104:6 — 111
106:19 — 110

4 Ezra — 115
6:6 — 62
12:32 — 63
13:22–24 — 111
13:25–26 — 63

Letter of Aristeas
254 — 101

Sibylline Oracles
2.243 — 47
3.309 — 101
3.545–72 — 90
3.556 — 101
3.561 — 101
3.632 — 101
5.75–89 — 90
12.110–12 — 90

Testament of Job
33:3 — 47
33:9 — 47

Testament of Moses
1:14 — 63

DEAD SEA SCROLLS

1QH 4:34–37 — 79
1QH^a 12:22–37 — 110
1QIsa^a — 110
1QS 11:12 — 79
1QS 11:13–15 — 79
4Q204 — 110

PHILO
— 113, 114

In Flaccum
1–107 — 7

Legatio ad Gaium
114–39 — 7

Quis rerum divinarum heres sit
199 — 62

Quod deterius potiori insisari soleat
54 — 62

JOSEPHUS

Contra Apion
1.161 — 7

TALMUD AND OTHER RABBINIC WORKS

b. Yoma
85b — 7

t. Sanhedrin
13.5 — 144

Pirqe Abot
3:16 — 7
5:18 — 144, 179–82

Sipre Deuteronomy
27 — 144

APOSTOLIC FATHERS

Barnabas
7.2 — 124
12.10 — 47

1 Clement
21.6 — 26
36.5 — 47
49.6 — 26

2 Clement
2.1 — 124

Didache — 7, 48, 56, 76, 82, 96–98, 129–31, 133–35, 137, 150, 152, 155, 161, 163
4.8 — 129, 163
7–10 — 136
7.1 — 56, 78
7.1–3 — 56
7.3 — 56, 76, 78
9–10 — 130, 133, 135, 136, 137, 154, 157
9.1 — 135
9.1–4 — 56

Index of Scripture and Other Ancient Texts

9.2	56	2.2	103	4.1.168–69	168
9.3	56	12.2	42		
9.4	130, 163			Epiphanius	5–6
9.5	76, 82				
10	134, 135, 136	**NEW TESTAMENT**		**Justin**	
10.1	136	**APOCRYPHA AND**		*1 Apology*	134
10.2	56, 130, 163	**PSEUDEPIGRAPHA**		66	134
10.2–3	76				
10.3	56, 130	Apocryphon of James		**Lucian**	
10.6	97, 130, 136, 163	14:30	47	*Dialogi deorum*	
14.1	48			4.2 (210)	85
		Apocryphon of Peter			
Ignatius		6	47	**Plato**	
To the Ephesians				*Theaetetus*	
10.1	101	Gospel of Thomas	2, 167	198B	138
To the Smyrnaeans				**Seneca**	
1.1	54	**OTHER ANCIENT**		*Epistulae morales*	
1.2	74	**WRITINGS**		24.6	168
To the Trallians					
9.2	42, 103	**Aeschylus**		**Theon of Smyrna**	
		Chorphori		*Expositio rerum*	
Polycarp		48	85	*mathematicarum*	
To the Philippians				1	138
2.1	42, 47, 118	**Epictetus**			
		Dissertationes			

www.ingramcontent.com/pod-product-compliance
Lightning Source LLC
Chambersburg PA
CBHW031253230426
43670CB00005B/165